PARTNERSHIP DEVELOPMENT

FOR THE FULLY FUNDED MISSIONARY

Rob Parker

FORERUNNER
PUBLISHING
KANSAS CITY, MISSOURI

Partnership Development for the Fully Funded Missionary by Rob Parker

Published by Forerunner Publishing
International House of Prayer
3535 E. Red Bridge Road
Kansas City, Missouri 64137
ihopkc.org/books

Forerunner Publishing is the publishing division of the International House of Prayer, which exists to partner in the Great Commission by advancing 24/7 prayer and proclaiming the beauty of Jesus and His glorious return.

ISBN: 978-1-938060-28-1

Cover design by Lala England
Interior design by Isaac Weisman and Jared Smith
Printed in the United States of America

CONTENTS

SESSIONS

SESSION ONE
Introduction to Partnership Development   1

SESSION TWO
The Current Crisis in Missions   7

SESSION THREE
Stewardship: Part One   17

SESSION FOUR
Stewardship: Part Two   25

SESSION FIVE
Old Testament Study   43

SESSION SIX
New Testament Study   53

SESSION SEVEN
Biblical Faith   67

SESSION EIGHT
A Modern Application   73

SESSION NINE
Letter and Postcard   81

SESSION TEN
The Phone Call   91
10.1 Supplement: Phone-Call Flowchart   99
10.2 Supplement: Mock Phone-Call Checklist   100
10.3 Supplement: Sample Phone Scripts   102

SESSION ELEVEN
Appointment: Prepare, Share, and Invite   109
11.1 Supplement: Appointment Flowchart   116
11.2 Supplement: Mock Appointment Checklist   117

SESSION TWELVE
Appointment: Excited Friends   119
12.1 Supplement: Excited Friends Flowchart   127
12.2 Supplement: Example Letters   128

SESSION THIRTEEN
Appointment: Multiple Strategies   133
13.1 Supplement: Sample Recommendation Letter   145

SESSION FOURTEEN
Your Assignment Has a Budget   147

SESSION FIFTEEN
Loving Your Team Well   153

HOMEWORK ASSIGNMENTS   **173**

HOMEWORK ASSIGNMENT #1
Meditation Questions   175

HOMEWORK ASSIGNMENT #2
Your Testimony   179

HOMEWORK ASSIGNMENT #3
Stewardship   185

HOMEWORK ASSIGNMENT #4
Old Testament Study   191

HOMEWORK ASSIGNMENT #5
New Testament Study   199

HOMEWORK ASSIGNMENT #6
Create Your Name List   213

HOMEWORK ASSIGNMENT #7
Financial Vision Plan   217

HOMEWORK ASSIGNMENT #8A
Your Vision Statement   219

HOMEWORK ASSIGNMENT #8B
Vision, Obstacles, and Goals Worksheet   221

HOMEWORK ASSIGNMENT #9A
Write Your Letter: First Draft   227

HOMEWORK ASSIGNMENT #9B
Write Your Letter: Second Draft   231

HOMEWORK ASSIGNMENT #10A
Written Phone Call: Yes   233

HOMEWORK ASSIGNMENT #10B
Written Phone Call: No, With an Additional Ask   235

HOMEWORK ASSIGNMENT #10C
Written Phone Call: Have Not Read the Letter Yet   237

HOMEWORK ASSIGNMENT #10D
Practice Phone Calls: Yes   239

HOMEWORK ASSIGNMENT #10E
Practice Phone Calls: Various Responses   241

HOMEWORK ASSIGNMENT #11A
Thinking It Through   245

HOMEWORK ASSIGNMENT #11B
Appointment Script   247

HOMEWORK ASSIGNMENT #11C
Appointment Script: Yes 249

HOMEWORK ASSIGNMENT #11D
Appointment Script: Excited-Friends Ask 253

HOMEWORK ASSIGNMENT #12A
Practice Appointment #1 257

HOMEWORK ASSIGNMENT #12B
Practice Appointment #2: Including Ask 259

HOMEWORK ASSIGNMENT #12C
Practice Appointment #3: Excited Friends 261

HOMEWORK ASSIGNMENT #12D
Practice Phone Call: Excited Friends 263

HOMEWORK ASSIGNMENT #13
Vision of Being Properly Funded 265

CAMPAIGN RESOURCES 269

Where to Begin 271

Before Your Campaign 275
Vision, Obstacles, and Goals Worksheet 277
Strategy Brainstorming Per Location 283
Grouping Your Contacts 291
Campaign Calendar 305
Instructions For Hosting A Small Group 307
Recommendation Letters & Emails 309

During Your Campaign 313
Partnership Commitment Cards 315
Giving Instructions Cards 317
Excited Friends Brainstorming Sheet 319
Gathering Contact Information Cards 321
Weekly Run Sheet 323

After Your Campaign 325
Tracking Monthly Partnership 327
Thank-You Chart 329
Cultivating Relationship Chart 331
83 Ways To Say Thank You 337

Other Resources 343
My Confession 345
Challenges to Partnership Development 347
The Please Do's & Please Don'ts 355

SESSION 1

- Values & convictions ⟶ WHAT we believe SHAPES OUR **WORLD** VIEW
  - ⟶ CAUSE US TO TAKE ACTION
- WHAT DO YOU BELIEVE ABOUT GLOBAL MISSION

KINGDOM WORLD VIEW:
- Letting God rule Matthew 4 5 6

Introduction to Partnership Development

Overview: In this session we will examine the perspective of partnership development—the benefits of raising a team, how partnership development trains you for ministry, and some common barriers to the process. Our intention is for you to rediscover the story of God in your life, gain confidence in God's call, and understand that partnership isn't a new model. It is a more than 3,500-year-old means by which God has funded His ministry workers.

Partnership development: The call to being a missionary

God, in His infinite wisdom and power, could have chosen a number of ways to financially supply His workers, but He chose the giving of the saints as the primary means.

The giving and financial stewardship of God's people advances almost every aspect of Christian ministry. Churches, missions, Christian schools, and para-church organizations are almost 100 percent funded 100 percent of the time by God's people. Even when ministries are funded by sales, those sales are most often for Christian products or Christian services purchased by Christians.

God owns all the gold and silver and the cattle on a thousand hills, and the earth is the Lord's and the fullness thereof; so, no matter who we are, whether Christian or unbeliever, and no matter what we do, whether righteous or unrighteous, we are using the Lord's money.

It is God's desire to redeem and restore the earth, and He will do this with His resources and His people. He will build His house, but He wants it built in a certain way. He wants to build it with us as we agree with Him about who He is and His plan. He wants us willingly and fully submitted to Him and to one another as good stewards throughout the entire process.

His building plan requires partnership: *people with people, and people with God.* Inviting people to partner in ministry is giving them an opportunity to steward the Lord's resources, advance His mission, and build His house.

Partnership development starts with a conversion in our thinking

Few, if any, enter occupational ministry because they like to raise money, but most quickly discover that partnership development is essential to fully complete their assignment with longevity. Obedience has a price tag.

Currently, in most mission circles, there is an aversion to asking about financial partnership. Most would rather not deal with the subject. They often fear rejection, think they don't have biblical permission, or have an understanding that missionaries are supposed to be poor. Several organizations do not allow their missionaries to raise support, believing it is contrary to faith.

Almost all fear, disagreement, or hesitation around the subject of raising support is rooted in our culture—not in the kingdom of God. We have believed many lies about finance, missions, missionaries, asking, faith, and income levels. This cultural stronghold often keeps us from even starting the process.

The number one hindrance to successful partnership development lies between our ears.

To be successful in partnership development, we must first have a paradigm shift from a *cultural mindset* to a *biblical mindset*. Our current cultural mindset is driven by fear, lack of understanding, opinion, "mammon," and tradition. It has sidelined thousands of workers, leaving their assignments largely undone, and it has resulted in a tremendous negative impact on global missions.

In Scripture there is a culture of partnership: the saints work together as they join God's will for the earth. Scripture has much to say about workers and their wages, the Church's commission, the stewardship of every believer, and the rewards of giving. He wants the Body of Christ submitted to Him and to one another as we work together in humility.

Perspective leads to action

Partnership development is 90 percent perspective. Without a proper perspective we will *not* enter into this ministry with any clarity, confidence, or conviction. Wrong perspective is a key reason why many never enter into partnership development or full-time ministry. They feel called and have a burden, but they cannot see how it could be financially viable.

Perspective (positive and negative) leads to *attitude,* which determines *action.* You will do what you believe. We *must* have the right perspective concerning biblical partnership.

We must renew our minds with the Word of God. We must welcome the Holy Spirit to enlighten our eyes and set our hearts free so that we no longer serve mammon and are delivered from the fear of men.

Biblical partnership is a team of people working together to engage in the Great Commission in a way that could not be done otherwise. The team will accomplish far more than one missionary could alone.

Person-to-person partnership could be defined as:

Two separate but equal parties with separate but equal responsibility working together to achieve a common goal.

The language of partnership development

We need to shift our thinking from culturally-based to biblically-based. When we make this shift, our language will change as well. Additionally, we need to shift from *fundraising* to *biblical partnership*. Fundraising has its place, but partnership is very different, and this is the focus of this course.

If a worker feels *forced* into fundraising because of financial needs, the whole process is often negative for everyone involved: fundraising becomes "a necessary evil." On the other hand, if the worker becomes involved in *partnership development* as a ministry to the Body of Christ, then the journey is fulfilling and fruitful.

Let me say it again: partnership development is *not* the same as fundraising. The focus of this course is partnership development.

Compare these different mindsets:

Fundraising	Biblical Partnership
Unpleasant and difficult	Spiritual ministry
Transactional	Transformational
Technique	Body of Christ in Relationship

Donor	Partner
Donate	Invest
Short-term	Long-term
Need-focused	Vision-focused
Pressure to give (sales)	Invitation to join God

Fundamental concepts of successful partnership development

Have the right master

Matthew 6:24 (ESV) says:

> *No one can serve two masters, for either he will hate the one and love the other, or he will be devoted to the one and despise the other. You cannot serve God and money.*

Jesus makes it very clear—idolatry is a real possibility.

Even though we would say that being a "faithful servant" of money is evident in the world today, most believers would not consider themselves guilty of this form of idolatry. Serving mammon is not just a love for money but rather obedience to a monetary value system that has engulfed the earth. Mammon is not rooted in stewardship because it is a worldview that ignores the sovereign rule of our Creator King. Mammon says things like: "I have worked hard for my money," "God doesn't need my money," "You can give but don't get carried away," "Pay yourself first," and "I need a little fallback money." Who is our master? Whom are we obeying? Who's providing for you?

Unless we are free from the love of money, stop trusting in it for our security, and break any allegiance to mammon, it will be impossible to walk in joy-filled obedience, let alone be successful in partnership development.

Observe the motivation of your heart. Don't look at people as dollar signs. God is your provider—not people. This is very important to remember:

God has always been your provider, and in partnership development He will continue to be your provider.

Be confident of your calling

People want to give to people who have a clear sense of calling and who are confident about where God is leading them. If you are excited and confident about the assignment that God has given you, people around you can also become excited with you and for you. You can't fake it! Real confidence in your calling will stimulate others to have confidence in you. If God has called you, it doesn't matter how much you need to raise. He *will* provide.

Giving often requires asking

Most giving is prompted by an *ask*. When we take the offering on Sunday morning at church, that is an *ask*. We receive asks in the mail, we hear them at conferences, and asking is a normal part of our faith. Most of the time, people who enjoy giving aren't thinking about giving, but when asked they are happy to participate. *People are more willing to give than we are willing to ask.*

People mostly give to faithful servants before they give to the ministry or organization

People are interested in you first—and secondarily in your ministry focus or organization. Share yourself first and then your ministry focus or organization. Allow people an opportunity to know you. Begin your new partnership rooted in relationship with them. The more they get to know you and develop a heart value for your ministry, the more likely they are to partner long term.

Benefits of raising a team

Building a partnership team is also a ministry and can be one of the most satisfying experiences you will ever have. It is exhilarating to help other Christians realize how they can be part of a team that is making an impact for the kingdom. You are not simply raising funds for yourself; you have received a vision from the Lord, and His work needs to be done. You will be providing members of the Body of Christ a stewardship opportunity.

Your being properly funded will strengthen your mission organization and therefore strengthen the missions movement. You will be providing opportunities for the Body of Christ to participate in God's global mission.

Partnership development will help you build a prayer base for your ministry as well as provide a number of relationships that would not have happened otherwise. Your being in full-time ministry will help develop the prayer culture within the Church.

While you are developing partners, you are engaged in real ministry to God's people. Partner development is not something you do in order to be in ministry; rather, *it is part of your ministry.* It is critical to understand that partnership development is not a means to an end, but is actually a key part of your assignment. Because developing partners is part of our ministry, we prepare our hearts with the same intensity as any other aspect of our ministry. We also prepare our materials, invitations, and sharing points with as much prayer, diligence, and practice as we do for any preaching, church planting, or discipleship ministry.

Support raising trains you for ministry

As you start to build your team, you will gain confidence in yourself and your calling, as well as confidence in God's willingness and ability to provide. The more you share your vision, the clearer it will become to you. Clarity brings confidence, and as the Lord stirs hearts around you and starts to build a team, you will feel your faith begin to rise.

You will also learn time management and flexibility as you raise your team, because you will have to be organized, focused, and disciplined. Many impromptu speaking or serving opportunities will come your way—often at inconvenient times. Being a missionary is our lifestyle, and therefore partner development is our lifestyle. Meeting people, sharing our vision, and inviting them into partnership will become a continuous and consistent part of our life.

Patience

» Patience is part of our lifestyle in God, and few things will teach us this lesson as well as partner development. When we feel financial pressure, we may be tempted to rush into partner development prematurely. This can, and often does, have a negative impact on our contact base. Team-building takes time and cannot be rushed. Therefore:

» We must be willing to take time to learn all we can about partnership development.

» We must be willing to get prepared and organized.

» We must wait until we have enough money to do partnership development correctly.

» We must be willing to "push pause" or reduce our daily ministry responsibilities in order to do our partnership development campaign. This will vary depending on the proximity between our ministry and our contact base.

» We must be willing and prepared to invest several months in the partnership development season for the sake of our long-term assignment.

People skills

In your team-building process, you are going to meet with a lot of people, *many of whom you do not yet know.* You will learn how to communicate effectively, how to listen well, and how to answer questions.

Prayer

Not only will you be praying and asking God to open doors, but you will also pray for the people you meet. In the process of partnership development, you will encounter situations where you have an opportunity to minister to people's needs. In my own experience, face-to-face appointments have turned into ministry times on more than one occasion.

Service

Life in the kingdom is all about service. No matter how far you climb your organizations work chart, you will never be promoted beyond the position of a servant. Your ministry and your mission organization are primarily responsible for serving God and serving other people.

Key ingredients of successful partnership development

Faith

Successful partnership development starts with the revelation that God is the one who meets all our needs, even while He requires us to work hard. Hard work is our act of faith, trusting God to honor and bless the labor of our hands and bring His provision. Having faith means rising above discouragement, being sure of your calling, and believing God at all times. *We must believe that God has called us, that partnership is His preferred way, and that He has a team for us.*

Strategy

If you fail to plan, you plan to fail. If you aim at nothing, you are sure to hit it. God is a visionary! He has given you the gift of vision, and our hearts are stirred by vision. Every vision must have a strategy. Fulfilling the calling and assignment of God won't just happen on its own. We must have a strategy for success.

> [5]*The plans of the diligent lead surely to abundance, but everyone who is hasty comes only to poverty. (Prov. 21:5, ESV)*

Diligence

Those who succeed in partnership development are those who know how to push themselves when they do not feel like it. It is a time-intensive ministry that requires we stick to the plan, make commitments to core concepts, and faithfully walk out best practices every day.

> [4]*The soul of the sluggard craves and gets nothing, while the soul of the diligent is richly supplied. (Prov. 13:4, ESV)*

Improvisation

In this training you will learn a clear model and the steps to follow, but be aware that sometimes life, work, and schedules get in the way and make it difficult to reach your potential partners. You must be willing to improvise and determine for yourself to have an overcoming, *can-do* attitude. While being careful to stick with the important concepts of partnership development, we often have to move to plan B on the fly.

Developing a partnership team will challenge you to grow as a Christian. If you are faithful, strategic, diligent, and willing to improvise, it will be an incredibly formative and maturing process for you.

Resources

» *Funding Your Ministry*, Scott Morton

» *People Raising*, William P. Dillon

» *Raising More Than Money*, Doug Carter

» *A Spirituality of Fundraising*, Henri Nouwen

» *Growing Givers' Hearts: Treating Fundraising as a Ministry*, Thomas H. Jeavons and Rebekah Burch Basinger

» *Friend Raising*, Betty J. Barnett

» *Getting Sent*, Pete Sommer

Summary

1. *Saints giving to saints is God's primary way of funding gospel workers.*

2. *Partnership development is essential to fulfilling your assignment with longevity.*

3. *Without the proper perspective, we will not enter into this ministry with great clarity, confidence, or conviction.*

4. *Partnership development builds a prayer base, strengthens the Church and your organization, and develops important job skills.*

5. *Successful ingredients include faith, strategy, diligence, and improvisation.*

The Current Crisis in Missions

Overview: Today many ministries and missionaries serve God from a place of financial weakness rather than strength. In this session we will be looking at the current crisis the field of missions is facing, myths related to partnership development, and the need to be delivered from unbiblical and cultural strongholds. Our hope for you is that you will be freed from every stronghold, and free to run with endurance, completing your assignment in full-time ministry. Workers are needed.

Introduction: Where are all the workers?

The full-time workers I have come into contact with are some of the most amazing people I have ever met. I'm surprised, stunned, and blessed time and time again by the lives my ministry friends lead. They give, serve, and labor over and over—compelled by the love of God. Many countless times they have exchanged the visible, easier, more profitable and prestigious high road for the hidden, often hard, modest, occupationally damaging low road of humility and meekness. They do this just to remain at the feet of Jesus a little while longer. I am often overwhelmed by a profound sense of privilege as I look around at the collection of people among whom the Lord has set me.

It is disheartening to see these incredible, called, gifted, and humble servants have to leave their field of service over the issue of consistent lack. I have seen missionaries come and go—often within a couple of years—due to a lack of financial support. Many divine assignments have come to a screeching halt because there wasn't enough money to continue.

I'm not talking about people who have jumped into ministry prematurely, operating out of enthusiasm more than divine call. I'm talking about men and women who have divine assignments on their lives, who have heard the Lord in the right timing and moved into ministry under the Lord's leadership.

I have seen a number of my friends go through very intense, emotional struggles over the lack of finance, often questioning their calling, questioning God, and occasionally getting upset with people they thought should support their work—not to mention the stress that it brings to a marriage or family.

If a worker remains in this situation for too long, a number of negative thoughts and behaviors begin to manifest. Consistent lack will cause us to make decisions that we would not normally make. Often, we will resort to secular techniques in our ministry, such as marketing, sales, promises of blessing—or worse, an unbiblical pressure to give. All of this is very bad for the Body of Christ and has a direct negative impact on the mission of the Church.

There are about 450,000 to 500,000 full-time, occupational *missionaries* on the earth. This does not include pastors or church staff. The number may be as high as 600,000 if we also consider the few thousand unknown cases of missionaries in poor regions, where there are no records of their work. Let's assume that there are a lot more than we know of, and round the number to one million non-Church staff missionaries on our planet.

> *It is disheartening to see these incredible, called, gifted, humble servants have to leave their field of service over the issue of lack.*

Let's consider a few other important numbers. There are about seven billion people on the earth with about 550–650 million of them born-again, evangelical Christians. That means there are about 550 million believing Christians called by Jesus to do the work of reaching the other 6.5 billion unbelieving people. Let me ask you this question: does the number of occupational missionaries (1 million) in relation to the number of professing Christians (550 million) sound right to you? This means that only about one-fifth of 1 percent of the Body of Christ is presently engaged in occupational missions.

If only 1 percent of the Body of Christ was called into full-time missions work that would be five million workers. This number is ten times the number we are currently seeing. Let's say only half of 1 percent of the Body of Christ is called to the missions field. That would still mean 2.75 million missionaries, which is five times more than we are now seeing in active service.

I believe that on the low end, a few million Christians are not active in full-time missions, and that on the high end it may be as many as 10 million.

I understand that many missionaries are doing an outstanding job in the marketplace, schools, communities, and so forth, who are also supported by their trade or vocation of some kind. My point is that I do not believe that half of 1 percent, or even 1 percent, is the *real* number of Christians that God would call to full-time missions work.

I believe that on the low end, a few million Christians called to the missions field are not active in full-time missions, and on the high end maybe as many as ten million. I see them far too often, people with a call of God upon their lives, yet they have given their lives to something else. When I talk to them, their response is typically the same, "I would love to go into full-time missions, but I just don't see how I can financially."

People feel a pull toward missions and they do the only thing they know how to do: raise just enough for the one short trip or finance a trip on their own. Please do not misunderstand me; I thank the Lord for the missionaries who are in the field and I thank the Lord for short-term trips. Many have come into the kingdom through these trips. *But I do believe millions more believers are called than are presently in active service, and I believe a major reason—if not the main reason—is the issue of financial support.*

If God has all the gold and silver, why is there such a dilemma over financial support? Jesus said, "*The harvest truly is great*" (Lk. 10:2), and the need was for workers. The need was the same then as it is now; the Great Commission needs a fully available, fully equipped, and properly empowered work force. Jesus didn't highlight a lack of funds as the problem; He pointed to the lack of available people.

This stronghold either contributes to or is directly responsible for about 95 percent of our mythical thinking concerning support raising.

You might ask, "How can this be? If they are called and they are obeying the Lord, the funding should be there." I couldn't agree more. So why are so many called men and called women leaving the field—or never going into the field to begin with? Mostly, it is due to perspective and attitude.

The stronghold

Currently, there is a large and powerful stronghold in the minds of those in the Church. This stronghold either contributes to or is directly responsible for about 95 percent of our unbiblical thinking concerning support raising, giving, and partnership in the harvest.

All the way through this course, we are going to work on our wrong thinking, but here I want to address some myths that have developed over time about missions, including support, asking or not asking, faith or the lack thereof, lifestyle, sources, ethics, and so forth. What follows is not an exhaustive list, but it comes from my own experience as I have taught the subject of support raising in a classroom setting on several occasions. I normally open the class by asking the students to list their objections to raising support. This is what they have shared. Most are in their 20s, but several are in their 30s, 40s, 50s, and 60s.

» I feel like I am begging; it's not biblical.

» I should work a real job.

» Why would anyone pay me to pray? I wouldn't pay anyone to pray.

» Making tents is the right way for missions.

» The ministry should pay me a salary.

» I'm afraid I will lose my friends if I ask them for money.

» My family is embarrassed that I ask; my family has told me not to ask them or their friends.

» I don't know anyone; all my friends are missionaries.

» My friends don't have any money; I don't know rich people.

» I don't want to ask; if God has called me, then the money should just come.

» Raising support shows a lack of faith; I should just trust God.

» I don't want to be broke; I don't want to live poor.

» It is irresponsible of me as a provider.

» My friends hate my ministry.

» My denomination doesn't give to missions.

» I should talk with churches.

» The house of prayer is not biblical, because everyone should be praying.

» So what makes me special?

» The economy is bad.

» I don't want to be obligated to people because of money.

» Real missions are overseas.

» Everybody thinks I'm in a cult.

» No one will support me; there are better things to give their money to.

» No one will support a student.

» I should walk by faith.

» I'm waiting on the ravens.

» I have debt.

» I'm already working.

» I could never raise enough.

» I want to get married.

» Elijah and George Muller didn't ask!

» I should be supported by the people I minister to.

» Asking is wrong.

» The shame!

» My home country is very poor.

» My job at ABC ministries is too important to stop and raise support.

» My church said I cannot ask anyone at church.

» My friends think I should join a real missions organization.

» I sent out a letter and nothing happened.

» I don't have faith for it

» I don't want the stress.

» People don't give.

» I fear rejection.

» I hate sales.

» I don't have the right personality.

» I don't want to be the "used car" salesmen.

» I feel like a telemarketer.

» All my friends live far away.

» I don't have time to learn how.

» I'm about to lose my house now.

» I tried it, hated it, and won't do it again.

» I don't want to treat my friends like an ATM.

» I'm not really a laborer.

» I'm not called to raise support.

» I just got saved.

» It's too hard with my late hours.

» I have no money to raise support.

» It makes me feel creepy.

» I should wait on the Lord.

» Jesus was poor.

» If I ask, then how can I live modestly?

» God will take care of me.

» Isn't being poor more holy? (Someone really said that.)

» I want a financial history in God, and raising support won't let me get that.

» The Lord said I'm not to raise support.

» I don't feel like it.

» It's not very spiritual.

» I want nice things, and I can't ask other people to pay for them.

» I want to have a real life.

» I have heard the stories about missionaries, and I don't want to live like that.

» I don't see the Levites doing it in the New Testament.

» The money hasn't come; I don't think I'm called.

» I could do it if people knew me, but I'm a nobody.

» I don't think it is right and ABC ministry shouldn't teach people to do so.

» Can't I get a job on the missions base?

» I would like to, but my spouse doesn't want to.

» If you don't work, you don't eat.

With the exception of a few items listed above, the majority of these comments are rooted in fear, shame, and unbelief. The Holy Spirit did not author any of them. This list is shaped by our culture more than by the Bible. It is very important that our worldview is shaped by Scripture and nothing else.

Understanding strongholds

[3]For though we walk in the flesh, we are not waging war according to the flesh. [4]For the weapons of our warfare are not of the flesh but have divine power to destroy strongholds. [5]We destroy arguments and every lofty opinion raised against the knowledge of God, and take every thought captive to obey Christ, (2 Cor. 10:3–5, ESV)

i. Paul is making a point about warfare, and part of our warfare involves strongholds.

ii. In the above verse, a stronghold is indicated by arguments and lofty opinions raised against the knowledge of God.

iii. This verse communicates the need for us to take these lofty thoughts captive and obey Christ. In other words, if we don't take these lofty thoughts and arguments captive we will end up disobeying.

Are strongholds always bad?

From the above verse we can get the impression that strongholds are always bad. However, the Bible uses words like *refuge, strong tower*, and *fortress* to describe strongholds and often does so in a positive sense, even describing the Lord Himself. Consider the following.

[9]The LORD is a stronghold for the oppressed, a stronghold in times of trouble. (Ps. 9:9, ESV)

[2]The LORD is my rock and my fortress and my deliverer, my God, my rock, in whom I take refuge, my shield, and the horn of my salvation, my stronghold. (Ps. 18:2, ESV)

[1] The LORD is my light and my salvation; whom shall I fear? The LORD is the stronghold of my life; of whom shall I be afraid? (Ps. 27:1, ESV)

[39] The salvation of the righteous is from the LORD; he is their stronghold in the time of trouble. (Ps. 37:39, ESV)

[2] He is my steadfast love and my fortress, my stronghold and my deliverer, my shield and he in whom I take refuge, who subdues peoples under me. (Ps. 144:2, ESV)

[1] The name of the LORD is a strong tower; the righteous man runs into it and is safe. (Prov. 18:10, ESV)

Also see Psalm 94:22; Proverbs 10:29; 21:22; Jeremiah 16:19; Nahum 1:7.

From a brief glance of Scripture, we can see that strongholds can be negative or positive. The stronghold itself is neither positive nor negative. What makes a stronghold negative or positive is the one who builds it and their intention for building it.

Definition of a stronghold

A fortified place, a fortress (like a castle or walled city), a place for survival or refuge, or a place chosen for strategic military purposes.

The negative strongholds listed in Second Corinthians are strongholds of the mind. ***Simply put they are a collection of thoughts.*** Strongholds are built when we repeatedly agree with thoughts of either *truth* or *lies*. Thoughts lead to attitude, and attitude leads to action. In other words, strongholds lead to action. Refer to the list of comments above; would you say this is a collection of thoughts? Yes, for sure. Who has influenced these thoughts? Is their intent righteous or otherwise? Are these thoughts submitted to the lordship of Christ? What kind of action will these strongholds lead to?

The strongholds we are fighting are not righteous and not shaped by Scripture. The thoughts listed above are not submitted to the lordship of Christ. This is a demonic stronghold in rebellion to the kingdom of God with evil intentions resulting in wrong attitudes and inaction.

Paul states that we are fighting against negative strongholds of the mind. On a daily basis every believer faces a spiritual battle that begins and ends with the thought patterns of our mind. That is why Paul emphasized the importance of Christians renewing their minds with the truth in order to avoid being conformed to this world.

[2] Do not be conformed to this world, but be transformed by the renewal of your mind, that by testing you may discern what is the will of God, what is good and acceptable and perfect. (Rom. 12:2, ESV)

PASTOR'S NEED A SALARY, MISSIONARIES ARE POOR!

We are always agreeing. What are you agreeing with?

Stronghold of lies

By agreeing with the enemy we allow him to build a stronghold of lies in our mind. This leads to a worldly mindset, which in turn leads to bad behavior patterns. Every time we agree with a demonic lie we help the kingdom of darkness build a stronghold in our mind. Fifteen years later, what seemed like an insignificant lie has become a huge fortress. Ultimately, *we give authority to what we agree with.*

Stronghold of truth

Once the Holy Spirit exposes a lie in our mind, it is crucial that we break our agreement with that lie. Then we want to ask the Holy Spirit to show us the truth, and we want to agree with it quickly.

By agreeing with the Holy Spirit, we allow Him to build up a stronghold of truth in our minds, which leads to right perspective, a holy attitude, and obedience.

We are creatures of habit and we tend to repeat patterns that are familiar to us. This tendency could lead to not wanting to give up our old thought patterns. However, we *must* allow God's Word to shape our thinking and form our attitudes. We must have our minds renewed.

Myths abound

Unfortunately, the missions movement has a number of myths concerning support raising and the lifestyle that accompanies it. (Please keep in mind when I talk about partnership development that I'm often talking about the whole process: raising support, the giver, the Church's role, lifestyle, the missionary's role—all of it). *Opinions and ideologies abound. A few have some wisdom, but most are harmful, causing many misunderstandings and much unnecessary hardship.*

It is impossible to measure the amount of damage caused by myth and misconception. I know of nothing that has contributed more directly to hindering the progress of the Great Commission than our lack of biblical understanding concerning the financial support of missions and missionaries.

Funding is not the problem, but rather a lack of biblical understanding of how to find, gather, and receive those funds. Many called missionaries know that God will provide, but very few understand the biblical pattern of how God does the providing. This lack of understanding is a large reason many never go into missions or don't stay in missions long-term. This lack of understanding is the area we need to grow in and will be the focus of this class.

> *The issue of a person's deliverance is the issue of Truth and the Knowledge of God. We must ask the Holy Spirit to reveal what lie we have believed, break agreement with that lie, and replace the lie with the truth of God's Word.*

Myth 1: I don't know enough people who will give.

You know enough people. You actually know between 250 and 400 people. Granted, most will never give to missions, but you have a lot of people you can share your vision with and a lot of people who would pray for you. We will focus more on your list later.

Some of the people the Lord is going to put on your team you have not met yet. You may meet them in the process of raising your support or in the midst of your ministry. God has partners for you all over the place.

Myth 2: No one will support me as a student.

You are a full-time gospel worker, but still obtaining training or education as a student. In other words, you see yourself as a missionary in training. Being that you are laboring in the training part of your calling, you may not feel it is suitable to be funded as a worker.

A disciple is a student. The twelve disciples traveled with Jesus, doing very little direct ministry, but they were being prepared for ministry, and they were provided for. (See Luke 8:1–3 in several versions and use the word *them*. NKJV uses the word *Him*.)

> ¹*Soon afterward he went on through cities and villages, proclaiming and bringing the good news of the kingdom of God. And the twelve were with him, ²and also some women who had been healed of evil spirits and infirmities: Mary, called Magdalene, from whom seven demons had gone out, ³and Joanna, the wife of Chuza, Herod's household manager, and Susanna, and many others, who provided for them out of their means. (Lk. 8:1–3, ESV)*

Myth 3: I'm not sure that I have enough faith to live on support.

This myth is a large subject and we will address it more at length in a later session. You have had enough faith to respond to the call of God on your life. You have had enough faith to pray for the sick, witness, and trust God for food, rent, tuition, and so forth. The faith required to live with support is the same faith that you are exercising every day.

Myth 4: I shouldn't ask, I should just pray. (ASKING IS PRAYER IN ACTION)

This is actually a part of the stronghold talking to you. Asking is biblical. Jesus has been promised the nations, yet He has to ask for them. Praying *is* asking. It is agreeing with what the Lord wants to do. He wants to provide for you and He wants to do it through people. Asking becomes easy when you see that *you're not asking for yourself,* but asking for *others.*

Myth 5: I will never be able to raise enough to live on.

There are over 250,000 missionaries on the earth right now working with support teams. Many have families, homes, insurance, retirement, and so forth. I personally have been working within a financial partnership team since 2006.

Myth 6: Raising support is contrary to faith.

As we mentioned before, the issue of faith is possibly the largest stronghold to overcome. Raising support is not contrary to faith; it is faith in action. It takes faith to believe God and step out. Raising support is possibly one of the greatest steps of faith I have ever taken. Partnership development continues to build my faith.

Myth 7: If I raise support, I will be broke all the time.

This kind of statement comes from what I call "poor talk." When we have a *poverty* mindset and talk with a poor mindset, we will focus on our lack and what we don't have. This must be broken off of us, and we must develop right thinking.

Who told you that raising support meant you would be broke all the time? Did Jesus say this to you? Isn't it interesting that our first thought about support is that it won't be enough or that it will just barely be enough? Where did we get these thoughts?

Myth 8: Support raising Is not biblical.

Support-raising is *very* biblical. There are about a dozen verses in the New Testament alone that speak directly about support. We all understand that it takes money to build the kingdom, because ministries have to be funded. Support raising is really just a thoughtful way to go about gathering those funds.

As we look at several verses about support, we will see a pattern develop. We will use this scriptural pattern as an outline to our approach. This approach to partnership development will be based on what we see in the Word and *not* what we see on Wall Street. Partnership development is not "sales." I do have to admit, however, that much of what I see going on in the arena of support-raising circles smacks more of sales, business, and marketing than it does the kingdom of God.

The kingdom of God has its own government and its own laws. It has its own set of standards and its own economy. The kingdom of God is not advanced, run, governed, or lived in based on worldly principles. As citizens of God's kingdom, we want to be totally biblical in the way we raise and use God's funds.

All things that pertain to God's kingdom impart life. If we are really touching the kingdom and its truth, then we should be touching life. If we touch finance in a biblical way, then life will be imparted. This is when all the *weirdness* leaves the issue of money. What I am suggesting to you is that there is a place in partnership development where we can touch the kingdom, so that the whole process becomes a great source of life for you and for those who partner with you.

> *The kingdom of God has its own government and its own laws. It has its own set of standards and its own economy. The kingdom of God is not advanced, run, governed, or lived in based on principles from the world. As citizens of the kingdom we want to be totally biblical in the way we raise and live with support.*

Eleven facts about partnership development

1. **Thousands of missionaries are doing it already.**

   There are presently about 250,000–300,000 known missionaries on the planet in full-time ministry who are funded through partnership. What you are doing is nothing new; the Lord has been supporting full-time workers through the giving of the saints for thousands of years.

2. **People need to give.**

   The ministry of partnership development is providing opportunities for God's people to become involved in God's work. Partnership development helps the Christian/steward answer the all-important question, "What do I do with what God has entrusted to me?"

3. **Partnership development is an invitation to be part of a team and to accomplish something that can't be done alone.**

God determined that the funding of His work be done through the giving of His people. He has always done this. A yes from a potential partner is really a statement in which they are saying yes to God's ways and will. Partnership is agreeing with God.

4. **Partnership development is building partnership teams, not fundraising!**

In fundraising, once the donation has been made, the transaction is done. In contrast, we are building teams that will work together for years to build the Lord's house. Partnership development is an ongoing relationship of trust and mutual encouragement. Both parties have equal parts to play.

5. **Partnership development is a vital aspect of your ministry.**

It is ministry to the Body of Christ, not what you to have to do to get into ministry. You will find numerous opportunities to walk in Jesus' second commandment to love people. Your partners are real people whom the Lord has stirred to partner with you in ministry; He added them to your partnership team. They are not just a source of income.

6. **Partnership development is a testimony of God's faithfulness to us.**

Walking into someone's home or place of business and walking out with their partnership, trust, and friendship is a true act of God. God loves biblical partnership, evidence of His children working together with Him. Partnership is a sign of spiritual health.

7. **God has given you all the time you need to do all that He's called you to do.**

You have time for partnership development. You will always make time for those things that hold highest priority in your life. Your other ministry responsibilities are important, but without partnership development, you may not stay in ministry long-term. If *you* don't schedule your time, someone or something else will.

8. **Everyone is a potential partner, so open up your thinking.**

God will connect you with all kinds of people from different backgrounds. Some you will have a history with and others you will not. You will have great relationships with some and no relationship with others. Relationship is not a prerequisite for asking, but it is necessary for a continued, long-term partnership. You may run out of family and friends, but you will never run out of people to invite into partnership.

9. **Partnership development is about good stewardship and trusting God for your provision.**

If you are faithful to plan and live within your means, you will have more than enough.

10. **Partnership development is about walking in the second commandment, not just asking "donors" when you are in need.**

Partnership development is the lifestyle of a faithful, humble servant who loves God and people. Ministry is always about people.

11. **People who give are more likely to give again.**

God is always stirring people and has created them to be stewards. Keep people informed about all that God is doing through your ministry, and give them recurring opportunities to join you in your assignment. Don't worry, if you love them well you won't wear them out.

Conclusion

Raising support is 90 percent perspective. Without the proper perspective, you will not enter into the process with any clarity, confidence, or conviction.

A wrong perspective about money is one of the reasons many never enter into full-time ministry. They feel called, have a burden to go, but just can't see how it is going to work financially.

Perspective—positive or negative—leads to attitude, which leads to action. You will only do what you believe. Therefore, we must have the right perspective and attitude concerning partnership development. This is important for both the goer and the sender.

Summary

1. *Due to a lack of funding, many people who once said yes to Jesus are no longer walking in their calling.*

2. *When it comes to partnership development, many myths abound in the Church, which have created significant strongholds.*

3. *Receiving deliverance from wrong thinking is essential to being successful in partnership development.*

4. *The negative strongholds that we have built must be torn down by renewing our minds with the truth of God's Word.*

5. *Our worldview must be shaped by the Word of God, not by culture or circumstances.*

Please complete the following homework assignment:

Homework #1: Meditation Questions

Homework #2: Your Testimony

Stewardship: Part One

Overview: Our stewardship responsibility before the Lord touches every facet of our lives. In this session we will look at stewardship as something more than money management, citing Biblical pictures of stewards and God's ownership through creation and redemption. Our desire is that you would see God enthroned, ruling and reigning over all of His creation—that He owns everything and we own nothing and our stewardship flows out of God's ownership.

Introduction

God gives humanity the privilege of being managers of His workmanship, keepers of His creation, and servants within His household. When servants act in love-filled obedience to their Master, that action is called stewardship. There is considerable dignity in possessing the role of a steward (God's manager). For the business owner, housewife, teacher, lawyer, or construction worker, we all become co-laborers with God when we have the perspective of stewardship and live as stewards.

Stewardship is more than wise money management, more than being conscious of the environment, and more than marketplace Christianity. Stewardship encompasses all of life. It is the biblical basis for living life skillfully and is the lifelong calling of every Christian, regardless of occupation. Stewardship is the foundation for the Christian life. Stewardship is acknowledging God as owner, trusting Him as provider, and faithfully managing all that He entrusts to you for His glory.

We have an incredible privilege and responsibility, and our stewardship goal is to stand before the Lord on that Day and hear Him say, "Well done, good and faithful servant."

A definition

The responsible management of wealth, possessions and property of another that has been entrusted to someone; can include thoughtful care that is similar to a shepherd to his sheep or the raising of someone else's children.

Biblical pictures of stewards

A steward could also be seen as overseer:

> [15]*Thus says the Lord* GOD *of hosts, "Come, go to this steward, to Shebna, who is over the household, and say to him . . ." (Isa. 22:15, ESV)*

Abraham had a slave named Eliezer of Damascus, and his service role was that of a household manager. This would have included oversight of other slaves, management of resources, and making sure that all of Abraham's personal interests were properly represented and met. Abraham trusted him to find Isaac a wife, which Eliezer did successfully, making his master very happy.

Jacob served Laban for several years and had a management role over Laban's flocks. Jacob did this well and caused Laban to prosper. The first job that Joseph had in Egypt was working for Potiphar as household manager. After his promotion Joseph had his own household manager.

⁴So Joseph found favor in his sight and attended him, and he made him overseer of his house and put him in charge of all that he had. ⁵From the time that he made him overseer in his house and over all that he had, the L ORD blessed the Egyptian's house for Joseph's sake; the blessing of the L ORD was on all that he had, in house and field. (Gen. 39:4–5, ESV)

¹Then he commanded the steward of his house, "Fill the men's sacks with food, as much as they can carry, and put each man's money in the mouth of his sack." (Gen. 44:1, ESV)

⁴They had gone only a short distance from the city. Now Joseph said to his steward, "Up, follow after the men, and when you overtake them, say to them, 'Why have you repaid evil for good?'" (Gen. 44:4, ESV)

Biblical stewardship flows out of God's ownership. God's ownership is shown in two ways. One is creation and the other is redemption.

Creation

Aside from the fact that all of creation testifies to the existence of a creator, we have a biblical account in Genesis 1:1–2:4. The opening words of the Bible make it clear that the Godhead as Trinity acted alone and of their own will: "Let Us make man . . ." (v. 26) .

From the text, it is clear that there was a time when creation did not exist. Creation came about only through His will and the spoken Word of God. No one or thing contributed to creation: He acted alone.

The fact that there was nothing and then there was something places ownership fully in the hands of the Lord, the Creator, and nowhere else. His divine right of ownership is the foundation of our stewardship.

*Where there is no divine ownership, there cannot be **true** biblical stewardship.*

God owns everything—He is the creator

In a very real sense, God owns us.

God owns us in a way that only a creator can—completely and rightfully. He owns us in a way that creation and other humans will never be able to enter into or participate in.

⁵"It is I who by my great power and my outstretched arm have made the earth, with the men and animals that are on the earth, and I give it to whomever it seems right to me." (Jer. 27:5, ESV)

¹⁴"Behold, to the L ORD your God belong heaven and the heaven of heavens, the earth with all that is in it." (Deut. 10:14, ESV)

²³"The land shall not be sold in perpetuity, for the land is mine. For you are strangers and sojourners with me." (Lev. 25:23, ESV)

⁸"The silver is mine, and the gold is mine, declares the L ORD of hosts." (Hag. 2:8, ESV)

¹⁰"For every beast of the forest is mine, the cattle on a thousand hills. ¹¹I know all the birds of the hills, and all that moves in the field is mine. ¹²If I were hungry, I would not tell you, for the world and its fullness are mine." (Ps. 50:10–12, ESV)

¹The L ORD owns the earth and all it contains, the world and all who live in it. (Ps. 24:1, NET)

[16]For by him all things were created, in heaven and on earth, visible and invisible, whether thrones or dominions or rulers or authorities—all things were created through him and for him. (Col. 1:16, ESV)

[11]"Yours, O Lord, is the greatness and the power and the glory and the victory and the majesty, for all that is in the heavens and in the earth is yours. Yours is the kingdom, O Lord, and you are exalted as head above all." (1 Chr. 29:11, ESV)

[11]"Who has first given to me, that I should repay him? Whatever is under the whole heaven is mine." (Job 41:11; ESV)

[5]Thus says God the Lord, who created the heavens and stretched them out, who spread forth the earth and that which comes from it, who gives breath to the people on it, and spirit to those who walk on it . . . (Isa. 42:5)

This complete, sovereign, authoritative ownership of God is potentially offensive to a person with a spirit of independence. But the Word says, *"Thus says the Lord, God who created the heavens . . . who gives breath to the people who are on it, and spirit to those who walk on it."* (Isa. 42:5) God creates the planet, then creates the human race, and then puts breath and spirit into us. We only exist because He decided to create us.

Humanity's unique role within the creation

Humans have a unique role within creation—they are part of it but also have a management responsibility over it.

They were created lower than angels, but higher than the ape, a part of creation, yet stewards over it. **Man is a part of creation unlike any other part, for he can choose a close personal relationship with his Creator.**

It's not enough to simply understand we have been created by God. We must have a clear conviction about the dignity that God has given man in appointing us as stewards over His creation. This is not connected to our occupation or how much education we have, but we have the greatest job of all: we get to enter into this dynamic of stewardship, and we get to play a part with God in managing His creation.

God created the planet, created the seas, vegetation, and animals, then creates man and invites the first man to participate with Him in completing this creation: He allows Adam to name the animals.

What was the first role and responsibility that Adam had in the garden? He had stewardship of the land. He had to take care of a piece of real estate called the Garden of Eden, and his stewardship had responsibilities, expectations, parameters, and guidelines. There was work to do before the fall. Adam stepped out of his job description, however, and made a decision based upon his own desire rather than God's desire for his wellbeing. As a result, sin entered the earth. The original fall of man is directly connected to a failed stewardship.

When a man or woman chooses to use his or her resources according to their own will, he or she is making a management decision that's not connected to the will of the Lord—it's a management decision connected to personal will. In light of God's plan, Adam's self-motivated decision was mismanagement—a failed stewardship.

We are men and women in relationship with the God of creation and all that He created. The way we relate to all of His creation—including humans—is the very foundation of stewardship.

We must pay attention to this because God cares about how you relate to the environment; it is part of His creation. God cares about how you relate to your neighbor because your neighbor is part of His creation. It's important that we walk in the second commandment not only for love's sake, but because it is part of understanding the place we have in creation and our responsibility for it. We must keep our eyes fixed on our enthroned Creator and act as proper stewards of everything within His kingdom.

We must remain in a place of humility, understanding that we are creations, yet given the role of stewards over creation. We must relate to all of creation as its stewards, including human beings. *Our relationships with friends, family, the lost, and the poor are all part of our calling to stewardship.* God is always calling us to good stewardship, and we must respond to that call.

God creates and owns Israel

Israel exists because God went to a man named Abraham and essentially said, "I am going to start a new nation which is going to be a light to the earth and a light to the nations. I am going to create this new nation out of your descendants who will be my own special people. I'm going to start with you, Abraham." This was around 1700 BC. This is how the nation of Israel was birthed.

Then, around 600 BC, God said to Abraham's descendant, Jeremiah, regarding his nation, that they only existed as a nation because He chose for them to exist.

> ⁶*"O house of Israel, can I not do with you as this potter?" says the LORD. "Look, as the clay is in the potter's hand, so are you in My hand, O house of Israel!" (Jer. 18:6)*

Something that we see with the Hebrew people is God's ownership: once through creation and once through redemption. God went to a Gentile named Abraham and started a new group with him. The nation of Israel only exists (was created) because God acted of His own will. Also, through the great Exodus, God brought them out of their 430 years of slavery in Egypt—a redemption.

> ⁵*"Now therefore, if you will indeed obey My voice and keep My covenant, then you shall be a special treasure to Me above all people; for all the earth is Mine." (Ex. 19:5)*

> ¹²*Blessed is the nation whose God is the LORD, the people He has chosen as His own inheritance. (Ps. 33:12)*

> ⁴*For the LORD has chosen Jacob for Himself, Israel for His special treasure. (Ps. 135:4)*

> ⁶*"For you are a holy people to the LORD your God; the LORD your God has chosen you to be a people for Himself, a special treasure above all the peoples on the face of the earth." (Deut. 7:6)*

> ²*"You are a holy people to the LORD your God, and the LORD has chosen you to be a people for Himself, a special treasure above all the peoples." (Deut. 14:2)*

> ¹⁸*"Also today the LORD has proclaimed you to be His special people, just as He promised you, that you should keep all His commandments." (Deut. 26:18)*

> ¹⁷*"They shall be Mine," says the LORD of hosts, "on the day that I make them My jewels. And I will spare them as a man spares his own son who serves him." (Mal. 3:17)*

> ⁸*But now, O LORD, You are our Father; we are the clay, and You our potter; and all we are the work of Your hand. (Isa. 64:8)*

Impact of the Enlightenment

With the coming of the Enlightenment period, the view of an all-knowing creator God began to be opposed in our universities and social settings. The Church began to pull back into a position of accommodation, giving in to the spirit of the age.

Starting about the early 1800s, our Christian theology began to shift from the foundation of an all-knowing creator God who sits on His throne to that of man and his situation. This gave birth to a man-centered gospel, which is currently at an all-time high mark.

A man-centered gospel will always diminish the understanding and conviction of biblical stewardship. Along with focusing more on the human condition, a man-centered gospel brings a corresponding loss of focus on an all-knowing, creator God seated upon His throne. Because we have largely lost an understanding of a coming theocratic kingdom, *we have also lost awareness of our role as stewards.*

There is a great king on a throne

Biblical theism lies at the root of stewardship. God is and He speaks. The Bible is the Word of God and through it, the Lord introduces Himself and makes His will known. Apart from the Bible, stewardship makes little sense. Only biblical theism provides an adequate foundation for practicing personal stewardship.

There is no such thing as natural or human stewardship. If our stewardship is not flowing from the reality that God is and has made His will known to us, then mankind will steward according to self-interest. This is not true stewardship. Any stewardship that does not come by revelation from above will cheapen true biblical stewardship and lead to a self-interest management.

Any other religious, humanistic mindset or false ideology that does not find its roots in an understanding of divine ownership will never touch true stewardship. When we do not walk out our faith from a position of divine ownership, we will not walk in stewardship. We will then have no choice but to walk in a way that is contrary to the full purpose for which God created us.

In Genesis we were created to be stewards, and this sense of stewardship is still in humans. Most of humanity has forgotten its creator king and thus lives life detached from its stewardship role, all the while the DNA of stewardship is still within the human frame. The result is humanity has a sense of stewardship, but because they're no longer looking at an enthroned creator king, their stewardship becomes self-motivated and everyone does what's right in their own eyes.

The steward is always on duty. We daily answer the call to enter into that personal relationship between the created and the Creator. A steward responds consistently to the call of God with a yes and lives as an image-bearer, walking in His will. We have the opportunity to live in a dynamic, interactive relationship with our creator God. With a daily understanding of our call to stewardship, we are lifted out of the boredom and depression of our fallen nature and given purpose and dignity.

Our stewardship must include all of creation. We were given the responsibility to tend the garden, which means cultivating it. Only God could create the garden, but we must tend it.

We were given authority and dominion over all of His creation, but in our fallen state that authority can run wild into self-indulgence. Biblical stewardship keeps us on track and within the boundaries of our original design.

Conclusion

As we have seen, we are simply stewards over God's creation. He owns all things, and He is the very One who created us, yet He gave us a unique role to play in the earth. Though we are created like everything else we see around us, we are the pinnacle of God's creation. There is nothing else in all of creation that relates to God in the way we do—voluntarily submitting ourselves to His authority. Stewardship is simply how we live from that place of submission to God.

Additional study on stewardship

1. **Individuals who acted as stewards**

   i. Adam in the Garden of Eden

   ¹⁵Then the LORD God took the man and put him in the Garden of Eden to tend and keep it. (Gen. 2:15)

   ii. Joseph in Potiphar's household

   ⁴So Joseph found favor in his sight, and served him. Then he made him overseer of his house, and all that he had he put under his authority. ⁵So it was, from the time that he had made him overseer of his house and all that he had, that the LORD blessed the Egyptian's house for Joseph's sake. (Gen. 39:4–5)

   iii. Daniel as administrator in Babylon

   ¹It pleased Darius to set over the kingdom one hundred and twenty satraps, to be over the whole kingdom; ²and over these, three governors, of whom Daniel was one, that the satraps might give account to them, so that the king would suffer no loss. (Dan. 6:1–2)

2. **Groups acting as stewards**

   i. The priests serving in the tabernacle

   ⁹"They shall therefore keep My ordinance, lest they bear sin for it and die thereby, if they profane it: I the LORD sanctify them." (Lev. 22:9)

   ii. The seven chosen by the Jerusalem church

   ¹Now in those days, when the number of the disciples was multiplying, there arose a complaint against the Hebrews by the Hellenists, because their widows were neglected in the daily distribution. ²Then the twelve summoned the multitude of the disciples and said, "It is not desirable that we should leave the word of God and serve tables. ³Therefore, brethren, seek out from among you seven men of good reputation, full of the Holy Spirit and wisdom, whom we may appoint over this business." (Acts 6:1–3)

3. **Household stewards**

   ¹⁶When Joseph saw Benjamin with them, he said to the steward of his house, "Take these men to my home, and slaughter an animal and make ready; for these men will dine with me at noon." (Gen. 43:16)

¹And he commanded the steward of his house, saying, "Fill the men's sacks with food, as much as they can carry, and put each man's money in the mouth of his sack. ²Also put my cup, the silver cup, in the mouth of the sack of the youngest, and his grain money." (Gen. 44:1–2)

¹When David was a little past the top of the mountain, there was Ziba the servant of Mephibosheth, who met him with a couple of saddled donkeys, and on them two hundred loaves of bread, one hundred clusters of raisins, one hundred summer fruits, and a skin of wine. (2 Sam. 16:1)

¹⁷There were a thousand men of Benjamin with him, and Ziba the servant of the house of Saul, and his fifteen sons and his twenty servants with him; and they went over the Jordan before the king. ¹⁸Then a ferryboat went across to carry over the king's household, and to do what he thought good. (2 Sam 19:17–18)

Summary

1. *Stewardship is more than just good money management.*

2. *Stewardship is the biblical basis for living life skillfully. It is the lifelong responsibility and privilege of every Christian, regardless of their occupation.*

3. *Because God is Creator, He owns everything.*

4. *Biblical theism is the root of stewardship; if God is not enthroned, then you do not have true stewardship.*

5. *God owns us twice; once through creation and once through redemption.*

6. *Living in biblical stewardship lifts our life from boredom and gives purpose to everything we touch.*

Stewardship: Part Two

Overview: All of our life revolves around biblical stewardship and our reward in Christ is directly related to how we manage what we've been given regardless of the quantity. In this teaching we will examine stewardship as the foundation for Christian living, various parables on stewardship, and the fact that stewardship is the topic of conversation at the judgment seat. Our goal is to move you beyond theological speculation and into action.

New Testament stewardship

God is the creator and owner of the earth, and has made us His managers. What we see in the New Testament is that we have a different reflection of God's ownership of us. We begin to see the Lord redeeming His people, redeeming the earth, and we see this issue of ownership reflected in redemption.

Stewardship in the New Testament can be seen as a continuation of what God began in the Old Testament, while at the same time having several distinct features. Our creator God reveals Himself as Christ the redeemer in the New Testament. Through Jesus we see the created order becoming redeemed.

In the Old Testament we see that God created the heavens and the earth, and therefore has ownership of all things. A major theme of stewardship begins in the Garden of Eden in Genesis 2:15, but as His people fail, we see Christ the redeemer in the New Testament buying back His people who have been lost to sin. *We see this redemption theme clearly in the incarnation, the cross, and the bodily resurrection of Jesus.*

Personally, some of the most powerful words I have ever read are John 1:14: "and the Word became flesh." The incarnation of Christ is something I love to meditate on, and every time I do I become overwhelmed by the thoughts of God becoming a man. God becoming a man speaks of stewardship. *Jesus, the second person of the Trinity, functions in stewardship, knowing the will of His Father, and acting upon it by becoming flesh. His incarnation is overflowing with stewardship.*

In the incarnation we see the eternal entering the temporal. We see that which is spirit entering the physical for the purpose of redeeming it. The incarnation made several things possible and also gave us an incredible model of stewardship. Jesus is the premier model of a servant, essentially a manager of God's will.

> ⁵*Let this mind be in you which was also in Christ Jesus, ⁶who, being in the form of God, did not consider it robbery to be equal with God, ⁷but made Himself of no reputation, taking the form of a bondservant, and coming in the likeness of men. ⁸And being found in appearance as a man, He humbled Himself and became obedient to the point of death, even the death of the cross. (Phil. 2:5–8)*

God is often invading our space. He is always reaching out toward us, sending a messenger, a dream, or a prophetic word. The incarnation is a picture of what is to come. When God comes and redeems humanity, He creates something new. He is not going to snatch us off of a dying planet and whisk us away to an everlasting life in the clouds. No! Just as He did before, He is coming here. He is coming to restore all things, and He is bringing with Him a "new heavens and a new earth." *God has been and always will be an excellent steward of His own purposes.*

God taking on a body of flesh is proof that He can use the temporal and physical for the purpose of redemption. In this we can see a foundation for stewardship: God used the material for His purpose and will; therefore, we can use the material according to His purpose and will.

If God entered into time and space to take on flesh for the purpose of redemption, to what degree will He continue to do so in our own lives? In other words, how does God want to use my body, my mind, and my will? How does He want to use my house and my food for the purpose of His own perfect will? How does He want to use my property, automobiles, money, relationships, time, and skills?

Because of the incarnation, we are now stewards with a new opportunity, in which all that we see and touch can be used for the purpose of redemption and for the fulfillment of His perfect will.

We can see the two foundation stones of stewardship, creation and redemption, repeated throughout the Word.

» God *created* a new nation through Abraham and his descendants, and *redeemed* them through the Exodus.

> [5]*"No longer shall your name be called Abram, but your name shall be Abraham; for I have made you a father of many nations." (Gen. 17:5)*

> [13]*"You in Your mercy have led forth the people whom You have redeemed; You have guided them in Your strength to Your holy habitation." (Ex. 15:13)*

» God *created* man and has *redeemed* him through the cross.

> [5]*But He was wounded for our transgressions, He was bruised for our iniquities; the chastisement for our peace was upon Him, and by His stripes we are healed. (Isa. 53:5)*

» God *created* the heavens and the earth and will *redeem* and restore them, and we will live in a new heaven and a new earth forever.

> [13]*Nevertheless we, according to His promise, look for new heavens and a new earth in which righteousness dwells. (2 Pet. 3:13)*

We can see a portion of God's plan in three gardens and the role that stewardship plays in these three instances.

» Eden was the first garden; God entrusted its management to Adam (Gen. 2:15). Through disobedience Adam lost his privilege of stewarding the Garden of Eden (Gen. 3:23–24).

» Gethsemane was the second garden. We see Jesus walking in the fullness of stewardship and "winning" back the privilege of stewardship for man (Lk. 22).

» The third garden is the New Jerusalem of Revelation 21 and 22. Redeemed man will ultimately end up back in a beautiful garden. What we see is the fulfillment of God's original intention: men and women walking in stewardship and acting as servants in the midst of God's plan.

The cross

When we meditate upon the cross, we must keep in mind that Jesus was on the cross because of our sin; He bought us back and His blood made a way for us. *Sin entered the earth through a failed stewardship.* Of all the sins Jesus paid for, many are our failures to steward well—and all sins have their roots in a failed stewardship.

What happened at the cross

We can see stewardship in the cross. Jesus had an assignment; He was to offer Himself as a sacrifice for the sins of others. God's plan had always been the restoration of all things. The cross was His means to bring about global redemption. Through this one event of the cross we see several things happen: first, Jesus atoned for our sins; our sins were washed away. Second, the head of the serpent was finally crushed. Third, we see the curtain of separation from God torn in two, now giving us access to the Holy of Holies.

The cross was a tremendous act of spiritual warfare. Jesus made a spectacle of the satanic powers and principalities who thought they had conquered Him on the cross. When you enter into a message or a ministry that is proclaiming the cross, and bringing that scenario into human lives, what are you doing? You are helping to proclaim the message, actually bringing light, pushing back darkness, and furthering God's global plan of redemption.

Through our giving, we could be putting a messenger of God's light and freedom in the 10/40 window. The message of global redemption can go forward with the kingdom being advanced. We are actually inviting people to play a part in this global advancement of the kingdom.

Love displayed

Romans 5:8 says that *God demonstrated His own love toward us*. In other words, God the Father is demonstrating His love through the death of His Son. Who killed Jesus, the Romans, the Jews, or us? It seems that His Father actually did it. It was prophetically spoken long ago that the Father would crush the Son, and that it pleased the father to bruise Him:

> *¹⁰Yet it pleased the Lord to bruise Him; He has put Him to grief. When You make His soul an offering for sin, He shall see His seed, He shall prolong His days, and the pleasure of the Lord shall prosper in His hand. (Isa. 53:10)*

> *²⁰For you were bought at a price; therefore glorify God in your body and in your spirit, which are God's. (1 Cor. 6:20)*

In these verses you see the two major components of Gods ownership: *creation and redemption*. We were bought with a price through redemption, and your body and spirit are God's through creation. We were first created by God and then purchased by God with His very own blood. We are therefore a twofold possession of God; He owns us completely.

Bondservants

During His time on earth, Jesus says much about only doing the Father's will: "My food is to do the will of Him who sent Me" (Jn. 4:34) and "[Father,] it is finished!" (Jn. 19:30). You know who says it's finished? A servant who knows what the master's will is and when it's done. Jesus' incarnation is the epitome of stewardship.

The word *servant* is the Greek word *doulos*, which actually means "slave" not "servant." About ninety-nine out of one hundred Bibles will translate that word *slave* as *servant*.

Bondservant actually speaks of a voluntary—because of love—slave. In the Old Testament when a servant had served his master and his time was up, he could go to the doorpost of the house where the master would pierce the slave's ear with an awl to become a bondservant. In other words, out of his love, the slave was pronouncing his master's ownership over him. Once a bondservant, or *doulos*, one was considered the owner's personal property with no rights. One could even be killed with impunity by his master.

"Servant" is not a good translation of this word *doulos*, because it implies that you have options in what you are or are not going to do. A slave or bondservant, however, doesn't speak of the quality of life the individual had, it speaks of their master's ownership. Slaves were bought or born in their master's house. They were like purchased property.

Paul is speaking in a cultural setting in which everybody understood that slavery did not mean you were poorly treated, but that you were fully available only to serve the master. And because of this trusted relationship between the slave and the owner, the slave carried the authority of the master to buy and sell in the market under the master's name.

When a slave spoke in public representing the interest of his master, other masters responded to him as though his master was there in their midst. This wasn't colonial America or Europe. This was a complete bond of ownership to a master.

Jesus wasn't dreading being a slave to His Father, but rather expressed a measure of delight in the duty and responsibility He was given. Similarly, Paul said he was a voluntary "bondservant of Jesus Christ" (Rom. 1:1). He saw himself as fully owned and possessed by another. This whole process does not cheapen my relationship with God or my job as His steward; rather, it is full of love and honor.

Jesus did not just die in order to satisfy the wrath of God for the sins of man. He was also demonstrating the love that was already in the heart of God. Jesus' stewardship of the cross is motivated by love and should inspire us as well to be good stewards, equally motivated by love. Jesus was engaged with the Father's redemptive global mission, and His stewardship of that mission led Him to a cross where tremendous love was shown. Love was making a way for us. We take our lead from Jesus and imitate Him. Therefore, *let's steward well because of love; steward well because of the global mission.*

Christianity is an invitation to share in the cross. We are to renounce all, take up our cross, and follow Him. We live in such a way that we carry within us the death of the cross, a death to self. We deny ourselves certain things, but even more, we are in a position of standing apart from ourselves and standing as wholehearted servants: "Not our will be done, but Your will be done." Understanding this simple yet profound truth and walking in it is the very foundation of stewardship. The cross was for us. Jesus became a curse for us. His stewardship was living and dying for others. Are we living for ourselves, or are we living for others?

We are bondservants of the One who bought us. If we are not our own but created by another and redeemed by another, then nothing is our own! Our time, bodies, property, gifts, relationships, jobs, callings, and any other aspect of our lives all belong to our Lord.

The cross: warfare and stewardship

> [15]*Having disarmed principalities and powers, He made a public spectacle of them, triumphing over them in it. (Col. 2:15)*

We have already stated that the cross was part of Jesus' stewardship, and that in it He demonstrated His love for us, redeemed us, and made a way for us. Additionally, He engaged in heavenly warfare. He disarmed principalities and powers. Through the act of the cross, Jesus came against all the powers that imprison, defile, and humiliate us. This has great implications for us as stewards. Since the redeeming act of the cross has disarmed all the forces of hell, when we engage in our stewardship connected with His message, we also partake in disarming every evil force.

What God uses

God uses very tangible things that we can see, touch, and smell for the purpose of global redemption. God enters into time and space, and through the frame of a human named Jesus Christ, He brings about global redemption. Through things like water, fish, and bread God brings about global redemption. He uses temporal items to bring about His will and His way. God has always used yielded human beings to bring about global redemption. He will use your house in the same way that He used Peter's house.

God has always used real things—real houses and real creation—to bring about global redemption. You can play a major role in this plan as you surrender your will to serve God's purpose for your life: yield your pocketbook, your cupboard, your car, your job, your time, your house, your spiritual gifts, and any other resources.

When we give our time in service and our money to ministries that are proclaiming the gospel of the kingdom, we are partnering with the victory Jesus has already begun. Good Bible schools, missions work, and various other ministries are all playing a part in extending the victory of the cross. The kingdom of God, its message and its victories, are all advanced on the earth when we function in our roles as His stewards. If we were to fully function this way, we would be the most satisfied people on the planet and a million other woes would also be dealt with.

Repentance marked by a changed stewardship

When we come to see Jesus as our Creator King, we understand that this world and all that is in it belongs to Him. We see a transfer of ownership, from us to Him. Any life that is fully given over to our King will be marked by changed behavior, including how we handle money.

> *[7]He said therefore to the crowds that came out to be baptized by him, "You brood of vipers! Who warned you to flee from the wrath to come? [8]Bear fruits in keeping with repentance. And do not begin to say to yourselves, 'We have Abraham as our father.' For I tell you, God is able from these stones to raise up children for Abraham. [9]Even now the axe is laid to the root of the trees. Every tree therefore that does not bear good fruit is cut down and thrown into the fire." [10]And the crowds asked him, "What then shall we do?" [11]And he answered them, "Whoever has two tunics is to share with him who has none, and whoever has food is to do likewise." [12]Tax collectors also came to be baptized and said to him, "Teacher, what shall we do?" [13]And he said to them, "Collect no more than you are authorized to do." [14]Soldiers also asked him, "And we, what shall we do?" And he said to them, "Do not extort money from anyone by threats or by false accusation, and be content with your wages." (Lk. 3:7–14, ESV)*

They are coming out to John to be baptized, and John rebukes them saying, "Who warned you to flee from the wrath to come?" First, we must bear the fruits of repentance. What are these fruits?

>   »   Share your food and clothing with those who have none.

>   »   Collect no more taxes than what are due you.

>   »   Stop extorting money for gain and be happy with your wages.

John knew that they were not repentant. How can he know this? He knew because their management of money and resource had not changed. They had not transferred full ownership over to the Lord and become stewards. What would John say to us? Does our spending reflect the Lordship of Christ? When we see that it all belongs to the King, we will manage His money in a way that He likes. The King likes the poor, and He likes honesty and contentment.

⁵And when Jesus came to the place, he looked up and said to him, "Zacchaeus, hurry and come down, for I must stay at your house today." ⁶So he hurried and came down and received him joyfully. ⁷And when they saw it, they all grumbled, "He has gone in to be the guest of a man who is a sinner." ⁸And Zacchaeus stood and said to the Lord, "Behold, Lord, the half of my goods I give to the poor. And if I have defrauded anyone of anything, I restore it fourfold." ⁹And Jesus said to him, "Today salvation has come to this house, since he also is a son of Abraham." (Lk. 19:5–9, ESV)

He sought Jesus, and so Jesus calls out to Zacchaeus. But when he sees Jesus, he essentially says, "Lord, I will sell what I have and give back to the poor four times what is owed."

It is as if Jesus said to Zacchaeus, "You have heard me rightly," and his repentance reaches into his stewardship. The first words out of his mouth are that he is going to sell what he has, give it to the poor, and pay back what is owed.

Jesus basically says, "That guy repented." What does the word *repent* actually mean? It means to turn, to change our mindset, to take action in another direction. When I change direction, my wallet goes with me. You can't repent from your former lifestyle and not change the style in which you have stewarded money. Our spending must reflect His Lordship.

Notice that in this verse Jesus finds the type of repentance that John was looking for in Luke, chapter three. Zacchaeus saw who Jesus really was, and it demanded a change in his behavior; the first change was how he managed his money. Seeing the Lord caused a shift in Zacchaeus' thinking. He now moves forward, determined to manage his finances according to Jesus' desire and no longer by his own.

¹⁶And behold, a man came up to him, saying, "Teacher, what good deed must I do to have eternal life?" ¹⁷And he said to him, "Why do you ask me about what is good? There is only one who is good . . . ²⁰The young man said to Him . . . What do I still lack?" ²¹Jesus said to him, "If you would be perfect, go, sell what you possess and give to the poor, and you will have treasure in heaven; and come, follow me." ²²When the young man heard this he went away sorrowful, for he had great possessions. (Mt. 19:16–22, ESV)

It is difficult for a rich man to enter the kingdom. It is far more difficult for a rich man than it is for a camel to go through the eye of a needle. Why? It's hard for the rich man because He has so much more to let go of.

The rich man has to let go of his stuff to be able to enter the kingdom—there has to be a transfer of ownership. If he doesn't understand that he really isn't the owner—that he's just a manager and a steward—he won't enter into the things of the kingdom. When Jesus becomes Lord, He becomes owner. This is a conversation about a steward coming into understanding his stewardship. Who was his master, Jesus or mammon?

When the rich man comes to Jesus—"What must I do to inherit . . . ?"—he is searching.

In so many words, Jesus is responding: "You are calling me good teacher, yet only God is good. So are you calling me God right now? Well then, sell all you own and give it to the poor." But the Bible tells us that he went away sad because he was a rich man.

This passage also tells us that he wasn't looking at Jesus as Lord. If he had been, he would have been willing to obey. When God asks *me* to let go, am I able to? Is it possible to acknowledge Jesus as Lord, but to let "master mammon" win in some situations? Is there a scenario that we could call *limited lordship*?

The man was searching for something. The text is not clear as to the man's thoughts about Jesus, whether He was the Lord or just a great teacher, but what we know for sure is that the man was aware of his need. He approaches Jesus hoping to find an answer to his questions, but is unable to receive Jesus' instructions. His revelation and understanding of Jesus did not provoke real change in behavior—not real repentance. Seeing Jesus as He really is will always lead to a change in lifestyle, behavior, and spending habits. When servants come into relationship with their master, they no longer exercise a will of their own. This man's actions indicate that for him Jesus was not Lord.

Note: Everyone must let go of their stuff, the rich and the poor alike. Now with that said, it's still possible to be fully repentant, fully let go, and be wealthy. Letting go does not necessarily equate to selling and giving away everything. Letting go means there is a full transfer of ownership; we become stewards, and we will faithfully obey everything Jesus asks us to do.

The kingdom and stewardship

Without question, the main message of Jesus' ministry is that of the kingdom of God.

> *14Now after John was put in prison, Jesus came to Galilee, preaching the gospel of the kingdom of God, 15and saying, "The time is fulfilled, and the kingdom of God is at hand. Repent, and believe in the gospel." (Mk. 1:14–15)*

> *23And Jesus went about all Galilee, teaching in their synagogues, preaching the gospel of the kingdom, and healing all kinds of sickness and all kinds of disease among the people. (Mt. 4:23)*

> *19The LORD has established His throne in heaven, and His kingdom rules over all. (Ps. 103:19)*

God sits on a real throne. Throne implies a kingdom, and a kingdom implies government. By this verse kingdom could, *in very simple terms*, be understood as the place where God rules or reigns. There would be no doubt that God founded His rule and reign in the earthly life of Jesus.

> *28"But if I cast out demons by the Spirit of God, surely the kingdom of God has come upon you." (Mt. 12:28)*

Not just in the above verse but also in all that He did, Jesus demonstrated the presence of a kingdom. When He moved in power, it was in the power of that kingdom. When He taught, it was about the kingdom or some aspect of it. All of Jesus' life was one of a steward, and that stewardship included the present and coming kingdom.

Jesus taught about the kingdom in a very direct way, often through parables. Church history is full of different understandings of these parables, trying to grasp the point(s) of them and their meanings. I think in recent years the Church has started to return to an understanding of parables that Jesus intended. *They are stories that not only teach, but they are a call to action for the hearer.*

When talking about stewardship, Jesus would do it in the form of a parable. It is a great and helpful teaching method for this particular subject. Many parables are real life stories with real people and places that He used to communicate a kingdom truth. This is a picture of stewardship itself—real people in a real kingdom. Even though all of Jesus' teachings touched the topic of the kingdom in some way, and therefore stewardship, we are going to look closely at the parables that deal more directly with stewardship.

Don't get tripped up on Jesus' teaching of parables: here are some things to keep in mind when looking at them.

First, Jesus rarely speaks in parables through allegory. Allegory is a poor method for understanding parables, because there isn't a standard plumb line and you can end up with a hundred different interpretations.

Second, Jesus often covers multiple things in His parables. Sometimes He is making one point and at other times there are two. On a rare occasion the parable is making three points. Most of Jesus' parables make one and occasionally two points.

Third, Jesus is often quite literal about the point that He is making in the parable, although He might use a story or a little allegory to communicate the parable. The point He is making is not a mystery.

Jesus is engaged in a conversation with real people in a real situation. Something is taking place in that circle that provokes Jesus to share the parable, which means there is a specific reason why Jesus is sharing what He is sharing. The context in which Jesus introduces the parable is the key to understanding His meaning.

> [44]*"Again, the kingdom of heaven is like treasure hidden in a field, which a man found and hid; and for joy over it he goes and sells all that he has and buys that field.* [45]*Again, the kingdom of heaven is like a merchant seeking beautiful pearls,* [46]*who, when he had found one pearl of great price, went and sold all that he had and bought it." (Mt. 13:44–46)*

Both of these parables have a measure of risk, and both of them have great joy. Both are about the kingdom of God. In the first one we have a man working in a field who runs across something buried, possibly uncovered to some degree. This was not an uncommon situation; hiding treasure in a field was done often.

In a day when there was no central banking system, you were forced to find some other way to protect your wealth. Often if a land was about to be invaded, a man would take all of his wealth, place it in clay jars, and bury it in a field. Sometimes a household servant would be asked to bury his landlord's wealth. In some situations, the treasure would be forgotten or the landowner would die, or maybe the servant would die or be captured by an invading army.

Finding treasure in a field was not unheard of in Jesus' day and the burials and discoveries still continue. In this story, a man plowing the field uncovers the treasure—maybe a clay jar. He takes a look inside and sees the treasure. He leaves the field, goes and sells everything he has to come up with enough money to buy the field, and as he is selling his stuff, he carries a great joy. In Jesus' day, the law of the rabbis permitted this man to do just this.

The man knew the worth of the treasure and it made really good business sense to sell all he had. We don't know the amount of the treasure, but it could be like selling your $30,000 house and $25,000 worth of personal property to buy a field that is worth $55,000. But the field has an oil reserve in it and overnight you become a millionaire. At that point, no one regrets selling his or her house or property; in fact, you would gladly sell it to gain something of far more value.

Where the rule of the King is, you have kingdom. Having the rule of God in us and around us is priceless. When we find the treasure of the rule of God, we must be willing to sell off everything that is of far less value. This is requisite for having the treasure and His rule within us. When we really see the King, we will understand that all belongs to Him. Our degree of willingness to let go of our stuff will be an indication of how well we see the King. What we receive in return will be far greater than what we gave up. This is really a twofold lesson. First, we must be willing to give up our personal property in exchange for something of far greater value. Secondly, there is great joy in the giving up!

The parable of the pearl is a little different. Here we have a pearl merchant. He isn't a little shopkeeper, but an expert buyer and seller of pearls. While he has a considerable inventory of pearls, one day in his trading he finds the greatest pearl he has ever seen. Without hesitation, he sells every pearl he has to buy this one of great value. As far as eternal stewardship goes, the kingdom of God offers us a once-in-a-lifetime opportunity. *The call of God always creates a crisis of belief.* "Do I let go of what I have to gain something greater?" There is no comparison between the kingdom of God and the greatest earthly possession.

In Matthew 25:14–30 we have a situation where the master, or lord, is going away for a while. Before he leaves, he entrusts a considerable amount of his resources to three of his servants. The word talent should not throw us off. At this time in history, it was not a word to describe a personal skill, but a unit of weight with allotted monetary value. A talent is similar to an ounce of gold or ounce of silver. A talent of gold in that day was equal to five thousand days' wages. In this parable, as well as many other parables, Jesus is making a comparison between two people groups, those who steward and those who do not. We can glean several points from this story but I feel the main focus is on the one-talent servant. Even though he has less to lose, he refuses to risk what has been entrusted to him and he buries his talent in a field.

> [14]*"For the kingdom of heaven is like a man traveling to a far country, who called his own servants and delivered his goods to them. [15]And to one he gave five talents, to another two, and to another one, to each according to his own ability; and immediately he went on a journey. [16]Then he who had received the five talents went and traded with them, and made another five talents. [17]And likewise he who had received two gained two more also. [18]But he who had received one went and dug in the ground, and hid his lord's money."* (Mt. 25:14–18)

The real turning point in this story is verse 19:

> [19]*"After a long time the lord of those servants came and settled accounts with them. [20]So he who had received five talents came and brought five other talents, saying, 'Lord, you delivered to me five talents; look, I have gained five more talents besides them.' [21]His lord said to him, 'Well done, good and faithful servant; you were faithful over a few things, I will make you ruler over many things. Enter into the joy of your lord.' [22]He also who had received two talents came and said, 'Lord, you delivered to me two talents; look, I have gained two more talents besides them.' [23]His lord said to him, 'Well done, good and faithful servant; you have been faithful over a few things, I will make you ruler over many things. Enter into the joy of your lord.'"* (Mt. 25:19–23)

The servants with the five and the two talents both acted with good stewardship and doubled all that they had been given. Because of their good stewardship, they are given more to steward and can enter into the joy of their master. Faithfulness at one level opens the door to a new level of stewardship. The greatest joy of a true servant is the opportunity to serve more. Good stewardship will provide us with endless opportunities to serve.

> [24]*"Then he who had received the one talent came and said, 'Lord, I knew you to be a hard man, reaping where you have not sown, and gathering where you have not scattered seed. [25]And I was afraid, and went and hid your talent in the ground. Look, there you have what is yours.'"* (Mt. 25:24–25)

The one-talent servant is bound by fear. When he is confronted, he accuses his master. He blames his lord for hardness and lofty expectations. His lord, however, was anything but a tyrant; he actually liked to reward his servants. Fear is never an adequate excuse for poor stewardship.

> [26]*"But his lord answered and said to him, 'You wicked and lazy servant, you knew that I reap where I have not sown, and gather where I have not scattered seed. [27]So you ought to have deposited my money with the bankers, and at my coming I would have received back my own with interest. [28]So take the talent from him, and give it to him who has ten talents.'"* (Mt. 25:26–28)

The master calls him wicked and lazy because not fulfilling his stewardship is a serious matter. The master takes from him what he had given him and gives it to the one with ten. In the same way, if we will not steward what the Lord has entrusted to us, He will give it to someone else. If we are not willing to seize opportunities in stewardship, then the Lord will pass them on to someone who is willing to risk.

²⁹"'For to everyone who has, more will be given, and he will have abundance; but from him who does not have, even what he has will be taken away. ³⁰And cast the unprofitable servant into the outer darkness. There will be weeping and gnashing of teeth.'" (Mt. 25:29–30)

Stewardship will always lead to personal accountability; we all will stand before the Lord to give an account of what He has entrusted to us.

In Matthew 25:31–46 is another parable, shared on the same day as the one on the talents, possibly as back-to-back parables. The talent parable addressed the issue of managing resources to build and advance the kingdom, whereas this parable has to do with the stewardship of human treatment. In both parables we end up before a judge.

³¹"When the Son of Man comes in His glory, and all the holy angels with Him, then He will sit on the throne of His glory. ³²All the nations will be gathered before Him, and He will separate them one from another, as a shepherd divides his sheep from the goats. ³³And He will set the sheep on His right hand, but the goats on the left." (Mt. 25:31–33)

All the nations will gather before the King, and this isn't like a scene from the United Nations. All the people of the earth will be standing before the Lord. No one is excluded: all will stand before Him. In this parable there are only two people groups: sheep and goats. On the left will be the goats and on the right will stand His sheep. The message is simple: the sheep will have shown compassion toward the needy, and the goats will have not.

³⁴"Then the King will say to those on His right hand, 'Come, you blessed of My Father, inherit the kingdom prepared for you from the foundation of the world: ³⁵for I was hungry and you gave Me food; I was thirsty and you gave Me drink; I was a stranger and you took Me in; ³⁶I was naked and you clothed Me; I was sick and you visited Me; I was in prison and you came to Me.' ³⁷Then the righteous will answer Him, saying, 'Lord, when did we see You hungry and feed You, or thirsty and give You drink? ³⁸When did we see You a stranger and take You in, or naked and clothe You? ³⁹Or when did we see You sick, or in prison, and come to You?' ⁴⁰And the King will answer and say to them, 'Assuredly, I say to you, inasmuch as you did it to one of the least of these My brethren, you did it to Me.'" (Mt. 25:34–40)

In this passage Jesus introduces Himself as the Son of Man, which was how He referred Himself the most. Full of meaning from an Old Testament perspective, the title means one who is exalted by way of humiliation.

⁴¹"Then He will also say to those on the left hand, 'Depart from Me, you cursed, into the everlasting fire prepared for the devil and his angels: ⁴²for I was hungry and you gave Me no food; I was thirsty and you gave Me no drink; ⁴³I was a stranger and you did not take Me in, naked and you did not clothe Me, sick and in prison and you did not visit Me.' ⁴⁴Then they also will answer Him, saying, 'Lord, when did we see You hungry or thirsty or a stranger or naked or sick or in prison, and did not minister to You?' ⁴⁵Then He will answer them, saying, 'Assuredly, I say to you, inasmuch as you did not do it to one of the least of these, you did not do it to Me.' ⁴⁶And these will go away into everlasting punishment, but the righteous into eternal life." (Mt. 25:31–46)

Jesus makes it clear that a measure of judgment will be based on the degree of compassion shown. This is the only place in the synoptic gospels where Jesus refers to himself as King.

The righteous sheep lived life well: they made good use of opportunities that came before them, and they lived from a position of service. In short, they were good stewards of their time, treasure, bodies, and so forth. The unrighteous goats did not live life from a place of service; they did not spend their time on other people. We are left with an impression that they lived for themselves. Notice that with the sheep there are six different acts of compassionate service:

» Feeding the hungry

» Clothing the naked

» Giving water to the thirsty

» Welcoming strangers with hospitality

» Visiting the sick

» Visiting the prisoner

Good stewardship, which is living from a position of a faithful servant, will always lead to compassion toward others. In this parable, the only distinction between sheep and goats—the righteous and the unrighteous—is their stewardship decisions toward the poor and needy. Jesus was a servant of all. Notice that the good-stewarding sheep are not conscious of their good deeds.

> *[30]"A certain man went down from Jerusalem to Jericho, and fell among thieves, who stripped him of his clothing, wounded him, and departed, leaving him half dead. [31]Now by chance a certain priest came down that road. And when he saw him, he passed by on the other side. [32]Likewise a Levite, when he arrived at the place, came and looked, and passed by on the other side." (Lk. 10:30–32)*

An important point within this parable is that the two Hebrew religious people passed over the person in need. It is often taught that they passed by him because they thought him to be dead and therefore unclean. Regardless, Jesus is still making a point here as He often does with His parables.

> *[33]"But a certain Samaritan, as he journeyed, came where he was. And when he saw him, he had compassion. [34]So he went to him and bandaged his wounds, pouring on oil and wine; and he set him on his own animal, brought him to an inn, and took care of him. [35]On the next day, when he departed, he took out two denarii, gave them to the innkeeper, and said to him, 'Take care of him; and whatever more you spend, when I come again, I will repay you.' [36]So which of these three do you think was neighbor to him who fell among the thieves?" [37]And he said, "He who showed mercy on him." Then Jesus said to him, "Go and do likewise." (Lk. 10:33–37)*

Jesus always speaks of living with compassion, and this parable requires us to show compassion to those we encounter who are in need. Stewardship is often walked out in the context of human need. This is not a story about being a "good person," but about managing our time and resources for the glory of our King. It is about loving well because we were first loved. This is not just a story about how humanity should act toward one another, but a story about how we should serve our King.

What you may have been teaching and doing is not always the right thing. This parable shows us that the "good steward" might be the most unlikely person. In this situation, Jesus does not allow the philosophical questions to remove the responsibility of stewardship. He moves the hearer from a place of theory to action and from a place of theological ideas to ethical behavior.

We are likely moving in stewardship when we care for the one in front of us, even if the situation demands much. This parable requires us to show compassion to *all people all the time*, and this lesson is one that is repeated throughout the Word. Jesus is asking us to do what He has done, and we can only do it because He has done it first. We cannot allow good stewardship to die at the hands of philosophical questions.

We all love the idea of being a good Samaritan but are we willing to walk in it as far as Jesus did? Is the Christian missionary willing to show compassion and take care of the violent Muslim who thirty days ago killed his seven-year-old son and wife? If we really understand the compassion the Lord has already shown us and we are committed to living as servants, our love for Him and others will lead us into some of the most unlikely places.

Other parables

Luke 16:1–13

> ¹*He also said to His disciples: "There was a certain rich man who had a steward, and an accusation was brought to him that this man was wasting his goods. ²So he called him and said to him, 'What is this I hear about you? Give an account of your stewardship, for you can no longer be steward.'" (Lk. 16:1–3)*

Vv. 1–3 show us that there are stewards, an account must be given, and that losing our stewardship is a serious matter.

> ³*"Then the steward said within himself, 'What shall I do? For my master is taking the stewardship away from me. I cannot dig; I am ashamed to beg. ⁴I have resolved what to do, that when I am put out of the stewardship, they may receive me into their houses.'" (Lk. 16:3–4)*

V. 4 is the key to understanding this often misunderstood parable. The steward is about to act shrewdly in order to benefit himself in his future.

> ⁵ *"So he called every one of his master's debtors to him, and said to the first, 'How much do you owe my master?' ⁶And he said, 'A hundred measures of oil.' So he said to him, 'Take your bill, and sit down quickly and write fifty.' ⁷Then he said to another, 'And how much do you owe?' So he said, 'A hundred measures of wheat.' And he said to him, 'Take your bill, and write eighty.'"* (Lk. 16:5–7)

Vv. 5–7: The steward takes action and reduces the bills that debtors have with his master.

> ⁸*"So the master commended the unjust steward because he had dealt shrewdly. For the sons of this world are more shrewd in their generation than the sons of light." (Lk. 16:8)*

V. 8: He still loses his job, but the master commends him on his shrewdness, then adds that the sons of the world are more shrewd then the sons of light, implying that the sons of light should be more shrewd.

> ⁹ *"And I say to you, make friends for yourselves by unrighteous mammon, that when you fail, they may receive you into an everlasting home." (Lk. 16:9)*

V. 9: Jesus gives instruction that part of our stewardship should include using money to strengthen relations so that later we will be received into everlastings homes (dwellings).

[10]"He who is faithful in what is least is faithful also in much; and he who is unjust in what is least is unjust also in much. [11]Therefore if you have not been faithful in the unrighteous mammon, who will commit to your trust the true riches? [12]And if you have not been faithful in what is another man's, who will give you what is your own?" (Lk. 16:10–12)

Vv. 10–12: We must be faithful with everything we have been trusted with. These lessons are taught in a few other scriptures as well.

[13]"No servant can serve two masters; for either he will hate the one and love the other, or else he will be loyal to the one and despise the other. You cannot serve God and mammon." (Lk. 16:13)

V. 13: Jesus gets to the heart of the matter. We cannot serve two masters. Who is our master and whom are we serving? Our answer is not what our mind tells us, but what our actions tell us. I believe our obedience to mammon is what lies behind the widespread resistance to Christian teaching on giving and generosity. We should exercise control over the tool of money and make it work our King, versus money having control of us.

Bottom line, we're all servants and therefore stewards. We must be faith as well as shrewd, for there will be a settling of accounts.

Luke 16:19–31

[19]"There was a certain rich man who was clothed in purple and fine linen and fared sumptuously every day. [20]But there was a certain beggar named Lazarus, full of sores, who was laid at his gate, [21]desiring to be fed with the crumbs which fell from the rich man's table. Moreover the dogs came and licked his sores." (Lk. 16:19–21)

Another parable with comparison. Two men: one a man of means the other a man in need. The rich man had several opportunities to steward resources and show compassion

[22]"So it was that the beggar died, and was carried by the angels to Abraham's bosom. The rich man also died and was buried." (Lk. 16:22)

Everyone dies.

[23]"And being in torments in Hades, he lifted up his eyes and saw Abraham afar off, and Lazarus in his bosom." (Lk. 16:23)

The rich man is very aware of his torment.

[24]"Then he cried and said, 'Father Abraham, have mercy on me, and send Lazarus that he may dip the tip of his finger in water and cool my tongue; for I am tormented in this flame.'" (Lk. 16:24)

The rich man is now wanting to be served in a way that he himself refused to serve.

[25]"But Abraham said, 'Son, remember that in your lifetime you received your good things, and likewise Lazarus evil things; but now he is comforted and you are tormented. [26]And besides all this, between us and you there is a great gulf fixed, so that those who want to pass from here to you cannot, nor can those from there pass to us.'" (Lk. 16:25–26)

37

In verse 25, he is reminded that he had plenty of time to act and make wise decisions but chose not to. We must make good decisions now; there will be no options later.

> 27"Then he said, 'I beg you therefore, father, that you would send him to my father's house, 28for I have five brothers, that he may testify to them, lest they also come to this place of torment.'" (Lk. 16:27–28)

The rich man is living with regret.

> 29"Abraham said to him, 'They have Moses and the prophets; let them hear them.' 30And he said, 'No, father Abraham; but if one goes to them from the dead, they will repent.' 31But he said to him, 'If they do not hear Moses and the prophets, neither will they be persuaded though one rise from the dead.'" (Lk. 16:29–31)

New Testament pictures

The understanding of household stewards would have been clear to the people of Christ's day. Families who had financial means could have, and most likely did have, household stewards. Herod had a steward, Chuza, who was married to Joanna, who was part of the financial team that supported Jesus' ministry.

> . . . 3and Joanna, the wife of Chuza, Herod's household manager, and Susanna, and many others, who provided for them out of their means. (Lk. 8:3, ESV)

It is possible that Chuza was responsible for Herod's children.

In Matthew 20:1–16, the parable of laborers in the vineyard, a parable about the kingdom of heaven, it is the steward who at the end of the workday is distributing wages to the workers. In Luke 16:1–13 is the parable about the unjust steward. He is not a slave but a free man whose occupation is household manager. Within his job description he had freedom with his employer's resources; he could use them for his own gain but would have to give an account of his management decisions. Luke 19:12–27, the parable of the minas, Matthew 25:14–30, the parable of the talents, and Matthew 21:33–46, the parable of the wicked tenants, all teach the truth that while our Master Jesus is away we need to show love and respect by being wise and faithful stewards of all He has entrusted to us.

> 42And the Lord said, "Who then is the faithful and wise manager, whom his master will set over his household, to give them their portion of food at the proper time?" (Lk. 12:42, ESV)

A household steward's role was to faithfully manage all of his master's personal and business interest. This could have included overseeing his children, bookkeeping, paying the staff, and possibly making business decisions. Leaders, pay attention to the above verse.

Stewardship of the apostles

Paul, his co-laborers, and the other apostles regarded themselves as "stewards of the mysteries of God."

> 1This is how one should regard us, as servants of Christ and stewards of the mysteries of God. 2Moreover, it is required of stewards that they be found faithful. (1 Cor. 4:1–2, ESV)

Paul understood what he had been entrusted with, and he took great care in dispensing it according to his master's will. We see here that there is a stewardship that pertains to leadership.

⁷For an overseer, as God's steward, must be above reproach. He must not be arrogant or quick-tempered or a drunkard or violent or greedy for gain. (Titus 1:7, ESV)

Peter saw himself and all other Christians as "stewards of the manifold grace of God."

⁸Above all, keep loving one another earnestly, since love covers a multitude of sins. ⁹Show hospitality to one another without grumbling. ¹⁰As each has received a gift, use it to serve one another, as good stewards of God's varied grace: ¹¹whoever speaks, as one who speaks oracles of God; whoever serves, as one who serves by the strength that God supplies—in order that in everything God may be glorified through Jesus Christ. To him belong glory and dominion forever and ever. Amen. (1 Pet. 4:8–11, ESV)

Jesus taught about thirty-eight parables; sixteen of them speak of stewardship and of those, eleven point to the judgment seat. This means that what we do with our resources, giftings, assignments, and relationships will be the basis of our conversation at the judgment seat.

When we say faithful stewardship it doesn't mean we won't have anything. But first, we have to let go of it all and make the transfer of ownership. We will not fall into poverty when we live with an open hand before Jesus, our open-handed King.

God used a human being to bring about global redemption, and He continues to use humans to further this message. He used bread, salt, gifting, and houses—and He continues to use them through us. God advances His kingdom through us, the very kingdom that Jesus proclaimed.

As servants of our great Creator God and Redeemer, we all have a stewardship. This stewardship is our privilege and highest honor. The stewardship that we have been entrusted with is the basis of our conversation with the Lord at the judgment seat of Christ. Our decisions matter! Our stewardship is not optional! Good stewardship cannot be determined by a percentage or a formula, it can only be found when we walk in a close, personal relationship with our Master. As good stewards, we must give great care to carrying out the daily duties that our King and His gospel ask of us. If we really see Jesus as He is, stewardship will be of the highest concern

Additional teaching of Jesus on stewardship

Jesus used parables that emphasized each individual's accountability. See Luke 19:12–27 for the story of the *minas*, which Jesus concludes this way:

⁴⁸"But he who did not know, yet committed things deserving of stripes, shall be beaten with few. For everyone to whom much is given, from him much will be required; and to whom much has been committed, of him they will ask the more." (Lk. 12:48)

The apostles continued this teaching

So then each of us shall give account of himself to God. (Rom. 14:12)

⁴In regard to these, they think it strange that you do not run with them in the same flood of dissipation, speaking evil of you. ⁵They will give an account to Him who is ready to judge the living and the dead. (1 Pet. 4:4–5)

Christians are entrusted with the stewardship of the gospel

¹Let a man so consider us, as servants of Christ and stewards of the mysteries of God. ²Moreover it is required in stewards that one be found faithful. (1 Cor. 4:1–2)

¹⁷For if I do this willingly, I have a reward; but if against my will, I have been entrusted with a stewardship. (1 Cor. 9:17)

¹⁹God was in Christ reconciling the world to Himself, not imputing their trespasses to them, and has committed to us the word of reconciliation. ²⁰Now then, we are ambassadors for Christ, as though God were pleading through us: we implore you on Christ's behalf, be reconciled to God. ²¹For He made Him who knew no sin to be sin for us, that we might become the righteousness of God in Him. (2 Cor. 5:19–21)

¹⁵But when it pleased God, who separated me from my mother's womb and called me through His grace, ¹⁶to reveal His Son in me, that I might preach Him among the Gentiles, I did not immediately confer with flesh and blood. (Gal. 1:15–16)

⁷But on the contrary, when they saw that the gospel for the uncircumcised had been committed to me, as the gospel for the circumcised was to Peter . . . (Gal. 2:7)

⁴But as we have been approved by God to be entrusted with the gospel, even so we speak, not as pleasing men, but God who tests our hearts. (1 Thes. 2:4)

. . . ¹¹according to the glorious gospel of the blessed God which was committed to my trust. (1 Tim. 1:11)

²⁰O Timothy! Guard what was committed to your trust, avoiding the profane and idle babblings and contradictions of what is falsely called knowledge. (1 Tim. 6:20)

¹⁴That good thing which was committed to you, keep by the Holy Spirit who dwells in us. (2 Tim. 1:14)

. . . ³but has in due time manifested His word through preaching, which was committed to me according to the commandment of God our Savior. . . ⁷For a bishop must be blameless, as a steward of God, not self-willed, not quick-tempered, not given to wine, not violent, not greedy for money. (Titus 1:3, 7)

We are to use our gifts in order to benefit others.

¹⁰As each one has received a gift, minister it to one another, as good stewards of the manifold grace of God. ¹¹If anyone speaks, let him speak as the oracles of God. If anyone ministers, let him do it as with the ability which God supplies, that in all things God may be glorified through Jesus Christ, to whom belong the glory and the dominion forever and ever. Amen. (1 Pet. 4:10–11)

We are to develop our gifts.

¹⁴Do not neglect the gift that is in you, which was given to you by prophecy with the laying on of the hands of the eldership. ¹⁵Meditate on these things; give yourself entirely to them, that your progress may be evident to all. (1 Tim. 4:14–15)

We are to care for our bodies.

18Flee sexual immorality. Every sin that a man does is outside the body, but he who commits sexual immorality sins against his own body. 19Or do you not know that your body is the temple of the Holy Spirit who is in you, whom you have from God, and you are not your own? 20For you were bought at a price; therefore glorify God in your body and in your spirit, which are God's. (1 Cor. 6:18–20)

We must remember where our prosperity comes from and why.

17"You say in your heart, 'My power and the might of my hand have gained me this wealth.' 18And you shall remember the Lord your God, for it is He who gives you power to get wealth, that He may establish His covenant which He swore to your fathers, as it is this day." (Deut. 8:17–18)

Jesus' teaching on sharing possessions

22So when Jesus heard these things, He said to him, "You still lack one thing. Sell all that you have and distribute to the poor, and you will have treasure in heaven; and come, follow Me." (Lk. 18:22)

1"Take heed that you do not do your charitable deeds before men, to be seen by them. Otherwise you have no reward from your Father in heaven. 2Therefore, when you do a charitable deed, do not sound a trumpet before you as the hypocrites do in the synagogues and in the streets, that they may have glory from men. Assuredly, I say to you, they have their reward. 3But when you do a charitable deed, do not let your left hand know what your right hand is doing, 4that your charitable deed may be in secret; and your Father who sees in secret will Himself reward you openly." (Mt. 6:1–4)

38"Give, and it will be given to you: good measure, pressed down, shaken together, and running over will be put into your bosom. For with the same measure that you use, it will be measured back to you." (Lk. 6:38)

1And He looked up and saw the rich putting their gifts into the treasury, 2and He saw also a certain poor widow putting in two mites. 3So He said, "Truly I say to you that this poor widow has put in more than all; for all these out of their abundance have put in offerings for God, but she out of her poverty put in all the livelihood that she had." (Lk. 21:1–4)

35"I have shown you in every way, by laboring like this, that you must support the weak. And remember the words of the Lord Jesus, that He said, 'It is more blessed to give than to receive.'" (Acts 20:35)

Sharing of possessions in the early church

32Now the multitude of those who believed were of one heart and one soul; neither did anyone say that any of the things he possessed was his own, but they had all things in common. 33And with great power the apostles gave witness to the resurrection of the Lord Jesus. And great grace was upon them all. 34Nor was there anyone among them who lacked; for all who were possessors of lands or houses sold them, and brought the proceeds of the things that were sold, 35and laid them at the apostles' feet; and they distributed to each as anyone had need. (Acts 4:32–35)

¹Brethren, we make known to you the grace of God bestowed on the churches of Macedonia: ²that in a great trial of affliction the abundance of their joy and their deep poverty abounded in the riches of their liberality. ³ . . . According to their ability, yes, and beyond their ability, they were freely willing, ⁴imploring us with much urgency that we would receive the gift and the fellowship of the ministering to the saints. ⁵ . . . They first gave themselves to the Lord, and then to us by the will of God. (2 Cor. 8:1–5)

The apostle Paul's teaching on sharing possessions

³⁵"I have shown you in every way, by laboring like this, that you must support the weak. And remember the words of the Lord Jesus, that He said, 'It is more blessed to give than to receive.'" (Acts 20:35)

⁶But this I say: He who sows sparingly will also reap sparingly, and he who sows bountifully will also reap bountifully. ⁷So let each one give as he purposes in his heart, not grudgingly or of necessity; for God loves a cheerful giver. ⁸And God is able to make all grace abound toward you, that you, always having all sufficiency in all things, may have an abundance for every good work. ⁹As it is written: "He has dispersed abroad, he has given to the poor; his righteousness endures forever." ¹⁰Now may He who supplies seed to the sower, and bread for food, supply and multiply the seed you have sown and increase the fruits of your righteousness, ¹¹while you are enriched in everything for all liberality, which causes thanksgiving through us to God. (2 Cor. 9:6–11)

Summary

1. *Stewardship in the New Testament is simply a continued conversation from the Old Testament.*

2. *Because of the price Jesus paid for our redemption, our response must be to live as righteous stewards before Him.*

3. *Our stewardship in a reflection of His lordship.*

4. *Good stewardship will always lead to compassion for others.*

5. *Biblical stewardship leads us beyond philosophical speculation and into direct action.*

6. *Our conversation with Jesus at His judgment seat will be about our stewardship.*

7. *Successful stewardship is rewarded with greater stewardship opportunities.*

Please complete the following homework assignment:

Homework #3: Stewardship

Old Testament Study

[handwritten: TRUTH REPEATEDLY → mindset starts to change!]

Overview: Throughout the pages of the Old Testament, a pattern emerges of how various leaders raised the funds needed to fulfill a God-given mandate, as well as a model for the first full-time, occupational ministers. During this session we will discuss 1) the biblical pattern for building a partnership team, 2) that God considers worship and intercession real work, and 3) the first occasion that God commands an offering to be taken. Our intention is to give you confidence from the Scriptures that team ministry is an age-old pattern of God.

IMPORTANT NOTE: We are trying to look at the Bible as a whole and see what the Lord has done throughout biblical history in the area of funding His workers and advancing His purposes. We want to know what the Bible says about offerings, ministry support, building budgets, etc. We may look at some verses that do not directly pertain to ministry support, yet reflect an important truth. We are not trying to "prove our case," but want to know what the Word of God says and operate within the freedom and boundaries Scripture gives us.

> *There is no confidence like biblical confidence.*

Tabernacle, temples, and workers

> ¹*Then the LORD spoke to Moses, saying:* ²*"Speak to the children of Israel, that they bring Me an offering. From everyone who gives it willingly with his heart you shall take My offering." (Ex. 25:1–2)*

> ⁴*And Moses spoke to all the congregation of the children of Israel, saying, "This is the thing which the LORD commanded, saying:* ⁵*"Take from among you an offering to the LORD. Whoever is of a willing heart, let him bring it as an offering to the LORD: gold, silver, and bronze.'" (Ex. 35:4–5)*

In Exodus 25, God commanded the Israelites to bring Him an offering to build a tabernacle where He would dwell among them. Therefore, Israel brought the first corporate offering ever given to God, which was dedicated to building the tabernacle, where the Levites would minister to the Lord (Ex. 35:21–29).

> ²¹*Then everyone came whose heart was stirred, and everyone whose spirit was willing, and they brought the LORD's offering for the work of the tabernacle of meeting, for all its service, and for the holy garments.* ²²*They came, both men and women, as many as had a willing heart. (Ex. 35:21–22)*

Moses shared the vision God had given him and the people responded. *Moses shared, God stirred.*

Vision that starts with God and is shared by His servants connects with those who have ears to hear, and God will stir their hearts. When you share the vision for your ministry, many will have their hearts stirred but some will not. Don't take anything personally—not everyone will respond the way you might expect. *[handwritten: DON'T TAKE IT PERSONAL]*

> *It has always been in the heart of God to make a way for people to be fully available to Him.*

> ²¹*"Behold, I have given the children of Levi all the tithes in Israel as an inheritance in return for the work which they perform, the work of the tabernacle of meeting . . .* ²⁴*For the tithes of the*

children of Israel, which they offer up as a heave offering to the LORD, I have given to the Levites as an inheritance; therefore I have said to them, 'Among the children of Israel they shall have no inheritance.'" (Num. 18:21–24)

1.   Notice that the tithe was given by God to the Levites for the work they perform.

2.   The tithe was given as an inheritance. Other tribes had land they could pass down through the generations. The Levites passed down the priesthood and its means of provision, the tithe.

3.   The tithe is first given to God as an offering, and then God gives it to the Levites.

4.   The work of the tabernacle was real work.

5.   The tithe has always been a means of support for the Levites who worked in the tabernacle of meeting. It was their means of support and provision for all that was needed to do their job.

There was provision even for the non-Levite

⁶And he said to him, "Look now, there is in this city a man of God, and he is an honorable man; all that he says surely comes to pass. So let us go there; perhaps he can show us the way that we should go." ⁷Then Saul said to his servant, "But look, if we go, what shall we bring the man? For the bread in our vessels is all gone, and there is no present to bring to the man of God. What do we have?" ⁸And the servant answered Saul again and said, "Look, I have here at hand one-fourth of a shekel of silver. I will give that to the man of God, to tell us our way." ⁹(Formerly in Israel, when a man went to inquire of God, he spoke thus: "Come, let us go to the seer"; for he who is now called a prophet was formerly called a seer.) ¹⁰Then Saul said to his servant, "Well said; come, let us go." So they went to the city where the man of God was. (1 Sam. 9:6–10)

> *The first time God commands an offering to be taken was for the place where the Levite would minister unto the Lord and for the building of a place where God would dwell among them.*

⁸Now it happened one day that Elisha went to Shunem, where there was a notable woman, and she persuaded him to eat some food. So it was, as often as he passed by, he would turn in there to eat some food. ⁹And she said to her husband, "Look now, I know that this is a holy man of God, who passes by us regularly. ¹⁰Please, let us make a small upper room on the wall; and let us put a bed for him there, and a table and a chair and a lampstand; so it will be, whenever he comes to us, he can turn in there." ¹¹And it happened one day that he came there, and he turned in to the upper room and lay down there. (2 Kgs. 4:8–11)

How do you think it came about that Israel would support the prophets, even though they were not commanded by the Law to do so? It's obviously worked into their culture; they would not go unless they had a gift. Why? Where did this custom come from? Why would they want to take a gift to the prophet?

David had it in his heart to build a house of rest (1 Chr. 28–29)

Read both chapters to better understand the context. Listed below are the highlights.

David has something he wants to share and so he gathers all his leaders together to share it with them.

¹Now David assembled at Jerusalem all the leaders of Israel: the officers . . . captains over thousands and . . . over hundreds . . . and the stewards over all the substance and possessions . . . with the officials, the valiant men, and all the mighty men of valor. (1 Chr. 28:1)

David shares with them what he has in his heart.

²Then King David rose to his feet and said, "Hear me, my brethren and my people: I had it in my heart to build a house of rest for the ark of the covenant of the LORD, and for the footstool of our God, and had made preparations to build it." (1 Chr. 28:2)

> *David was carrying something in his heart, and he gathered the people together to hear his vision.*

✳ David had done considerable prep work before he ever shared this vision.

¹¹Then David gave his son Solomon the plans for the vestibule, its houses, its treasuries, its upper chambers, its inner chambers, and the place of the mercy seat; ¹²and the plans for all that he had by the Spirit, of the courts of the house of the LORD, of all the chambers all around, of the treasuries of the house of God, and of the treasuries for the dedicated things; ¹³also for the division of the priests and the Levites, for all the work of the service of the house of the LORD, and for all the articles of service in the house of the LORD. (1 Chr. 28:11–13)

1. Notice that David gathered together the leaders, not all the men of Israel.

2. David is not working under the direct order of God but rather a deep desire that he had carried for years.

3. In David's deep desire the Holy Spirit gave him detailed blueprints.

David is inviting these men into his vision and asks them to help him; they all do so willingly.

¹Furthermore King David said to all the assembly: "My son Solomon, whom alone God has chosen, is young and inexperienced; and the work is great, because the temple is not for man but for the LORD God. ²Now for the house of my God I have prepared with all my might: gold for things to be made of gold, silver for things of silver, bronze for things of bronze, iron for things of iron, wood for things of wood, onyx stones, stones to be set, glistening stones of various colors, all kinds of precious stones, and marble slabs in abundance." (1 Chr. 29:1–2)

David made plans, carried them out, and prepared for the job with all his might. What does it look like for a king to prepare with all his might?

³"Moreover, because I have set my affection on the house of my God, I have given to the house of my God, over and above all that I have prepared for the holy house, my own special treasure of gold and silver: ⁴three thousand talents of gold, of the gold of Ophir, and seven thousand talents of refined silver, to overlay the walls of the houses; ⁵the gold for things of gold and the silver for things of silver, and for all kinds of work to be done by the hands of craftsmen. Who then is willing to consecrate himself this day to the LORD?" (1 Chr. 29:3–5)

David gave vast amounts of gold out of his own private treasure.

We gather it, what God has already provided!

⁵Who then is willing to consecrate himself this day to the Lord?" ⁶Then the leaders of the fathers' houses, leaders of the tribes of Israel, the captains of thousands and of hundreds, with the officers over the king's work, offered willingly. ⁷They gave for the work of the house of God five thousand talents and ten thousand darics of gold, ten thousand talents of silver, eighteen thousand talents of bronze, and one hundred thousand talents of iron. ⁸And whoever had precious stones gave them to the treasury of the house of the Lord, into the hand of Jehiel the Gershonite. (1 Chr. 29:5–8)

David clearly states his desire and plans and asked the men to commit to it as well. David asks and calls it a consecration. The men respond willingly and extravagantly.

⁹Then the people rejoiced, for they had offered willingly, because with a loyal heart they had offered willingly to the Lord; and King David also rejoiced greatly. (1 Chr. 29:9)

The men rejoiced and gave extravagantly. David is rejoicing over their willingness to give.

¹²"Both riches and honor come from You, and You reign over all. In Your hand is power and might; in Your hand it is to make great and to give strength to all." (1 Chr. 29:12)

¹⁴"But who am I, and who are my people, that we should be able to offer so willingly as this? For all things come from You, and of Your own we have given You." (1 Chr. 29:14)

¹⁶"O Lord our God, all this abundance that we have prepared to build You a house for Your holy name is from Your hand, and is all Your own." (1 Chr. 29:16)

¹⁷"I know also, my God, that You test the heart and have pleasure in uprightness. As for me, in the uprightness of my heart I have willingly offered all these things; and now with joy I have seen Your people, who are present here to offer willingly to You." (1 Chr. 29:17)

Cyrus and the building of the second temple (Ezra 1:1–11)

¹In the first year of Cyrus king of Persia, that the word of the Lord by the mouth of Jeremiah might be fulfilled, the Lord stirred up the spirit of Cyrus king of Persia, so that he made a proclamation throughout all his kingdom, and also put it in writing. (Ezra 1:1, ESV)

To fulfill a prophecy and to get the temple built, God stirred the heart of a non-believing king.

²Thus says Cyrus king of Persia: The Lord, the God of heaven, has given me all the kingdoms of the earth, and he has charged me to build him a house at Jerusalem, which is in Judah. (Ezra 1:2, ESV)

In verse 2, Cyrus uses the word *charged*. He definitely felt he had a responsibility to build the temple.

³Whoever is among you of all his people, may his God be with him, and let him go up to Jerusalem, which is in Judah, and rebuild the house of the Lord, the God of Israel—he is the God who is in Jerusalem. ⁴And let each survivor, in whatever place he sojourns, be assisted by the men of his place with silver and gold, with goods and with beasts, besides freewill offerings for the house of God that is in Jerusalem. (Ezra 1:3–4, ESV)

Cyrus' first declaration is to build the temple, and his second is for financing the building of the temple. We see God's order: *calling, vision, assignment first, and financing second.*

We see this process with Moses and David as well. God gives them a vision, or speaks to them in some fashion, and the next step immediately following is how to finance the assignment.

Notice in Cyrus' "building the temple" he requires Israel to share with each other: to give to those who are going to build and do the work in the temple.

Notice that their support is in addition to "freewill offerings" (v. 4). I believe this to mean that in restoring the temple there would also be a restoration of the priesthood as well as the tithe system with freewill offerings. The support Cyrus was requiring was in addition to, and not a replacement of, the tithes and offerings.

> *⁵Then rose up the heads of the fathers' houses of Judah and Benjamin, and the priests and the Levites, everyone whose spirit God had stirred to go up to rebuild the house of the Lord that is in Jerusalem. ⁶And all who were about them aided them with vessels of silver, with gold, with goods, with beasts, and with costly wares, besides all that was freely offered. (Ezra 1:5–6, ESV)*

Notice that it is God who is doing all the stirring: first stirring Cyrus to build the temple and make declarations, then secondly stirring Israel to go (v. 3).

> *⁷Cyrus the king also brought out the vessels of the house of the Lord that Nebuchadnezzar had carried away from Jerusalem and placed in the house of his gods. ⁸Cyrus king of Persia brought these out in the charge of Mithredath the treasurer, who counted them out to Sheshbazzar the prince of Judah. (Ezra 1:7–8, ESV)*

In cooperating with the building of the temple, Cyrus returns all the articles and vessels that Nebuchadnezzar had carried away from Jerusalem. They were needed for restoring all the sacrificial offerings in the temple.

Later in Ezra: Under a different king

> *³In the first year of Cyrus the king, Cyrus the king issued a decree: Concerning the house of God at Jerusalem, let the house be rebuilt, the place where sacrifices were offered, and let its foundations be retained. Its height shall be sixty cubits and its breadth sixty cubits, ⁴with three layers of great stones and one layer of timber. Let the cost be paid from the royal treasury . . . ⁸Moreover, I make a decree regarding what you shall do for these elders of the Jews for the rebuilding of this house of God. The cost is to be paid to these men in full and without delay from the royal revenue, the tribute of the province from Beyond the River. ⁹And whatever is needed—bulls, rams, or sheep for burnt offerings to the God of heaven, wheat, salt, wine, or oil, as the priests at Jerusalem require—let that be given to them day by day without fail. (Ezra 6:3–4; 8–9, ESV)*

Summary

» *God stirred the heart of Cyrus. Cyrus responded by saying yes to building the temple and commissioning the project.*

» *He called upon the neighbors and friends of those who were going to help them by sharing their gold, silver, cattle, etc., in addition to freewill offerings.*

» *Cyrus returned all the temple articles that had previously been stolen.*

» *Lastly, if we look at the larger context, especially chapter 6, it appears that Cyrus also set up a portion of public tax money to be sent toward the building project.*

» *All this was later enforced by the subsequent king, Darius.*

Nehemiah wants to rebuild Jerusalem and the temple

Nehemiah hears about the ruins of destruction in Jerusalem and becomes depressed. He responds to his captor king's inquiry about Jerusalem.

> *⁴Then the king said to me, "What do you request?" So I prayed to the God of heaven. ⁵And I said to the king, "If it pleases the king, and if your servant has found favor in your sight, I ask that you send me to Judah, to the city of my fathers' tombs, that I may rebuild it." ⁶Then the king said to me (the queen also sitting beside him), "How long will your journey be? And when will you return?" So it pleased the king to send me; and I set him a time. (Neh. 2:4–6)*

Nehemiah asks for further help:

> *⁷Furthermore I said to the king, "If it pleases the king, let letters be given to me for the governors of the region beyond the River, that they must permit me to pass through till I come to Judah, ⁸and a letter to Asaph the keeper of the king's forest, that he must give me timber to make beams for the gates of the citadel which pertains to the temple, for the city wall, and for the house that I will occupy." (Neh. 2:7–8)*

Nehemiah 3: describes the work and part each person played in the rebuilding.

Nehemiah 4: opposition comes against the rebuilding; Nehemiah prays and keeps on working with his sword in hand.

Nehemiah 5: he listens to the poor and rebukes the leaders for taking their fields. The work continues.

Nehemiah 6: threats of conspiracy against Nehemiah come.

> *¹⁰Now when I went into the house of Shemaiah the son of Delaiah, son of Mehetabel, who was confined to his home, he said, "Let us meet together in the house of God, within the temple. Let us close the doors of the temple, for they are coming to kill you. They are coming to kill you by night." . . . ¹⁹And Tobiah sent letters to make me afraid. (Neh. 6:10, 19, ESV)*

Nehemiah 7: the work is completed.

> *¹Then it was, when the wall was built and I had hung the doors, when the gatekeepers, the singers, and the Levites had been appointed . . . (Neh. 7:1)*

Nehemiah 8: the law is read publicly and the people worship. They gain understanding and start living correctly again. They continue to read the words of the law.

Nehemiah 9: they repent, worship, and remind the Lord of His works and recall their history.

Nehemiah 10: they commit to obey God's commandments and seal a covenant.

> *³²Also we made ordinances for ourselves, to exact from ourselves yearly one-third of a shekel for the service of the house of our God . . . ³⁵And we made ordinances to bring the firstfruits of our ground and the firstfruits of all fruit of all trees, year by year, to the house of the LORD; ³⁶to bring the firstborn of our sons and our cattle, as it is written in the Law, and the firstborn of our herds and our flocks, to the house of our God, to the priests who minister in the house of our God; ³⁷to bring the*

firstfruits of our dough, our offerings, the fruit from all kinds of trees, the new wine and oil, to the priests, to the storerooms of the house of our God; and to bring the tithes of our land to the Levites, for the Levites should receive the tithes in all our farming communities. (Neh. 10:32–37)

Nehemiah 11: they resettle the area, and several move to Jerusalem.

Nehemiah 12: dedication with worship and setting the priesthood in order.

> *⁴⁴And at the same time some were appointed over the rooms of the storehouse for the offerings, the firstfruits, and the tithes, to gather into them from the fields of the cities the portions specified by the Law for the priests and Levites; for Judah rejoiced over the priests and Levites who ministered . . . ⁴⁷In the days of Zerubbabel and in the days of Nehemiah all Israel gave the portions for the singers and the gatekeepers, a portion for each day. (Neh. 12:44–47)*

> *⁴Now before this, Eliashib the priest, having authority over the storerooms of the house of our God, was allied with Tobiah. ⁵And he had prepared for him a large room, where previously they had stored the grain offerings, the frankincense, the articles, the tithes of grain, the new wine and oil, which were commanded to be given to the Levites and singers and gatekeepers, and the offerings for the priests. (Neh. 13:4–5)*

> ***"Behold, I have given the children of Levi all the tithes in Israel as an inheritance in return for the work which they perform, the <u>work</u> of the tabernacle of meeting." (Num. 18:21)***

While Nehemiah the vision caster and reformer is away, Eliashib acts inappropriately and makes a room for Tobiah in the temple.

> *⁶But during all this I was not in Jerusalem, for in the thirty-second year of Artaxerxes king of Babylon I had returned to the king. Then after certain days I obtained leave from the king, ⁷and I came to Jerusalem and discovered the evil that Eliashib had done for Tobiah, in preparing a room for him in the courts of the house of God. ⁸And it grieved me bitterly; therefore I threw all the household goods of Tobiah out of the room. ⁹Then I commanded them to cleanse the rooms; and I brought back into them the articles of the house of God, with the grain offering and the frankincense. (Neh. 13:6–9)*

Nehemiah upon his return to Jerusalem cleans house and begins to put things back in order.

> *¹⁰I also realized that the portions for the Levites had not been given them; for each of the Levites and the singers who did the work had gone back to his field. ¹¹So I contended with the rulers, and said, "Why is the house of God forsaken?" (Neh. 13:10–11)*

Notice what Nehemiah is saying, that when the workers in the Temple are not given their portion that this is the same as forsaking the House of God.

> *¹¹And I gathered them together and set them in their place. ¹²Then all Judah brought the tithe of the grain and the new wine and the oil to the storehouse. ¹³And I appointed as treasurers over the storehouse Shelemiah the priest and Zadok the scribe, and of the Levites, Pedaiah; and next to them was Hanan the son of Zaccur, the son of Mattaniah; for they were considered faithful, and their task was to distribute to their brethren. (Neh. 13:11–13)*

Verses that show the work of the temple

⁴⁸*And their brothers the Levites were appointed for all the service of the tabernacle of the house of God.* ⁴⁹*But Aaron and his sons made offerings on the altar of burnt offering and on the altar of incense for all the work of the Most Holy Place, and to make atonement for Israel, according to all that Moses the servant of God had commanded.* (1 Chr. 6:48–49, ESV)

. . .¹²*and Adaiah the son of Jeroham, son of Pashhur, son of Malchijah, and Maasai the son of Adiel, son of Jahzerah, son of Meshullam, son of Meshillemith, son of Immer;* ¹³*besides their kinsmen, heads of their fathers' houses, 1,760, mighty men for the work of the service of the house of God.* (1 Chr. 9:12–13, ESV)

¹⁹*Shallum the son of Kore, the son of Ebiasaph, the son of Korah, and his brethren, from his father's house, the Korahites, were in charge of the work of the service, gatekeepers of the tabernacle. Their fathers had been keepers of the entrance to the camp of the Lord.* (1 Chr. 9:19)

³²*And some of their brethren of the sons of the Kohathites were in charge of preparing the showbread for every Sabbath.* ³³*These are the singers, heads of the fathers' houses of the Levites, who lodged in the chambers, and were free from other duties; for they were employed in that work day and night.* (1 Chr. 9:32–33)

³⁷*So he left Asaph and his brothers there before the ark of the covenant of the LORD to minister before the ark regularly, as every day's work required.* (1 Chr. 16:37)

¹*So when David was old and full of days, he made his son Solomon king over Israel.* ²*And he gathered together all the leaders of Israel, with the priests and the Levites.* ³*Now the Levites were numbered from the age of thirty years and above; and the number of individual males was thirty-eight thousand.* ⁴*Of these, twenty-four thousand were to look after the work of the house of the LORD, six thousand were officers and judges.* (1 Chr. 23:1–4)

²⁴*These were the sons of Levi by their fathers' houses—the heads of the fathers' houses as they were counted individually by the number of their names, who did the work for the service of the house of the LORD, from the age of twenty years and above.* (1 Chr. 23:24)

. . .¹³*also for the division of the priests and the Levites, for all the work of the service of the house of the LORD, and for all the articles of service in the house of the LORD.* (1 Chr. 28:13)

Summary

1. *The first offering that God commanded to be taken was for the tabernacle and the priesthood.*

2. *When God's vision is shared, He stirs hearts.*

3. *The biblical fourfold model of partnership includes receiving a vision, gathering the people, sharing the vision, and inviting others to be a part of the vision.*

4. *Moses, David, and Nehemiah incorporated God's fourfold model into their assignment.*

5. *In the Scriptures God calls worship and intercession work.*

Please complete the following homework assignment:

Homework #4: Old Testament Study

New Testament Study

Overview: What God has done in the Old Testament He continues to do in the New. God began a pattern for funding workers that carries right on through the New Testament and gives us a model for today. In this session we will discuss the numerous instances of partnership and its spiritual fruit, focusing in on Paul's relationship with his partners. The goal of this teaching is to show that there is a significant culture of partnership in the New Testament.

New Testament perspective of laboring—with partnership

The New Testament is a continuation of the unfolding story of the restoration of all things. God stewards His own purpose through the voluntary agreement of His people. His approach is the same; the giving of the saints is His preferred way of advancing His kingdom. Stewardship and partnership are natural byproducts when the family of God walks in spiritual health.

> *¹Soon afterward he went on through cities and villages, proclaiming and bringing the good news of the kingdom of God. And the twelve were with him, ²and also some women who had been healed of evil spirits and infirmities: Mary, called Magdalene, from whom seven demons had gone out, ³and Joanna, the wife of Chuza, Herod's household manager, and Susanna, and many others, who provided for them out of their means. (Lk. 8:1–3, ESV)*

> *Notice that Jesus, –God in the flesh– put Himself in a position of being dependent on other people. Why?*

Notice that Jesus—God in the flesh—put Himself in a position of being dependent on other people. He could have supported himself through His carpenter job but He didn't. Once he left secular work Jesus never returned to it. Neither did he support himself with daily miracles. We all have a need to give, and we all have a need to receive. The Lord has fashioned His Body to be interdependent upon one another.

Paul, his ministry and funding

> *²²I also have been much hindered from coming to you. ²³But now no longer having a place in these parts, and having a great desire these many years to come to you, ²⁴whenever I journey to Spain, I shall come to you. For I hope to see you on my journey, and to be helped on my way there by you, if first I may enjoy your company for a while. (Rom. 15:22–24)*

While working for the Lord, Paul makes plans. He shares those plans clearly and then asks people to help him. In verse 24, the Greek phrase "to be helped on my way" is the word *propempo*.

Propempo (*Pro-pem-po*)

In the New Testament there is an interesting Greek word: *propempo*. The word appears nine times in eight different verses within the New Testament. When we understand this Greek word and read it in its context, we begin to see more clearly how the early church worked together to accomplish the mission of God. The following is a list of various definitions of the Greek word *propempo*.

4311. προπέμπω **prŏpĕmpō**, *prop-em´-po*; from *4253* and *3992*; to *send forward*, i.e. *escort* or *aid* in travel—accompany, bring (forward) on journey (way), conduct forth.[1]

προπέμπω **propempō**; from *4253* and *3992*; to *send before, send forth*—accompanying (1), escorted (1), help (1), helped on my journey (1), helped on my way (1), journey (1), send . . . on his way (1), send . . . on my way (1), send . . . on their way (2), way (1).[2]

προπέμπω [*propempo* /prop·em·po/] v. From *4253* and *3992*; GK *4636*; Nine occurrences; AV translates as "bring on (one's) way" four times, "bring (forward) on (one's) journey" three times, "conduct forth" once, and "accompany" once. **1** to send before. **2** to send forward, bring on the way, accompany or escort. **3** to set one forward, fit him out with the requisites for a journey.[3]

In Acts 15:3 after the council met to discuss the situation about circumcision, they decided to send Paul and Barnabas up to Jerusalem. The phrase *sent on their way by the church* is the translation of propempo and here it means to send forward, aid in travel, help for the journey.

> *Paul clearly asks the Romans to help him with his assignment.*

In Acts 20:38 Paul was leaving Ephesus, and he told the church that he would not see them anymore. With real sadness they all knelt down together and prayed. Then they all *accompanied* him to the ship. Here the word means accompany or escort. It would have been a sad but also joyous sending, filled with moral support. It could have included money and food.

In Acts 21:3–5 Paul has been in Tyre for about a week, staying with disciples there. When it comes time to leave, the disciples with their families *accompanied* Paul to the ship. Paul had only known them a week, but you get the sense of a real loving relationship. Similar to Ephesus, they knelt down and prayed together.

In Romans 15:24 Paul is communicating that his ministry in the area is done and now he wants to travel to Spain. Paul has heard about the church in Rome and wants to pass through there as he makes his way to Spain, hoping to stay and visit with them for a while. In verse 24 the phrase *"and I hope to be helped on my way by you"* is the Greek word *propempo*. Paul is asking for assistance and possibly company on his journey.

In his *Notes on the Bible*, Albert Barnes explains this means, "To be assisted by you in regard to this journey; or to be accompanied by you. This was the custom of the churches."[4]

According to John Gill's *Exposition of the Bible*, "He not only hoped to see them, but that he should have the company of some of them along with him, in his way to Spain; from whose conversation he might expect much spiritual pleasure and refreshment; and by whom he might be directed in his way, as well as supplied with all necessaries for his journey; in which sense the phrase of bringing on in the way, is sometimes used."[5]

In First Corinthians 16, the word *propempo* is used twice. The chapter begins with Paul instructing the Corinthians to take up an offering for the church in Jerusalem. The saints there may not have been able to earn a living because of persecution. Paul then asks them to be ready to help Timothy and himself, likely also in a financial way, when they each come through the city to visit.

---

1. James Strong, *A Concise Dictionary of the Words in the Greek Testament and The Hebrew Bible* (Bellingham, WA: Logos Bible Software, 2009), s. v. "G4311."

2 Robert L .Thomas, *New American Standard Hebrew-Aramaic and Greek Dictionaries: updated edition* (Anaheim: Lockman Foundation Publications, 1998), s. v. "G4311."

3. James Strong, *Enhanced Strong's Lexicon* (Bellingham, WA: Logos Bible Software, 2001), s. v. "G4311."

4. Albert Barnes, *Notes on the Bible*, 1834, http://www.sacred-texts.com/bib/cmt/barnes/rom015.htm

5. John Gill, *Exposition of the Old and New Testament* http://sacred-texts.com/bib/cmt/gill/rom015.htm

⁶And perhaps I will stay with you, or even spend the winter, so that you may send me on my way wherever I may go . . . ¹¹So let no one despise him. But send him on his way in peace, so that he may come to me; for I expect him with the brethren. (I Cor. 16:6,11, NASB)

"So that you may send me on my way wherever I may go." The verb *propempō* is used as a technical term for supplying the travel needs of God's itinerant ministers. (1 Cor. 16:6, cf. v. 11).[6] Adam Clark's *Commentary on the Bible* interprets this phrase to mean, *"That ye may furnish me with the means of travelling.* It appears that, in most cases, the different Churches paid his expenses to other Churches."[7]

In Second Corinthians 1:16 the word *propempo* is translated into the phrase "to be brought forth." It means to aid in the journey, financial support.

Titus 3:13 is self-explanatory: "Make every effort to help Zenas the lawyer and Apollos on their way; make sure they have what they need." (NET)

From the different uses of the word *propempo* in their contexts we can see that the early church had an excellent relationship between goers and senders. The early church was a giving church. It was a missional church that was full of love and joy and did not have hang-ups about money or funding missionaries. Also, a brief study of this word *propempo* shows us that the early church felt a responsibility to work together and to each play their role to accomplish the mission of God.

Paul defends his apostleship

¹Am I not free? Have I not seen Jesus our Lord? Are you not my work in the Lord? ²If I am not an apostle to others, at least I am to you, for you are the confirming sign of my apostleship in the Lord. ³This is my defense to those who examine me. ⁴Do we not have the right to financial support? ⁵Do we not have the right to the company of a believing wife, like the other apostles and the Lord's brothers and Cephas? ⁶Or do only Barnabas and I lack the right not to work? (1 Cor. 9:1–6, NET)

» Notice in verse 3, Paul is about to give his defense.

» Paul uses the word *right* three times in verses 5, 6, and 7. Why do you think he does this? Is Paul being proud?

» In verses 4–6, Paul is drawing a contrast between two groups of people. Who are they?

Paul appeals to common sense and the law

⁷Who ever serves in the army at his own expense? Who plants a vineyard and does not eat its fruit? Who tends a flock and does not consume its milk? ⁸Am I saying these things only on the basis of common sense, or does the law not say this as well? ⁹For

> *"Do we not have the right to financial support? Do we not have the right to the company of a believing wife, like the other apostles and the Lord's brothers and Cephas? Or do only Barnabas and I lack the right not to work?" (1 Cor. 9:4–6)*

---

6. R. J. Utley, *Paul's Letters to a Troubled Church: I and II Corinthians* (Marshall, TX: Bible Lessons International, 2002), Vol. 6, p. 188.

7. Adam Clarke, *Commentary on the Bible* (1831), http://www.sacred-texts.com/bib/cmt/clarke/co1016.htm

it is written in the law of Moses, "Do not muzzle an ox while it is treading out the grain." God is not concerned here about oxen, is he? ¹⁰Or is he not surely speaking for our benefit? It was written for us, because the one plowing and threshing ought to work in hope of enjoying the harvest. ¹¹If we sowed spiritual blessings among you, is it too much to reap material things from you? (1 Cor. 9:7–11, NET)

In verse 7 Paul is comparing his apostleship to three natural examples: an army, a vineyard, and a flock. He is saying that every worker who sows or serves does so with an expectation of a return. What was Paul's *vineyard*? Who was Paul's *flock*? Was Paul serving in an *army*?

In verses 9 and 10 Paul turns to the Law and uses a verse about the care of oxen to illustrate his point. God cares about the treatment of animals that labor for man; how much more will He care about people who labor for the gospel?

In verse 12 Paul makes his point very clear.

¹²If others receive this right from you, are we not more deserving? But we have not made use of this right. Instead we endure everything so that we may not be a hindrance to the gospel of Christ. (1 Cor. 9:12, NET)

The church was supporting other workers but Paul was making it clear that he was entitled but chose not to receive their support.

¹³Don't you know that those who serve in the temple eat food from the temple, and those who serve at the altar receive a part of the offerings? (1 Cor. 9:13, NET)

Paul makes his point in verse 13 in the form of a question. He is referring to Leviticus 7:6, 8–10, 14, 28–36.

¹⁴In the same way the Lord commanded those who proclaim the gospel to receive their living by the gospel. ¹⁵But I have not used any of these rights. And I am not writing these things so that something will be done for me. In fact, it would be better for me to die than—no one will deprive me of my reason for boasting! (1 Cor. 9:14–15, NET)

In verse 14, where Paul says, "*In the same way the Lord commanded those who proclaim the gospel to receive their living by the gospel,*" he is most likely referring to Matthew 10:10 and Luke 10:7. The Greek word for command is *diatasso* (*dee-at-as-so*). It means to give detailed instruction, to command, ordain, set in order, give order, arrange, appoint.

¹⁶For if I preach the gospel, I have no reason for boasting, because I am compelled to do this. Woe to me if I do not preach the gospel! ¹⁷For if I do this voluntarily, I have a reward. But if I do it unwillingly, I am entrusted with a responsibility. ¹⁸What then is my reward? That when I preach the gospel I may offer the gospel free of charge, and so not make full use of my rights in the gospel. (1 Cor. 9:16–18, NET)

Paul is saying that his right to be supported makes sense in the natural, that it is written in the Law, that it is in the spirit of Leviticus 7, and that it is the very thing the Lord Jesus commanded.

Paul's second address to Corinth

⁵Indeed, I consider that I am not in the least inferior to these super-apostles. ⁶Even if I am unskilled in speaking, I am not so in knowledge; indeed, in every way we have made this plain to you in all things. ⁷Or did I commit a sin in humbling myself so that you might be exalted, because I preached God's gospel to you free of charge? ⁸I robbed other churches by accepting support from them in order to serve you. (2 Cor. 11:5–8, ESV)

In verse 8 Paul is probably referring to the financial partnership that he received from the brothers in Macedonia.

⁹And when I was with you and was in need, I did not burden anyone, for the brothers who came from Macedonia supplied my need. So I refrained and will refrain from burdening you in any way. ¹⁰As the truth of Christ is in me, this boasting of mine will not be silenced in the regions of Achaia. ¹¹And why? Because I do not love you? God knows I do! ¹²And what I am doing I will continue to do, in order to undermine the claim of those who would like to claim that in their boasted mission they work on the same terms as we do. (2 Cor. 11:9–12, ESV)

The reason Paul was not receiving support from the Corinthians is summed up in 2 Corinthians 11:12.

¹³For such men are false apostles, deceitful workmen, disguising themselves as apostles of Christ. ¹⁴And no wonder, for even Satan disguises himself as an angel of light. ¹⁵So it is no surprise if his servants, also, disguise themselves as servants of righteousness. Their end will correspond to their deeds. (2 Cor. 11:13–15, ESV)

Paul's reference in verses 8 and 9 is to the following:

¹After these things Paul left Athens and went to Corinth. ²And he found a Jew named Aquila, a native of Pontus, having recently come from Italy with his wife Priscilla, because Claudius had commanded all the Jews to leave Rome. He came to see them, ³and because he was of the same trade he stayed with them and they were working, for by trade they were tentmakers. ⁴And he reasoned in the synagogue every Sabbath, and trying to persuade Jews and Greeks. ⁵But when Silas and Timothy came down from Macedonia, Paul began devoting himself completely to the word, solemnly testifying to the Jews that Jesus was the Christ. (Acts 18:1–5, NASB)

Other New Testament verses that reflect supporting missionaries

⁵Dear friend, you demonstrate faithfulness by whatever you do for the brothers (even though they are strangers). ⁶They have testified to your love before the church. You will do well to send them on their way [propempo] in a manner worthy of God. ⁷For they have gone forth on behalf of "The Name," accepting nothing from the pagans. ⁸Therefore we ought to support such people, so that we become coworkers in cooperation with the truth. (3 Jn. 1:5–8, NET)

» In verse 5, John says that faithfulness is demonstrated by caring for the worker/messenger.

» You do well when you send a worker out in a manner worthy of God.

» When we support a worker/messenger, we share in the work they are doing; we co-labor with them. Where our money goes, we go. We are coming into agreement with the truth by supporting the messengers of truth.

¹⁰I have great joy in the Lord because now at last you have again expressed your concern for me. (Now I know you were concerned before but had no opportunity to do anything.) ¹¹I am not saying this because I am in need, for I have learned to be content in any circumstance. ¹²I have experienced times of need and times of abundance. In any and every circumstance I have learned the secret of contentment, whether I go satisfied or hungry, have plenty or nothing. ¹³I am able to do all things through the one who strengthens me. ¹⁴Nevertheless, you did well to share with me in my trouble. ¹⁵And as you Philippians know, at the beginning of my gospel ministry, when I left Macedonia, no church shared with me in this matter of giving and receiving except you alone. ¹⁶For even in Thessalonica on more than one occasion you sent something for my need. ¹⁷I do not say this because I am seeking a gift. Rather, I seek the credit that abounds to your account. ¹⁸For I have received everything, and I have plenty. I have all I need because I received from Epaphroditus what you sent—a fragrant offering, an acceptable sacrifice, very pleasing to God. ¹⁹And my God will supply your every need according to his glorious riches in Christ Jesus. ²⁰May glory be given to God our Father forever and ever. Amen. (Phil. 4:10–20, NET)

- »   Verse 10: Paul has joy because they have expressed love through giving.

- »   Verse 14: Paul says their giving was a job well done.

- »   Verse 15: Paul refers to the partnership (*koinōneō*) that he has had with them for years.

- »   Verse 16: Paul was supported by Philippians while in Thessalonica (one of the places where he worked with his hands).

- »   Verse 17: Paul is thinking of their benefit.

- »   Verse 18: Paul has everything he needs—plenty—because the saints gave.

Paul's relationship with the Philippians

Two verses in Philippians point toward Paul receiving support for his work in the gospel. Philippians 1:5 is speaking about relational support as well as financial support. When we see it in the context of the whole Philippians letter, I believe it lends itself toward financial support.

Koinonia

The word *koinonia* means: to share, to willingly contribute, to have fellowship, and to have close mutual association. It can also mean association, community, communion, and joint participation. Less common definitions of the word include: intimacy, a gift jointly contributed, or a collection. Below are some translations of the word *koinonia*.

> ⁵*. . . for your* fellowship *in the gospel from the first day until now. (Phil. 1:5)*

> ⁵*. . . because of your* participation *in the gospel from the first day until now. (Phil. 1:5, NET)*

> ⁵*. . . because of your* partnership *in the gospel from the first day until now. (Phil. 1:5, ESV)*

> ⁵*. . . for your* fellowship *in furtherance of the gospel from the first day until now. (Phil. 1:5, RV)*

Another use of the word *koinonia:*

³That which we have seen and heard we declare to you, that you also may have fellowship with us; and truly our fellowship is with the Father and with His Son Jesus Christ. (1 Jn. 1:3)

⁹God is faithful, by whom you were called into the fellowship of His Son, Jesus Christ our Lord. (1 Cor. 1:9)

Use of *koinonia* when translated "share" or "participation":

⁴They begged us earnestly for the privilege of participating in this ministry to the saints. (2 Cor. 8:4, ISV)

Use of *koinonia* when translated "willing contribution" or "gift":

²⁶For it pleased those from Macedonia and Achaia to make a certain contribution for the poor among the saints who are in Jerusalem. (Rom. 15:26)

¹⁵And you Philippians yourselves know that in the beginning of the gospel, when I left Macedonia, no church entered into partnership with me in giving and receiving, except you only. (Phil. 4:15, ESV)

Koinoneo: A second important word in Paul's relationship

This word is a little different in that it speaks of co-laboring, working together, teamwork, and partnership.

According to Strong's, κοινωνέω (*koinōneō*) means: to share, distribute, do together with, participate in. In eight occurrences it translates as "be partaker with" and five times as "communicate."

    i.   To come into communion or fellowship with, to become a sharer, to be made a partner.

    ii. To enter into fellowship, join one's self to an associate; make one's self a sharer or partner.[8]

¹⁵You Philippians also know that in the early days of the gospel, when I left Macedonia, no church participated with me in the matter of giving and receiving except for you. (Phil. 4:15, ISV)

Other New Testament verses

¹⁷Elders who provide effective leadership must be counted worthy of double honor, especially those who work hard in speaking and teaching. ¹⁸For the scripture says, "Do not muzzle an ox while it is treading out the grain," and, "The worker deserves his pay." (1 Tim. 5:17–18, NET)

¹³Make every effort to help Zenas the lawyer and Apollos on their way; make sure they have what they need [propempo]. ¹⁴Here is another way that our people can learn to engage in good works to meet pressing needs and so not be unfruitful. (Titus 3:13–14, NET)

Notice the language Paul uses in this passage: *make every effort* and *make sure they have what they need.*

Paul is saying that *supporting a gospel worker is a good work and therefore fruitful.*

Spiritual fruit of biblical partnership

You demonstrate faithfulness; you do well to send them on their way, become a coworker, and cooperate with the truth. (3 Jn. 1:5–8)

Partnership provides a context for *koinonia* (2 Cor. 8:4; Rom. 15:26).

Partnership allows us to credit another's spiritual account (Phil. 4:17).

Partnership enables and teaches the Body of Christ to engage in good works and bear spiritual fruit (Titus 3:14).

Paul's repentance

[12]Indeed, the signs of an apostle were performed among you with great perseverance by signs and wonders and powerful deeds. [13]For how were you treated worse than the other churches, except that I myself was not a burden to you? Forgive me this injustice! [The ASV, ESV, ISV, KJV and NKJV all say, "Forgive me of this wrong"!]

[14]Look, for the third time I am ready to come to you, and I will not be a burden to you, because I do not want your possessions, but you. For children should not have to save up for their parents, but parents for their children. [15]Now I will most gladly spend and be spent for your lives! If I love you more, am I to be loved less? (2 Cor. 12:12–15, NET)

Jesus sends out disciples

[5]Jesus sent out these twelve, instructing them [NKJV, "commanded them"] *as follows: "Do not go to Gentile regions and do not enter any Samaritan town. [6]Go instead to the lost sheep of the house of Israel. [7]As you go, preach this message: 'The kingdom of heaven is near!' [8]Heal the sick, raise the dead, cleanse lepers, cast out demons. Freely you received, freely give. [9]Do not take gold, silver, or copper in your belts, [10]no bag for the journey, or an extra tunic, or sandals or staff, for the worker deserves his provisions. [11]Whenever you enter a town or village, find out who is worthy there and stay with them until you leave." (Mt. 10:5–11, NET)*

Jesus gives a clear command. Verses 9, 10, and 11 are all part of that command. They are to leave their resources at home, travel, and when they enter a town find out who's worthy. This wasn't a command to "shoeless missions" but rather gives the sense that Jesus was not letting them use their stuff because a worker is worthy of his wage.

Jesus was saying to them, "I don't want you self-funding your assignment. You're working, and a worker deserves his pay." The reason for not taking money wasn't primarily about building super faith, although I'm sure their faith was built by the provision.

> *Jesus created a situation that forced the disciples to share their assignment with others.*

Part of the instruction was securing provision for themselves (v. 11). This was an order that can be compared to other types of ministries, like preaching the gospel of the kingdom or healing the sick (v. 7–8).

» Notice in verse 11 that the disciples are to find out where they are staying, and to do this they must ask. *Notice that verse 11 is part of the commission.*

» The provision was already there before they ever left. God always provides for the commission.

» If you are called and serving the Lord, the provision *is* there; we just do our part and find out who is worthy (v. 11). *Finding the provision that is already there is part of the assignment.*

> [3]*"Go! I am sending you out like lambs surrounded by wolves.* [4]*Do not carry a money bag, a traveler's bag, or sandals, and greet no one on the road.* [5]*Whenever you enter a house, first say, 'May peace be on this house!'* [6]*And if a peace-loving person is there, your peace will remain on him, but if not, it will return to you.* [7]*Stay in that same house, eating and drinking what they give you, for the worker deserves his pay. Do not move around from house to house.* [8]*Whenever you enter a town and the people welcome you, eat what is set before you."* (Lk. 10:3–8, NET)

In the sending of the seventy, the instructions are the same.

> [35]*And He said to them, "When I sent you without money bag, knapsack, and sandals, did you lack anything?" So they said, "Nothing."* [36]*Then He said to them, "But now, he who has a money bag, let him take it, and likewise a knapsack; and he who has no sword, let him sell his garment and buy one.* [37]*For I say to you that this which is written must still be accomplished in Me: 'And He was numbered with the transgressors.' For the things concerning Me have an end."* [38]*So they said, "Lord, look, here are two swords." And He said to them, "It is enough."* (Lk. 22:35–38)

Notice the contrast between this passage and the first assignment from Matthew 10. Jesus is contrasting the difference between the short mission He sent them on and the way life would be for them after His departure.

Jesus is not telling them they now have the responsibility of self-support, but rather they need a shift in their thinking. He is instructing them to think long term—to make provision for a longer, more dangerous mission. He is preparing them for the danger and hardship they are about to face in apostolic ministry.

Paul takes up an offering for the saints

> [1]*Now concerning the collection for the saints, as I have given orders to the churches of Galatia, so you must do also:* [2]*On the first day of the week let each one of you lay something aside, storing up as he may prosper, that there be no collections when I come.* [3]*And when I come, whomever you approve by your letters I will send to bear your gift to Jerusalem . . .* [10]*And if Timothy comes, see that he may be with you without fear; for he does the work of the Lord, as I also do.* [11]*Therefore let no one despise him. But send him on his journey in peace, that he may come to me; for I am waiting for him with the brethren.* (1 Cor. 16:1–3, 10–11)

At this point Paul is not talking about support for himself, but rather taking up an offering for the saints. But we still have something to learn from the way he does it.

> [15]*And with this confidence I intended to come to you first so that you would get a second opportunity to see us,* [16]*and through your help to go on into Macedonia and then from Macedonia to come back to you and be helped on our way into Judea by you.* [Paul may still be talking about the offering for the saints.] (2 Cor. 1:15–16, NET)

> »   Notice Paul has a pattern: vision, plan, share, and ask. (This is a good pattern—*hint!*).

> »   Paul does not hem and haw around; he comes right out and says it: *Will you help me get to Judea?*

> »   I think most of this verse is talking about the offering for the saints, but Paul also seems to include his own personal ministry.

You don't have to be a tentmaking missionary

Paul worked in tentmaking during three different seasons of his ministry: with the Thessalonians, the Corinthians, and while at Ephesus.

While in Thessalonica

> *[8]So, affectionately longing for you, we were well pleased to impart to you not only the gospel of God, but also our own lives, because you had become dear to us. [9]For you remember, brethren, our labor and toil; for laboring night and day, that we might not be a burden to any of you, we preached to you the gospel of God. (1 Thes. 2:8–9)*

I think from the verse above we can say that Paul worked with his hands while at Thessalonica.

> *[8]and we did not eat anyone's food without paying. Instead, in toil and drudgery we worked night and day in order not to burden any of you. [9]It was not because we do not have that right, but to give ourselves as an example for you to imitate. [10]For even when we were with you, we used to give you this command: "If anyone is not willing to work, neither should he eat." (2 Thes. 3:8–10, NET)*

We don't know if Paul made tents at Thessalonica or not. We do know that while at Thessalonica Paul worked with his hands and did not receive any kind of support from the young converts there.

Because of intense persecution and an overall tension, Paul stayed in Thessalonica only about six or eight weeks. This was hardly enough time to plant a church and bring them to maturity. It is possible that sufficient time had not passed for Paul to build mature relationships.

Paul was also dealing with a number of accusations that had come against him in those few weeks: two of them being that he was greedy and lazy. The Thessalonians had become quite idle themselves, and it was for all the above reasons that Paul worked with his hands.

Also, keep in mind the following verse.

> *[15]And as you Philippians know, at the beginning of my gospel ministry, when I left Macedonia, no church shared with me in this matter of giving and receiving except you alone. [16]For even in Thessalonica on more than one occasion you sent something for my need. (Phil. 4:15–16, NET)*

While he "worked with his hands" at Thessalonica, he was being supported by the church at Philippi.

While in Corinth

Paul made tents while with the Corinthians but was also supported by the church in Macedonia (2 Cor. 11:9).

> *[1]After these things Paul departed from Athens and went to Corinth. [2]And he found a certain Jew named Aquila, born in Pontus, who had recently come from Italy with his wife Priscilla (because Claudius had commanded all the Jews to depart from Rome); and he came to them. [3]So, because he was of the same trade, he stayed with them and worked; for by occupation they were tentmakers. [4]And he reasoned in the synagogue every Sabbath, and persuaded both Jews and Greeks. (Acts 18:1–4)*

Notice Paul works with his hands, and also notice he is in synagogue weekly.

[11]And he continued there a year and six months, teaching the word of God among them. (Acts 18:11)

Paul is at Corinth a year and a half.

[10]We are fools for Christ's sake, but you are wise in Christ! We are weak, but you are strong! You are distinguished, but we are dishonored! [11]To the present hour we both hunger and thirst, and we are poorly clothed, and beaten, and homeless. [12]And we labor, working with our own hands. Being reviled, we bless; being persecuted, we endure; [13]being defamed, we entreat. We have been made as the filth of the world, the off-scouring of all things until now. (1 Cor. 4:10–13)

A few other things we should know about Paul's stay at Corinth.

[9]And when I was with you and was in need, I did not burden anyone, for the brothers who came from Macedonia supplied my need. So I refrained and will refrain from burdening you in any way. (2 Cor. 11:9, ESV)

[3]Because he was of the same trade he stayed with them and worked, for they were tentmakers by trade. [4]And he reasoned in the synagogue every Sabbath, and tried to persuade Jews and Greeks. [5]When Silas and Timothy arrived from Macedonia, Paul was occupied with the word, testifying to the Jews that the Christ was Jesus. (Acts 18:3–5, ESV)

It appears that Paul started making tents while sharing in synagogues weekly, but later, when the support came from Macedonia, he gave himself to full-time ministry.

[5]But after Silas and Timothy came from Macedonia, he spent all his time preaching to the Jews about Jesus the Messiah. (Acts 18:5, CEV)

[5]But when Silas and Timothy arrived from Macedonia, Paul devoted himself entirely to the word as he emphatically assured the Jews that Jesus is the Messiah. (Acts 18:5, ISV)

Note: NIV translates this as "devoted himself exclusively"; NASB translates this as "devoting himself completely"

Paul and the Corinthians

The Wiersbe Bible Commentary says the following related to Paul's relationship with the Corinthians around the issue of support:

First, Paul shamed the Corinthians for their lack of commendation (2 Cor. 12:11–13). They should have been boasting about him instead of compelling him to boast. Instead, the Corinthians were boasting about the "super-apostles," the Judaizers, who had won their affection and were now running their church.

Was Paul inferior to these men? In no way! . . . He had cost the church nothing. Paul used his subtle irony again when he wrote, "How were you inferior to the other churches, except that I was never a burden to you? Forgive me this wrong!" (2 Cor. 12:13, NIV).

. . . It seemed that the more Paul loved them, the less they loved Paul! Why? The Bible states that they did not have a sincere love for Christ (2 Cor. 11:3). Paul was willing to "spend and expend" in order to help the church.

The Judaizers had used crafty methods in order to exploit the church (see 2 Cor. 4:2), but Paul had been open and without guile. The only "trick" Paul had played on them was his refusal to receive financial support. In this, he disarmed them so that they could never accuse him of being interested only in money. None of the associates Paul sent to them exploited them in any way or took advantage of them.[8]

[13]For how were you treated worse than the other churches, except that I myself was not a burden to you? Forgive me this injustice! (2 Cor. 12:13, NET)

Paul made tents while at Ephesus.

[31]"Therefore be alert, remembering that night and day for three years I did not stop warning each one of you with tears. [32]And now I entrust you to God and to the message of his grace. This message is able to build you up and give you an inheritance among all those who are sanctified. [33]I have desired no one's silver or gold or clothing. [34]You yourselves know that these hands of mine provided for my needs and the needs of those who were with me." (Acts 20:31–34, NET)

Is it possible that since so many were out of work, Paul chose not to receive support because of how it may have been perceived?

It is possible that there were some dynamics going on that are not recorded in the Word.

One thing we know for sure: Paul is not against receiving support. He is also not putting his tentmaking forward as the chosen model for his livelihood. Paul makes it clear that a worker is worthy of support. I feel it's safe to say that Paul made tents at Ephesus for similar reasons as before: for the sake of those he was ministering to.

Conclusion

Scripture does not require the worker to fund themselves in ministry. The priest didn't do it, Jesus didn't, and for most of Paul's ministry he didn't. Several positive biblical principles are derailed when we require ourselves and other to be self-funded "tentmakers". The more we work outside of our calling, the less we enter into the issue of giving and receiving and interdependence on one another. When we work outside of our call, we are denying our friends and family the opportunity to partner with us in ministry. There are many issues in our own hearts that can only be dealt with when we enter into that close relationship of interdependence.

For some, tentmaking is the open door for ministry in closed countries. They use their job as their place of missionary service. I say, "yes and amen" to them!

Most of what I have heard taught and what I have read in regards to tentmaking, however, is not rooted in biblical principles, but is rooted in tradition, opinion, ignorance, or some powerful strongholds about finances.

> *Out of 30+ years of ministry, we only have record that Paul made tents for about 4.5 years. And he was supported by other churches while he did it.*

---

8. James Strong, *A Concise Dictionary of the Words in the Greek Testament and The Hebrew Bible* (Bellingham, WA: Logos Bible Software, 2009), s. v. "G2841."

Please don't misunderstand me: I do believe there is a place and time for tentmaking. Sometimes the situation requires it, and in many cases it is the wisest way to get the gospel to people. But it has been my experience that many are making tents unnecessarily or for the wrong reasons.

Many may think that tentmaking is their only option. If this is you, I would encourage you to seek the Lord wholeheartedly on this issue. *If you are called to full-time ministry, believe that a worker is worthy of his wages and that God has a support team for you!* WOW & AMEN!

Something to remember as we begin to develop our partnership teams is this: we are not missionaries looking for a charitable handout; neither are we seeking to build up our economic strength or personal comfort. We are gospel workers in partnership with God's global mission. There is kingdom work that will not get done and will not continue if we are not there to do it. We will not be able to fully give ourselves to the work if we are not supported and made available. The prayer and worship movement—along with any other area of missions—will only be as strong as it has fully available and fully funded people.

Summary

1. *Jesus had a partnership team.*

2. *Paul made requests for financial partnership and celebrated the gifts he received.*

3. *Out of a 30-plus year ministry, Paul made tents for around 4.5 years and was being supported financially while he did it.*

4. *The primary model in Scripture for funding workers is giving that comes from the Body of Christ.*

5. *Paul experienced a high level of relationship with His partnership team.*

6. *The fruit of partnership includes faithfulness, co-laboring with others, and credit to our spiritual account, good works, and spiritual fruit.*

Please complete the following homework assignment:

Homework #5: New Testament Study

Biblical Faith

Overview: Our perspective and attitude of how the Lord supports His workers must withstand the test of Scripture. We want to move forward in our ministry with a confidence that comes from the written Word of God. Is "by faith alone"—that is, "just believe and go, and the money will find you"—the model of Scripture? What is biblical faith and what role does it have for the full-time worker?

Missions by faith

Historically in missions circles it has not been uncommon to hear the phrase "by faith alone." When this was spoken by a missionary, it generally meant that they did not have financial resources and were not planning on asking anyone for financial support. With the idea that God knows my needs, I don't need to tell anyone but simply trust God to take care of my needs.

This by-faith-alone model has been around for about two hundred years. It has ebbed and flowed in popularity and practice through the years. Some of the testimonies from this approach can be very inspiring, but for the overwhelming majority this approach has led to considerable heartache, disillusionment, dashed dreams, and incomplete assignments.

Typically, those who hold to the faith-alone model validate it with the following three passages of scripture.

> *Is the Great Commission an order to go without the support of the body of Christ, to go with nothing more than faith? Does the word of God teach us that finances are to come only through prayer and no other means? Is support raising really a lack of faith?*

> [5]*Jesus sent out these twelve, instructing them as follows: "Do not go to Gentile regions and do not enter any Samaritan town.* [6]*Go instead to the lost sheep of the house of Israel.* [7]*As you go, preach this message: 'The kingdom of heaven is near!'* [8]*Heal the sick, raise the dead, cleanse lepers, cast out demons. Freely you received, freely give.* [9]*Do not take gold, silver, or copper in your belts,* [10]*no bag for the journey, or an extra tunic, or sandals or staff, for the worker deserves his provisions.* [11]*Whenever you enter a town or village, find out who is worthy there and stay with them until you leave." (Mat. 10:5–11, NET)*

From the above verses, at first glance it would seem easy to build a case for a faith-only approach to ministry, but is this really what the Lord is saying?

Jesus gives a clear ministry assignment. Verses 9, 10, and 11 are all part of that assignment.

The key to understanding this passage is in verse 10; it's the word "for." The reason Jesus doesn't want the disciples taking their own money is because they "deserve their pay."

Part of their assignment was securing provision for themselves. In the same way that they were commanded to preach, heal the sick, and cast out demons, they were commanded to find out who was worthy and stay with them (v. 11). How do you find out who is worthy? You have to talk to people. What does "who's worthy" mean? He who has ears to hear.

This was not a command to go with nothing; it was a command to find out who was worthy and stay with them.

Jesus was not introducing the "no shoes, no money" model for ministry. Practical items like proper gear, tools, money, and so forth are good and needed for ministry. Jesus Himself was properly equipped and funded. Jesus had shoes and a money bag; Judas was the treasurer. Why do you have a treasurer? It's not because you're broke and don't deal with money.

> *¹And Elijah the Tishbite, of the inhabitants of Gilead, said to Ahab, "As the Lord God of Israel lives, before whom I stand, there shall not be dew nor rain these years, except at my word." ²Then the word of the Lord came to him, saying, ³"Get away from here and turn eastward, and hide by the Brook Cherith, which flows into the Jordan. ⁴And it will be that you shall drink from the brook, and I have commanded the ravens to feed you there." ⁵So he went and did according to the word of the Lord, for he went and stayed by the Brook Cherith, which flows into the Jordan. ⁶The ravens brought him bread and meat in the morning, and bread and meat in the evening; and he drank from the brook. ⁷And it happened after a while that the brook dried up, because there had been no rain in the land. ⁸Then the word of the Lord came to him, saying, ⁹"Arise, go to Zarephath, which belongs to Sidon, and dwell there. See, I have commanded a widow there to provide for you." ¹⁰So he arose and went to Zarephath. And when he came to the gate of the city, indeed a widow was there gathering sticks. And he called to her and said, "Please bring me a little water in a cup, that I may drink." ¹¹And as she was going to get it, he called to her and said, "Please bring me a morsel of bread in your hand." ¹²So she said, "As the Lord your God lives, I do not have bread, only a handful of flour in a bin, and a little oil in a jar; and see, I am gathering a couple of sticks that I may go in and prepare it for myself and my son, that we may eat it, and die." ¹³And Elijah said to her, "Do not fear; go and do as you have said, but make me a small cake from it first, and bring it to me; and afterward make some for yourself and your son. ¹⁴For thus says the Lord God of Israel: 'The bin of flour shall not be used up, nor shall the jar of oil run dry, until the day the Lord sends rain on the earth.'" ¹⁵So she went away and did according to the word of Elijah; and she and he and her household ate for many days. ¹⁶The bin of flour was not used up, nor did the jar of oil run dry, according to the word of the Lord which He spoke by Elijah. (1 Kgs. 17:1–16)*

Notice in verses 3 and 4 that Elijah was commanded to go and the ravens were commanded to feed him. Elijah is not headed out on some kind of faith mission trusting only the Lord to provide, and neither did he pray in the provision needed. Elijah was acting under direct orders from the Lord. He had not lived this way before and he did not live this way afterward. This was a short, onetime event. Most scholars agree that it was about a six-week period, hardly a lifestyle.

We see this same type of thing happen a few verses later with the widow. Again Elijah was acting under direct orders and so was the widow. This situation only works because God commanded it, not because anyone prayed it in. *In the more than two dozen times Elijah is mentioned in Scripture, not one time is it in the context of financial provision. This experience is not referred to by anyone in the Old Testament or the New Testament as an example of how we ought to walk by faith for finances; it seems to be a one-time event.*

Observations from 1 Kings 17:1–16

i.   Elijah is acting in direct response to the word of the Lord (vv. 2–3).

ii. The Lord commanded the ravens in v. 4.

iii. Elijah knew where the provision was coming from before he ever left.

iv. This season of provision was prompted by the Lord and had nothing to do with Elijah's faith or prayer life. He was under the direction of the Lord, and it was only for a short season.

v.   A new set of directions comes in vv. 8–9. Again it is the Lord: no one "prayed it in."

vi. This was a short season: Elijah did not live this way the length of his ministry. In v. 9 the provision was already waiting there, but Elijah had to cooperate. The widow was acting upon a command from the Lord as well.

What God does regularly we should do regularly. What God does infrequently we should do infrequently. Jesus and Peter both walked on water, but this doesn't make it our primary means of transportation.

> [25]*"Therefore I say to you, do not worry about your life, what you will eat or what you will drink; nor about your body, what you will put on. Is not life more than food and the body more than clothing?* [26]*Look at the birds of the air, for they neither sow nor reap nor gather into barns; yet your heavenly Father feeds them. Are you not of more value than they?* [27]*Which of you by worrying can add one cubit to his stature?* [28]*So why do you worry about clothing? Consider the lilies of the field, how they grow: they neither toil nor spin;* [29]*and yet I say to you that even Solomon in all his glory was not arrayed like one of these.* [30]*Now if God so clothes the grass of the field, which today is, and tomorrow is thrown into the oven, will He not much more clothe you, O you of little faith?* [31]*Therefore do not worry, saying, 'What shall we eat?' or 'What shall we drink?' or 'What shall we wear?'* [32]*For after all these things the Gentiles seek. For your heavenly Father knows that you need all these things.* [33]*But seek first the kingdom of God and His righteousness, and all these things shall be added to you.* [34]*Therefore do not worry about tomorrow, for tomorrow will worry about its own things. Sufficient for the day is its own trouble."* (Matt. 6:25–34)*

The main message of the passage isn't really about money or provision: it's about worry. Worry is mentioned at the beginning, in the middle, and at the very end of the passage. Jesus is talking about worry. Some have taken the point where Jesus says "you of little faith" and connected it with all the talk about necessities of life. From there, they conclude that we are to walk by faith and trust God for our provision. Trust here meaning you don't have to do anything about provision, just believe and God will find you.

I find it interesting that those who have this pattern of thought only apply it to missionaries. Missionaries are required to trust God for provision while all other Christians are expected to get a job and receive a salary. Even pastors are not expected to live by the faith-alone model. Additionally this passage, like the rest of the Sermon on the Mount, is directed at the multitudes, not just gospel workers.

God provides for the birds. He gives then worms, bugs, seeds, and all sorts of building material: sticks, grass, mud, and trees. God has provided it all for them, but He doesn't bring it to them; they have to go get it. When the bird goes, he will find all that he needs. Actually, the bird is acting in faith: things hoped for but not yet seen. He believes there is a worm in the ground, therefore he goes until he finds his worm. With us as well, God has given us everything we need, but he doesn't bring it to us. We have to believe, act in faith, and go gather what He has already provided.

The pitfalls of holding tightly to the by-faith-alone model, as it has been understood traditionally in mission circles, are as follows:

i. It lacks scriptural foundation. The three verses shared above are not about how to fund workers, and they don't lay a good foundation for the faith-alone approach. *Which full-time worker in Scripture used the faith-alone model for years of ministry? It wasn't the priest, prophets, Jesus, or Paul.* Who was it?

ii. It doesn't empower the worker, making them fully available for years of service, and it doesn't strengthen the Great Commission. Jesus said we need workers and that they are worth of a wage.

iii. It puts all the responsibility on the worker and doesn't engage the Body of Christ. The partnership between goer and sender is to be equal. "Two separate but equal parties, with separate but equal responsibilities, working together to achieve a common goal."

iv. When it doesn't work, it charges the worker with a lack of faith. This has led to a great deal of shame and condemnation. A lack of faith as the source of problems is more than most can bear. Unwilling to live with such a charge, they will rewrite the assignment, reducing it until it can be achieved with almost no resource. Or the rewrite will read something like, "the grace has lifted, the Lord is transitioning us back to the marketplace."

The by-faith-alone approach, as noble as it sounds, ends up putting a restriction on the worker that Scripture does not. It robs the Body of Christ the spiritual healthiness and fruit of partnership, as well as weakening the worker and denying the Great Commission the labor force it needs.

Our definition of faith must come from the Scriptures and it must be a definition that applies to every believer, in every culture, and in every time period of history. It cannot be a faith based on occupation, situation, or circumstances.

Faith in action: our part in laying hold of the Lord's provision

[1]*"Every commandment which I command you today you must be careful to observe, that you may live and multiply, and go in and possess the land of which the* Lord *swore to your fathers.* [2]*And you shall remember that the* Lord *your God led you all the way these forty years in the wilderness, to humble you and test you, to know what was in your heart, whether you would keep His commandments or not.* [3]*So He humbled you, allowed you to hunger, and fed you with manna which you did not know nor did your fathers know, that He might make you know that man shall not live by bread alone; but man lives by every word that proceeds from the mouth of the* Lord. [4]*Your garments did not wear out on you, nor did your foot swell these forty years.* [5]*You should know in your heart that as a man chastens his son, so the* Lord *your God chastens you.* [6]*Therefore you shall keep the commandments of the* Lord *your God, to walk in His ways and to fear Him.*

[7]*"For the* Lord *your God is bringing you into* a good land, a land of brooks of water, of fountains and springs, that flow out of valleys and hills; [8]a land of wheat and barley, of vines and fig trees and pomegranates, a land of olive oil and honey; [9]a land in which you will eat bread without scarcity, in which you will lack nothing; a land whose stones are iron and out of whose hills you can dig copper. [10]When you have eaten and are full, then you shall bless the* Lord *your God for the good land which He has given you." (Deut. 8:1–10)*

Verses 7–10, mentioned above, describe abundant provision. It is a lush, fertile land full of water. Take a close look at the provision. How do they lay their hands on it? With a lot of hard work. They have to carry water by hand or dig wells and canals. They have to break ground with a plow behind a team of oxen. Then they have to plant the seed and wait on the harvest. Then they have to gather the harvest by hand and thresh the wheat. They have to grind their own grain, bake their own bread, press their own olives and grapes. They have to dig into the hills to recover the copper. God has abundantly provided for us but we must do our part in gathering His provision.

> [11]*"Beware that you do not forget the* LORD *your God by not keeping His commandments, His judgments, and His statutes which I command you today,* [12]*lest—when you have eaten and are full, and have built beautiful houses and dwell in them;* [13]*and when your herds and your flocks multiply, and your silver and your gold are multiplied, and all that you have is multiplied;* [14]*when your heart is lifted up, and you forget the* LORD *your God who brought you out of the land of Egypt, from the house of bondage;* [15]*who led you through that great and terrible wilderness, in which were fiery serpents and scorpions and thirsty land where there was no water; who brought water for you out of the flinty rock;* [16]*who fed you in the wilderness with manna, which your fathers did not know, that He might humble you and that He might test you, to do you good in the end—*[17]*then you say in your heart, 'My power and the might of my hand have gained me this wealth.'* [18]*And you shall remember the* LORD *your God, for it is He who gives you power to get wealth, that He may establish His covenant which He swore to your fathers, as it is this day.* [19]*Then it shall be, if you by any means forget the* LORD *your God, and follow other gods, and serve them and worship them, I testify against you this day that you shall surely perish.* [20]*As the nations which the* LORD *destroys before you, so you shall perish, because you would not be obedient to the voice of the* LORD *your God." (Deut. 8:11–20)*

> ## The fulfillment of God's promise required their participation and labor.

For forty years Israel wanders in the desert eating only manna, not because of faith but because of unbelief. With the exception of about the first eighteen months, the manna was not God's will for Israel; it was a response to their lack of faith. Why does God respond to their unbelief this way? Because He is full of mercy, and He made a covenant with Abraham and could not let his descendants die.

Summary

1. *Our model must stand up to the test of Scripture.*

2. *God does provide for the birds of the air, and the birds work really hard gathering that provision.*

3. *Faith is always proactive.*

4. *Raising support is not contrary to faith; it is faith in action.*

5. *"I believe God has and will provide for me. I know that He primarily does it through people. I am convinced that the provision is there; it's my job to discover it."*

6. *We must do our part to lay hold of the Lord's provision.*

A Modern Application

Overview: In this session we want to introduce our modern application of the biblical pattern and make you aware of a couple of important elements of communication and what moves people to give. Additionally, none of us make financial decisions in an instant; we bring opportunities into our thinking several times before we make a decision. We will cover the need to keep our ministry invitation in front of people, introduce a four-step model for gathering and sharing, and discuss the importance of following the model. Our goals for you are that by the end of this session you know the "why" behind the model, are able to embrace it with confidence, recognize the importance of a face-to-face meeting, and understand the steps to get you there.

A pattern from Scripture

As we were doing our Bible study in the previous lesson, a pattern began to emerge from the Scriptures. We can see it with Moses, David, Nehemiah, Cyrus, and Paul, through his letters. When these servants had an assignment from the Lord and they understood their role within the assignment, they went before people, shared that assignment, and asked people to be a part of that assignment.

This pattern makes sense in the practical. *How are we going to obey God and advance His mission if we don't talk to people and make plans?* The second and, I believe, the more important point is that it engages God's people in God's missions.

>   »   This pattern puts the worker in a position where they must believe what the Lord has spoken, and they must take responsibility for the assignment by securing the resources, people, and tools needed for the job.

>   »   The pattern puts the assignment before God's people and makes an opportunity for their voluntary agreement, which they'll indicate by money, time, services, and prayer.

We are going to walk in the same pattern that we see from Scripture. We are going to get clarity on what the Lord has asked us to do. We are going to prepare and do all we can to get ready. Then we are going to share our assignment with people. Lastly we are going to invite them to be a part of God's mission. Scripture's pattern as well as ours is:

1. **Vision** (what has God placed in your heart or asked you to do?)

2. **Prepare** (strategize, plan, reduce debt, save money, learn skills, buy tools, etc.)

3. **Gather** (a systematic way to get in front of people)

4. **Share** (the assignment God has given)

5. **Invite** (to be a part of the assignment)

We want to take this biblical pattern and bring it into our current situation; we want to give it a modern application. This application we will call our "model". As it is with any model, we have to understand why the model was created and the fruit that it bears before we will embrace it confidently. The rest of this session is about understanding the why.

Two important components

Relationship and effective communication. As we move forward to develop funding for our ministry, we are *not* trying to figure out how to make money, and we are *not* trying to do spiritual telethons, product sales, or take offerings. Those things are fine in and of themselves, and there is a proper time and place for them. We, however, are learning how to raise a financial partnership team who will link arms with us and join us in walking out our vision together.

We will be using the most effective means of communication in the most personal way while remaining very practical. There are many forms of communication and some are better than others. *We want to use the best forms of communication to gather, share, and invite as we walk in love. Genuineness and clarity are the cornerstones of the model.*

Why we give

For most Christians most of the time, we give because our heart has been stirred by the Holy Spirit. *(According to Exodus 25 and 35, whoever's heart is stirred will give.)* We may or may not be aware of this stirring: it may be dramatic, or it may be so subtle that we barely notice at all. We might say *I felt led*, or *I had a peace about it*. Either way it's a work of the Holy Spirit.

The stirring of the Holy Spirit can come a number of ways but most of the time it comes as people hear. This can come through public speaking, a testimony, or when someone shares their ministry assignment. Often it's not until the sharing and thus the hearing with our own ear that we are stirred.

Trying to explain the stirring of the Holy Spirit is difficult, but in general when it occurs there are normally a few things present, mingled together. We need a measure of *confidence* and *trust*; we need to *see God at work* in the person and ministry, and fourth, is that intangible connection we can't explain, we just know it when we feel it.

Confidence in you

For people to partner with a missionary or ministry, they need confidence in the person or the people involved. Confidence can mean different things, but one certain key is confidence in the person. They need to believe that your mission assignment is from the Lord, that you're trying to obey, and that you're prepared to carry it out.

The ministry itself is not as important to them as confidence in you and your *clarity of vision.* They need confidence that you have thought this through and that this truly is your ministry assignment.

Don't underestimate the power of confidence. I was once in an appointment explaining the ministry that I was a part of, but the prospective partner said, *"I am more confused about ABC ministry now than when we started. But it is clear that you are called. I would like to partner with you for $200 a month."*

This is one of the reasons you need to be confident of your assignment. *Be able to communicate it in just a sentence or two.* When you can say it clearly and concisely, it will build confidence in you and in the heart of the other person.

Whether we use the term vision, calling, leading of the Lord, or burden of the Lord is not as important right now. What is important is that we are following the Lord the best we know how and heading into ministry full-time under His clear direction. We may not know every detail, but the general direction should be known and communicated clearly.

Trust

For anyone to sow into a ministry or partner with a missionary there has to be a level of trust. This is true with all of us; we have to have a level of trust before we will sow into someone. No one will regularly give to a ministry if they don't have financial confidence in the leadership of that ministry.

Neither will people sow into a ministry when they are being asked for money for one purpose, yet feel like it may be used for another. This lowers the trust level, which affects the sowing level. We must be forthright and honest about every aspect of our ministry.

Prospective partners need to know that your mission assignment is from the Lord and that you're prepared to carry it out. This confidence will unlock their heart and allow them to make a financial commitment.

Trust builders are:
honesty, clarity, humility, soberness of mind, conviction about your ministry or cause, patience, accuracy, faith in the Lord, sincere love for God, caring, listening well, courtesy, kindness, thoughtfulness, gentleness, showing respect, and consistency.

Trust killers are:
vagueness, lack of clarity, overly confident, sensational speech and goals, feeling rushed, not feeling heard, distracted during conversation, not being valued or respected, lack of sincerity, impatience, defensiveness, inconsistency, the know it all, the hard sale, story doesn't line up, lack of conviction, lack of eye contact, and lack of follow through.

When we are in face-to-face partnership meetings with someone we have little or no relationship with, we should take time to get to know them, and they you. Ask about their family, work, church, and their life in the Lord. Making good eye contact, listening, and asking good questions can all help to start to build rapport and trust.

People need to trust those they are giving to, and trust is always connected to character. It is easy for us to give to people who we have seen operate faithfully in ministry by taking the low road and walking in humility. When we see people showing the heart of a servant and faithfulness over a period of time, it makes it very easy for us to give to them. We want to be able to give this to our prospective partners as much as possible. Living out a lifestyle of service will give opportunities for people to see your character in ministry. Don't be out of sight and out of mind; have a plan for keeping yourself and your ministry in front of people.

Seeing God's involvement

People also love to give where they can see God at work, because we love to partner with God. The story doesn't have to be dramatic or the situation desperate for people to give, but they do want to see that God is involved. More than a cause, more than a ministry, and more than a person, people love to give to God.

Again, the evidence doesn't have to be substantial, but they do need to see God involved. They may have met you for the first time at a friend's small group and heard you share. They may have seen you working in the church for a number of years or heard you share your heart on a Sunday morning. Now your move into full-time ministry makes perfect sense. Or, maybe the ministry you are about to do full time is the same ministry in which you have invested your heart and labor for years.

Whatever the situation, people need to see that God has led you and that you have not come into your situation for any lesser reason. It may take time throughout your relationship with them or it can be communicated in just a few minutes in a face-to-face meeting. No matter what the case or its history, at some point they will need to believe that God's hand is on you and in your ministry. We must be mindful of this to build their confidence. Give them opportunities to see and hear how God Himself is at work in you and in the organization you are a part of.

When to ask

You can invite anyone, any time, to be part of your team. *People do not need as much relational equity in order to give as you think they do.* (Question: do you need a lot of relational equity in order to give?) However, if these three factors listed above are present in your contact or relationship with them, you may have an increased chance of receiving a yes to your invitation. *These three factors do not have to be present at a high level to start the partnership.* I know a number of missionaries who have raised ministry teams and the team was 50% or more made up of people the missionary did not know when they started their partner development.

We may not have a chance to meet someone face-to-face right away. Should this be the case, take advantage of the time and build these three aspects into your relationships via newsletters, phone calls, and social media. We want to be intentional about these relationships and provide a way for confidence, trust, and the encouragement that comes through seeing God at work, to be worked into the relationship.

Choosing the best communication medium

The *Harvard Business Review* studied and ranked the effectiveness of different forms of communication.[1] Face-to-face meetings are the most effective way to communicate and therefore should be the primary way we share God's assignment for us with others.

Appointments are also great for building relationship. The Christian life is always about loving well, which involves loving both the Lord and people. Appointments give us a chance to hear what's going on in the lives of people, ask questions, and pray. Face-to-face meetings can be the beginning place of years and years of fellowship.

In order for us to be successful in developing a ministry team, we need to start by connecting with the people we know, and we need to do it in a personal and time-effective way.

The best way and the fastest way to build a team of long-term, deeply committed partners is to talk with them face to face and invite them to be a part of your team. Your letter is the first step in a multi-step process to get a face-to-face appointment.

---

1. As discussed in William P. Dillon, *People Raising* (Chicago: Moody Publishers, 1993), 66–67.

The contact process

Because of limited time, we want to have an effective system that reaches a large number of people at the deepest heart level. We could do a mass mailing and contact two hundred people in a weekend, but this would be impersonal, ineffective in its communication, and fail to provide the important face-to-face meeting, resulting in very little partnership.

Meeting with people face to face is the best way to go. People respect the fact that you would take the time to talk with them, and the face-to-face interaction gives you a chance to communicate your heart and a chance for your prospective partner to hear your excitement and vision. This will play a major part in their having the confidence necessary to partner with you.

I recently read that in face-to-face meetings, the actual words we speak make up only about 7 percent of what we are communicating. Voice inflection, body language, the expressions on our face, and hand gestures make up the other 93 percent.[2] This dynamic is what makes face-to-face communication effective. You simply cannot duplicate this fully in a letter, over the phone, or even by video chat.

Contact Methods Ranked by Effectiveness

1. One-on-one meetings
2. Small-group discussion
3. Large-group discussion
4. Telephone
5. Handwritten letter
6. Typed letter
7. Mass letter
8. Newsletter
9. Brochure
10. News item
11. Advertisement
12. Handout[3]

Contact points

Most people need to hear about a ministry or a project a number of times before they make a decision of financial commitment. They can hear about it through a letter, an email, Facebook, a friend, a phone call, an article in a magazine, or a promotional video. In whatever way they hear about it, they will have to have contact with that ministry a number of times in order to move through the decision-making process.

I call these "touch points" or "points of contact." Everyone requires a certain number of contact points before they make a decision. These touch points help move our minds along and bring us to the point of decision. Even when we know the party we will be potentially partnering with, we still have to go through a mental process before we can make a decision. Most of us are not even aware that we do this, but we do. This is one reason why mass mailing doesn't work; it doesn't provide enough points of contact to move a person through this process into a decision.

You can invite anyone at anytime. But when confidence, trust, and evidence that God is at work are present, then you have an increased chance of receiving a yes to your invitation.

It has been my experience that most people need about four or five touch points to move them through the process of making a decision. I have had a couple of people who didn't wait for me to contact them. When they heard I was raising a team for full-time ministry, they wanted to jump on board right away. I also had a few people who needed a little more contact and a little more time—maybe six or seven contact points.

2. Ibid.
3. Ibid.

Now, keep in mind I am not talking about people having to wrestle with the idea of whether they want to partner with you or not: "Should I partner with Jim or not? Hmmm . . ." What I am saying is that a person normally has to have an opportunity or situations put before them a number of times before they engage mentally enough to make a decision or to take action.

For example, a teacher or instructor has to make an announcement three or four times after a break to get the class back in their seats. A flight attendant has to prepare passengers three or four times before we actually return to our seats, lock up the tray, stow our bag, and buckle our seat belt. It's not that people don't care or that they are being disrespectful, it's simple science. When our brains are engaged with one project or task and a second situation requiring our attention comes, this new task or project has to knock at the door of our brains a number of times before we will disengage with our first task and turn our attention to this new opportunity.

Decision making is a process. We cannot fight against this process. We must give our prospective partners the points of contact they need in order to make good decisions. Don't be alarmed if people aren't on board right away; they may need to go through this decision-making process.

> *Decision making is process.*

KEY CONCEPTS

1. People give to people they know, trust, have confidence in.

2. Face-to-face meetings are the most effective way to communicate.

3. Several touch points are needed in the decision-making process.

Everything that follows from here will be built on these three concepts.

What we want to do is give them the points of contact they need without our having to do a lot of running around and spending precious time. We want to make our points of contact in the most effective way, using our time and energy wisely.

The contact point doesn't have to be sophisticated; it just needs to be contact. A letter, a phone call, a post card, an email, a text, or even a thirty-second passing conversation are all sufficient points of contact. *We can use these as a means to help bring our prospective partner to a point of decision. Remember, it's all working toward the face-to-face appointment.*

Four-step model

A good model must provide multiple points of contact. It must provide an opportunity for the Holy Spirit to stir hearts. Our model must value the best forms of communication. A good model will reach the largest number of people at the deepest heart level, in a time effective way. We have found the following model to meet our criteria.

1. Send an invitation letter (about four or five weeks before you could meet face to face).

2. Send a follow-up post card (about seven days after the letter).

3. Make a phone call to ask for an appointment (five to seven days after the postcard).

4. Have a face-to-face appointment to share and invite (most times about four to seven days after the phone conversation).

As you see, the face-to-face connect is my fourth point of contact. I made three points of contact without ever leaving my house. But every point is important: four or five contact points help move people along in the decision-making process.

With this method you move through three points of contact before you ever talk face-to-face. The face-to-face meeting becomes the fourth point, and many times I had my *yes* right there in the appointment. By the way, the appointment is a great time to take care of contact information, instructions on the giving process, and so forth (more on this later). Remember, most people need at least four points of contact before they get to making a decision.

A few things about the four-step model:

» It helps start the conversation and removes the challenge of a cold call.

» When done weekly, it allows you to reach a large number of people.

» It keeps people from falling through the cracks.

» It gives a fair amount of time to start praying it over.

» Do not start the process unless you are ready and able to have the face-to-face meeting.

» Once you start the steps, you must remain consistent and finish the steps.

» Do not send the letter unless you already have your postcards.

	Week 1	Week 2	Week 3	Week 4	Week 5	Week 6	Week 7	Week 8	Week 9
Group 1	Letter	Postcard	Phone Call	Appt.	Follow Up				
Group 2		Letter	Postcard	Phone Call	Appt.	Follow Up			
Group 3			Letter	Postcard	Phone Call	Appt.	Follow Up		
Group 4				Letter	Postcard	Phone Call	Appt.	Follow Up	

Summary

1. *We give when we are stirred by the Holy Spirit.*

2. *Stirring includes confidence, trust, seeing God at work, and elements we can't explain.*

3. *According to a Harvard study on communication, the most effective form of communication is a face-to-face conversation.*

4. *Several touch points are needed in the decision-making process.*

5. *Your invitation letter is the first step in a multi-step process leading up to a face-to-face appointment.*

6. *The postcard is the second point of contact.*

7. *The phone call is the third point of contact that's working to establish your face-to-face appointment.*

8. *Sticking to the model will help move people toward making a well-informed decision.*

Please complete the following homework assignment:

Homework #6: Create Your Name List

Homework #7: Financial Vision Plan

Letter and Postcard

Overview: Making a first impression is important. For many of those you will interact with throughout your campaign, your invitation letter and postcard will be the first time they are hearing about God's story in your life. In this session we will be covering the need to be both professional and personal in your letter, the various sections of the invitation letter, and how to write and design your postcard. The aim of this teaching is to help you introduce your story and your call to ministry, followed by an invitation for others to be a part of it.

First point of contact: your letter

For many of the people you know this will be the first letter they have received from you. This is your chance to make a good first impression. We want to be sure to communicate the right message with clarity. This will be your first point of contact.

Remember that this letter is leading up to your face-to-face appointment. Important: your letter is not the place to tell them your whole story and life vision in great detail. It is also important to keep your letter short and on topic. Your letter is primarily an invitation to pray about financial partnership and to talk further. We are not going to do the full formal ask for partnership, but we will inform our prospective partner about the call of God on our lives and then invite them to be a part of it. I re-emphasize that the letter is an *invitation for them to pray* about being a part of your team through their prayers and financial partnership. The full formal invitation is done later in our face-to-face appointment.

Each section needs to be no more than one paragraph and maybe two if they are short.

The typical missions "ask letter" usually says something like this: "If you would like to support me, here's how you can: send your faith gift to 123 ABC St., Holy Town, MO." In contrast, *your* letter is asking them to *pray* about financial partnership *and letting them know that you will follow up with them to talk further.*

Be personal as well as professional

Most people will only spend a few seconds scanning a letter before deciding to read it or not. The first thing they will scan is the headline and the postscript (PS). Therefore, write your PS by hand. Make it personal and a concise summary of the whole letter.

Next, they will scan headlines, pictures, and anything that catches their eye before deciding to read the rest of the letter. Therefore, the letter must be *well written, concise, clear, and attention-grabbing.*

YOUR LETTER SHOULD BE:

1. Written on one page
2. Written on only one side
3. To one person
4. Covering one topic

Feel free to include a picture of yourself. This will depend on the last time you saw your potential partner, however, and may not be needed. Think this through before you automatically include a picture. Be sure to also *include all your contact information.* Don't be afraid to send a brochure or information about your ministry or organization. This will help them grasp what you do without having to take up space in the letter.

Make sure the layout is easy on the eye. Make good use of white space, using no less than one-inch margins. Use a comfortable font size, at least eleven-point font but twelve may be better. Leave yourself room at the bottom for your handwritten PS.

Write your letter with one person in mind to give it a more personal feel. Don't say things like, "Dear family and friends." Rather say, "Dear John and Jane." Don't say, "I hope to visit with all of you." Rather say, "I hope to visit with you."

In other words, write to one person and not a crowd. We want our friend to feel the personal nature of this important invitation.

Feel free to write a couple of different versions of your letter, depending on who is receiving one: family, non-family, close friends, not-so-close friends, conservative believers. The different versions of the letter should still be ninety-five percent the same.

In your letter, as well as any other written or verbal communication, do not be presumptuous and do not use manipulative language. For example, don't say, "I will be calling you in a few days to set an appointment." Rather say, "I will be calling you in a few days and I hope to have an opportunity to share with you."

Remember: this is an invitation. Invitation means they could decline. We are not going to assume that we already have an appointment or that they are going to partner with us. We are going to go low, honor them, show respect, allow them to pray, and be thankful when they give us their time. There is no need for the hard sell or dramatic language. We are on an assignment from the Lord, and He has given us a vision to walk out.

Four sections and a catchy introduction

Your letter will consist of a headline or hook, four basic sections, and a personalized handwritten PS. Each section should be no more than one paragraph or two if they are short.

Headline

Share an attention-getting opening line. Something like this:

God is on the move and so am I. In January I will be moving to Kansas City to enter full-time missions work at ABC Ministries.

God has led me to a new season in life. I will soon be entering full-time ministry in the Middle East.

After much prayer the Lord has made it clear: it's time for me to transition to full-time missions work.

God has changed our hearts and now we are changing occupations; we are moving to Florida to start a full-time campus ministry.

Sharing the love of Christ in the Chicago inner city

Speaking His name where it has never been heard

Lifting my voice for those who have no voice

OUTLINE OF LETTER

1. Headline or hook

2. Personal address ("Dear Jane")

3. Get them up to date

4. Calling, how you were called

5. Organization, vision/values, your role

6. Invitation to partnership

7. Handwritten PS

If you have been in ministry for some time, this opening line needs to be adjusted accordingly.

Try to keep the headline to a short sentence. The headline should communicate the move to full-time ministry or at least the basic nature of your ministry. After the PS, the reader's eyes will go right to the headline—so we want to get their attention and be clear, but don't go over the top or try to be sensational. When you print your letter, feel free to make this opening line bold or in a larger, different font style.

After your headline, personally address your letter: "Dear John and Jane Doe" (use a mail merger). Use a greeting that is appropriate for the relationship. Examples: Mr. and Mrs. Smith, John and Jane Smith, or John and Jane.

Section one

Section one is for catching them up on your life. Share concisely what you have been doing the last three months or so. This section is a conversation starter and gives the reader a sense of what your life currently looks like. If you have been in ministry for some time, adjust your language accordingly. Share the work or training you have been doing as well as some fruit of your labors. You could include a testimony. Express your excitement!

> *For the past (x amount of months) I have been enrolled in xyz internship at ABC Ministries in Smithville, Arkansas. The Lord has impacted me in a great way as I have served on local outreaches, served the poor, planted churches, and preached the gospel.*

Share a little more and make it personal, but keep it short.

Section two

Section two is for describing how the Lord has worked in your life. For most of you, this is an occupational change and it's your chance to inform your prospective partners how God led you to this shift in life direction. If you have already been in ministry, recast vision and share about the season you are in and where the Lord is currently taking you. Include any changes in ministry here as well.

If your reader is assured that you are following the leading of God, it will help them to be more confident in partnering with you. They need to know that the decision you are making to be in full-time ministry is one of obedience to God—not you just trying out something new. People will be encouraged that you are responding in obedience to the Lord's leadership.

Even though you may be writing to a friend, it's still very important you make the right impression about your occupational decision as well as your approach and attitude toward ministry. If you have already been in ministry, adjust your language. In short, share how God has led you to this decision and state the ministry assignment.

> *Over the last few months of this internship the Lord has awakened my heart to the need for workers among the inner-city youth. The need is great and the workers are few. My heart has been impacted by God's heart for the poor and oppressed. The Lord has spoken in a number of ways and confirmed it a number of times. He has made it clear: I am to give myself fully to the inner-city youth. Starting in January, I will launch out into ABC Ministries as a full-time missionary.*

Section three

Section three has two parts: the vision and values of your organization and your current role within it. You can start this section with either of the two parts, but in general I think it works best most of the time to lead with the vision and values of the organization.

Share their vision, the "why we exist": what we are doing, with whom, and the goal. Share the important values, the "three things we want everyone to know about our organization." I recommend that you use language that your organization has developed. This will help keep the message consistent and represent the organization correctly.

Second item: *Summarize what it is you will be doing.* This is a chance for you to paint a mini-picture of what your ministry work will look like in general. Don't just make a bullet point list; we want to give them a visual impression as best we can. *If you are in a supporting role, be sure to show how important this supportive role is to your department and the organization you work for.* If you have one, mention an enclosed brochure about your ministry in this paragraph.

A helpful tip for this section: remember, we want to paint a little picture.

Don't say, "I will be praying twenty-four hours a week," but rather say, "I will spend several hours a week engaged in the prayer room, impacting people and nations through prayer."

Don't say, "I will be doing evangelism," but rather say, "I will have several opportunities to share the love of Christ with inner-city youth."

Don't say, "I will work ten hours a week working with street kids," but rather say, "I will get to serve street kids several hours a week, sharing the love of God with them, speaking a kind word, and being their friend."

Section four

Section four is for explaining missionary support and partnership, and giving the invitation. Remember they need to hear that you are responding to God's leading and that this is a full-time ministry or a full-time occupational change for you. Consider these examples. Do not just copy and paste them, but glean from them and re-write them in your own words.

> *In order for me to fully give my time and energy to this calling, I need to build a team: a team of friends like you who will stand with me in prayer and financial partnership. Would you prayerfully consider being a part of my ministry team? I will be contacting you soon once you have had time to pray, and I look forward to talking with you.*

> *In January I will be a missionary with ABC Ministries and therefore have the responsibility and privilege of building my own financial partnership team. I want to invite you stand with us in prayer and financial partnership. I will be contacting you soon, once you have had time to pray. I look forward to talking with you.*

> *In order for me to fully invest my time and energy to this ministry, I need to partner with a team of friends who will stand with me in prayer and financial partnership. I want to invite you to partner with me in ministry to reach inner-city youth for Jesus. Would you prayerfully consider my invitation to ministry? I will be contacting you soon, once you have had time to pray. I look forward to speaking with you.*

We are committed to ministering to God and others, that they might know the Lord and spend their lives for Him. We are asking if you will prayerfully consider committing yourself as well to the purposes of God, with us through prayer and financial partnership. We invite you to ask the Lord what part He may have you play in this ministry. We look forward to speaking with you soon.

We are committed to ministering to others so that they might know the Lord and spend their lives for Him. As we sow into them, would you prayerfully consider sowing into us so that we might reap a harvest together? We invite you to ask the Lord what part He may have you play in this ministry. We look forward to speaking with you soon.

Handwritten note

After you have finished your letter, be sure to include a hand-written message for the postscript (PS). Address it to them personally; reveal your excitement and that you look forward to sharing more with them. The handwritten PS will help make the letter more personal and less formal. The PS can be a short summary of your letter.

Mike and Sue, I am excited to be moving into full-time ministry. I hope to have a chance to share with you what the Lord is doing in me and in ABC Ministries. I look forward to having an opportunity to share with you. I will be contacting you soon.

It's important they know you will be contacting them soon; this will help move them towards prayer in the decision-making process and remove the "cold call" feel when you phone in about two weeks.

Remember to gather your contact information well in advance of the invitation process. You don't want to be looking for an address when it is time to send letters and postcards.

Don't get lost in the mail

A letter can only be effective if it is read, but it's going to arrive on the same day as several other pieces of mail. There are a few things we can do to help increase our chances that our letter doesn't get lost among all the other mail. We want to do all that we can to help our letter get read.

When most people pick up an envelope, the first thing they do is look at the mailing address and then move their eyes to the return address. On this "Ask Letter," write their mailing address by hand. This will help your letter stand out from all the other mail. We are talking about your appointment letter only: there is no need to hand write addresses on newsletters. Feel free to use a stamp or sticker for the return address—this is much smaller and needs to be very clear.

We want our letter to have a *personal* appearance, unlike all the other mail they have that day. You may want to include a personal stamp; you can have one made online at the post office.

I recommend that you print your letter on heavier paper; maybe something like #28. You want it to feel good in their hands. You may want to buy some boxed stationary with matching paper and envelopes. Make it with something other than plain white, maybe an off-white or ivory. You want it to look distinct from the rest of their mail. Don't use regular copier paper and a regular #10 white envelope. You might consider using an invitation-size envelope (e.g., 5.25" x 7.25") as this could communicate "invitation" before they even open the letter. Again, these are suggestions for making your letter stand out from all the other mail.

Send your letter about four to five weeks before your opportunity for an appointment. This will play an important role in keeping momentum; don't send it too early and don't wait too long. If you send it about four or five weeks before the possible appointment date, your prospective partner will be hearing from you about once a week right up until the time they see you in the face-to-face meeting.

The last thing you want to do is send a letter two months before you have a chance to see them; this is way too early. You also don't want to send a letter two weeks before your visit; this would not allow enough time for you to follow up and for them to pray. If you wait too long, many times you will be in their town before you have contacted them. We want to avoid this. Four to five weeks is a perfect amount of time.

Letter outline template

Consider handwriting your first couple drafts. This exercise will make you choose your words more carefully.

Catchy opening line, headline, or hook:

Personal address:

Bring them up to date:

Your calling (include how you were called):

Your ministry's vision and values. Your work and role at your ministry:

Invitation to partnership. Be sure they know you will be contacting them soon:

Handwritten PS:

Second point of contact: the postcard

A point of contact does not have to be flashy; it just needs to be contact. A postcard is a great way to connect: it's easy, inexpensive, and *very effective*. If the organization you work with has a postcard, use it. If they don't, encourage them to consider developing materials for their staff. You can make your own postcard if you like; you just need a little creativity, a printer, and some card stock. Make sure it is heavy enough to hold up to mail service. There are also several online options as well.

> *Don't underestimate the power of a postcard. It is very effective, fun, inexpensive, and provides a crucial point of contact.*

You can use an online template or make your own. You can upload your pictures and graphics, write your text, and in about seven working days you have your postcards. You can also have postcards printed at a UPS store, Kinko's, Staples, postcards.com, Vista Print, etc. If you take time to make a nice postcard, be sure to include your contact info, a picture, and maybe a tag line. Another option is to pick up a local postcard.

This will be a handwritten postcard—only a couple of short sentences. You could send a card of some kind in an envelope but this will cost a little more. You can send a postcard with a postcard stamp; this is about sixty percent the cost of a regular stamp. Regardless of which method you choose, your message needs to be handwritten and personalized.

At this point they have already received your letter, so there's no need to tell your story again. The postcard is serving as a reminder and providing them an important second point of contact. You ended your letter saying that you would contact them soon and this is your next contact. You should borrow from the fourth paragraph of your letter and/or your PS to make the text of your postcard. *We want to keep our ministry and the invitation for them to be a part of it in front of them; this will help bring them to a point of decision.*

DO NOT skip the important postcard step in order to save a dollar or two; skipping this step will not save you a few dollars, but will end up costing you many more dollars.

Your postcard is a chance to be personal; think "high touch" not high-tech. Think it through; know what you want to say. Try to communicate these points: *God's leading, prayer, invitation, full-time ministry, calling soon, and looking forward to talking with them.*

> » We want to follow up, just like we said we would.

> » We want to remind them to pray. Be easy and go soft.

> » We want them to hear invitation or partnership or both.

> » We want them to hear our excitement.

> » We want them to know we would love to see them and talk with them.

> » We want them to know we will be contacting them soon. If they know you are going to call ,then they will be more apt to engage in prayer, which is what we want. This will actually help them start moving through the decision-making process.

Remember: do not be presumptuous and do not use manipulative language. Avoid the hard sell.

Hello John and Jane, I hope that you have had a chance to read the letter I sent you. I am really excited about God's call to full-time ministry and would love to have a chance to talk with you about it. I am going to call you in a few days once you have had a little more time to pray; I look forward to talking with you soon.

John and Jane, I hope that you have received my recent letter and have had a chance to prayerfully consider my invitation to partner with me in ministry. I look forward to having a chance to share with you what the Lord is doing in me and through ABC Ministries. I will be calling you in a few days; I look forward to speaking with you.

Hi John and Jane, we hope that you have received our letter and had a chance to consider our invitation to be a part of our ministry team. We are really excited about God's call on our life and we would love to have a chance to share with you. We will be calling you in a few days once you have had a little more time to pray. We look forward to talking with you soon.

Send your postcard out about seven days after your letter. Be mindful of the mail service and holidays. We would like them to have had their letter in hand about six to seven days when they get your postcard. This is enough time for them to start praying, talk about it with a spouse, and consider your invitation.

Do not wait longer than seven days—this would not be good. We want it all to stay fresh in their minds and we want to follow through on what we said we would do. Any excitement you spark in them can die down if your contact points are too far apart. There is a good chance that they will not have read your letter yet, or only one spouse in the marriage has read the letter. This postcard will serve as a good reminder.

Summary

Letter:

1. *This is the first point of contact with your potential partner—make a good impression. Communicate the right message with clarity.*

2. *Keep your letter brief, sharing only what's essential with the understanding that in your meeting you can share in greater detail.*

3. *The letter should be both personable and professional.*

4. *Your letter should have 7 key elements included in it: headline, personal address, one paragraph getting them up to speed, a paragraph stating your calling, a paragraph describing your organization, a paragraph with a clear invitation to partnership, and a handwritten postscript.*

5. *Do what you can to ensure your letter is read by handwriting their address, using attractive paper and envelope, non-white, one page, one side, one person, one topic.*

Summary

Postcard:

1. *Your second point of contact is a handwritten, creatively designed postcard that follows your letter a week later.*

2. *This postcard should include a personal photo of you or you and your family. Use a tagline similar to your invitation letter.*

3. *Contact information should be on the same side as the photo.*

4. *The handwritten note needs to be personable, express your excitement about God's call, and include a reminder to pray about your invitation, as well as a commitment to contact them.*

5. *We're reminding, not selling. Be friendly.*

Please complete the following homework assignments:

Homework #8a: Your Vision Statement

Homework #8b: Vision, Obstacles, and Goals Worksheet

Homework #9a: Write Your Letter: First Draft

The Phone Call

Overview: All of your previous preparation has led you to this opportunity to share directly with a potential partner. You want to make sure that you're ready, have a clear plan, and are personable and confident as you share. In this session you will learn how to prepare, how to make a proper greeting and conversation; how to move toward asking for an appointment, and how to navigate through a few challenges. The aim of this session is to prepare you for making a quality phone call that is personable and professional, and it offers a few ideas of how to work within our cell phone culture.

Third point of contact: phone call

The third point of contact, the phone call, is made to ask for a face-to-face meeting. Before making your calls, give yourself plenty of time to prepare. I suggest practicing several mock calls with friends in the days leading up to your first real call. Use your outline and have your friends present you with different scenarios to better prepare you. Use your outline until the calls become natural. Use a video or audio recorder for your mock calls to speed up the learning process.

You should know in advance the approximate date when you will make your first call. It should be about two weeks after your letter. Mark this date on your calendar, pray, and prepare.

1. **Do not hesitate when it's time to make the phone call!**

   When you sit down to make your calls, find a quiet place where there will be no distractions. Have your phone outline, contact call sheet, and contact information in front of you, along with your appointment book, your postcards, pen, and stamps.

2. **Dress the part**

   Get prepared for your calls by dressing properly—as though you were going to meet them in public. This will help put you in the right frame of mind, and you will sound and feel more professional.

3. **If you are using a cell phone, make sure there is no background noise**

   You want a very quiet place with a good signal. Don't make calls from a coffee shop or your car. Find a quiet corner of the house or an office—maybe the kitchen table if the house is empty. You may have to leave your house or apartment, but you will need a good writing surface with zero distraction.

4. **Have a way to organize your calls**

   When you are making several calls in a row, it is easy to forget whom you are calling. It's a terrible feeling, while the phone is ringing on the other end, to realize that you don't know who you just called! You never want the person on the other end to say, "You just called me five minutes ago!" I suggest you create a call sheet for each set of letters and postcards you send out. For example, the fifteen letters you sent out in group #1 would have their own call sheet with only those fifteen names and numbers on it.

Remember, the most effective way to build your partnership is through face-to-face meetings. That is the point of the phone call: to ask for a face-to-face appointment. While making your call, please remember why you want that face-to-face appointment. It is the most effective way to

» give you opportunity to become better acquainted,

» share your excitement about your ministry,

» build friendship,

» provide people with an on-ramp to your ministry through partnership,

» develop your prayer team, and

» build up the missions organization you are with.

5. **You must not hesitate**

When you come to the point of making your first call, you must not hesitate. You have to pick up the phone, dial the number, and ask for the important appointment. Mark your first call date on the calendar to take place five to seven days after you send the postcard. Mark the date, look forward to the day, pray, and be prepared. Look over your outline, role-play, and get organized. As you make your calls, review the above points—this will better equip you for each call. It will also help you to answer any potential questions your prospective partner may have.

Work through what you are going to say as well as what you *are not* going to say. You may want to create a little outline for your conversation. You will only need to use this outline a couple of times, and then your phone calls will become very natural.

Do not hesitate to make the first call. The first call is the hardest. The fear of the first call is far worse than the experience of the call itself. After the first call, they get really easy and really fun.

Remember; don't go into too much detail about your ministry. Instead, focus on working toward setting the appointment. You must stick to this plan. A number of your phone call recipients will want you to tell them all about the ministry right then on the phone. Some may even tell you they are going to partner with you. When either one of these conversations happen, just politely say:

> *John, there is so much to share and the Lord has led me in some incredible ways. It would really take more time than we have on the phone. It would really be better if we could meet and talk in person. Besides, we haven't had coffee together in months, and this would be a good chance to catch up and share with you.*

"We want to partner with you; where do we send the check?"

> *The phone call is the biggest place of hesitation. Many stumble in partnership development because of procrastinating when they get to the phone call. Once you start the process, you need to follow through on each step to completion.*

John, thank you so much for your willingness to partner with us in ministry; I look forward to working with you! There is a lot to share and I would love to have a chance to share more fully with you in person; could we do that next week?

Keep in mind that many people will try to help you by not bothering with the appointment. Because of the excellent communication in face-to-face meetings, keep reaching for that chance to share in person. Reach a couple of times.

You may want to consider sending a text message before you make your call. It is becoming much more common to not answer our phone when it rings. As a culture, we are starting to filter more and more of the communication that comes our way. *At this point, a text is another quick point of contact that presents you and your ministry to your potential partner, and prepares them for the call.* Identify yourself and ask if they have time for a two-minute call. Consider the following for your text:

Hi, John, this is Sally Singer. Do you have time for a quick three-minute call?

Hi, John, Bill Smith here. Do you have three minutes for a quick call?

Adjust your text based on the amount of relationship you have with the person you are calling. You may want to go ahead and include your name. I have texted several friends who I thought would have my number in their phone, but did not and they had no idea who was texting them. Including your name removes all doubt.

Why a phone outline?

When you get ready to make your calls, it will be important to know what you want to say as well as what you don't want to say. In all of our communication with prospective partners, we need to be able to speak clearly and concisely; our phone call is no different.

The last thing you want to do after you have sent a well-written letter and personal postcard is to stumble around on the phone, lacking direction, and failing to set an appointment. This is our first chance to really speak to our prospective partner, so we want to be clear and informative. We want to make a good impression. Here's a phone-call outline:

> *Don't give in to the temptation of telling the whole story or inviting over the phone. Reach for the face-to-face meeting.*

1. **Greeting**

   » Let them know who you are.

   » Make sure you have the person you want to talk to.

   » Ask if it's a good time to talk. Respond accordingly, set a time to call back if need be—be proactive, and don't leave it open-ended.

   » Never apologize for calling.

2. **Small talk only for a few minutes**

   » Review the person and your relationship before you call. Have a conversation point ready; make small talk if you have the chance.

» Keep your ears open and be sensitive to the Holy Spirit.

» Minister and pray when it's needed.

» Be a friend.

3. Let them know why you are calling: transition to asking for an appointment

"Hey John, the reason I am calling is that I recently sent you a letter sharing about our ministry (name of ministry)—how God is moving in our lives and ABC ministries. Did you have a chance to read it?"

If they didn't read your letter: move toward wrapping up the phone call and make plans to call back in four or five days, giving them time to read your letter.

If they ask you to go ahead and share about your ministry, encourage them to read the letter and pray. Set a time to call back; *do not leave* it open. Be sure to set a time to call.

Here is an example of what you might say:

> *How about if I call you back on Tuesday the 19th, four days from now. Would that give you enough time to read my letter?*

If they did read your letter: continue on. Share your excitement about going into full-time ministry. They should be hearing your excitement throughout the whole process: by letter, postcard, text, phone call, and appointment.

4. Ask for an opportunity

Ask them for an opportunity to talk and share more with them. If they say yes, express your appreciation and set a time, date, and location.

5. Set an appointment

If needed, let them know how long it will take (no more than one hour, unless their only availability is for a weekday lunch, then it might only be 30–40 minutes). Be flexible. Do what works for them. Be creative if you have to. Many of your friends will want to have dinner and I encourage you to do that. In the event of a dinner, your appointment may be a couple of hours or more. Sometimes I had two dinners in one night! (Going to dinner will always take longer.) Have your appointment book ready, and be prepared to meet anywhere and any time they can. Make it easy for them. When they suggest dinner or a time and place follow their lead as much as possible. When they aren't offering anything make a few suggestions of times and dates.

WHEN THEY SAY NO

If they say no, assure them that they have no financial obligation, but that you are excited about what the Lord is doing, what He has called you to, and that you would like to have an opportunity to share with them.

If they still say no, ask them if they would be prayer partners and if it's okay to share your newsletter with them.

6. For people who feel too busy

Consider the following options for busy people who think they don't have time to meet. Have a short list memorized and be ready to share when needed. Then try to book:

» Dinner or a late dessert

» Weekday breakfast (this works well for busy business people)

» Business lunch

» Evening coffee at a coffee shop

» Sunday lunch after church or a brunch between services

» A 40-minute appointment with a business person (possibly meet at their office)

» A shorter meeting after small group, house church, or youth group where you would spend a few more minutes

» If someone is going out of town, drive them to the airport—share on the way

» Jump onto their schedule, run errands with them if you need to

7. **Confirm the time, date, and location: remember to speak it back to them**

Wrap up the phone call, thank them for the opportunity to share, and mention how much you are looking forward to seeing them. Keep your calls short to honor their time. Also remember that you are going to be calling several people each day. Possibly you might sense a call needs more time to build the relationship, so by all means take the time to do it. In some calls, you may find yourself with an opportunity to offer pastoral care and prayer. When this happens, please take as much time as they need.

8. **Serve well**

To increase your chances of reaching your people, try calling at peak times (this paragraph mostly applies to people who may have a landline phone). We want to increase our chances of reaching them and we also want the time to be as convenient as possible: we want their attention. Evenings after dinner were the best times for me to call. I had the most success on Monday nights between 6:30 and 8:30 as well as Saturday mid-morning around 11:00. Peak times may differ depending on time zones, age group, occupation, culture, and regional circumstances.

9. **Use good judgment**

Don't call a couple that owns their own business on their home phone in the middle of the day. Don't call your church friends at 11:00 a.m. Sunday morning. Don't call when you know there is a good chance they are sitting down with their family over dinner. I would also avoid calling people while they are at work unless they own their own business.

» Try calling on weekday evenings first; Wednesday may be church night.

» Don't call after 9 or 9:15 p.m. their time.

> » Sundays work well from 2–9 p.m., but you may want to wait a little later (perhaps 4–5 p.m.); Sunday afternoons are a popular nap time.

> » If you are calling a family with small children, you may want to call later in the evening. Their bath and bedtime are often around 8pm, so you may want to make your call afterward.

> » Generally speaking, you could save the younger, single people for later calls.

When you are having a hard time reaching someone and you leave a message, don't go into detail. Just let them know that you look forward to talking with them and leave a time you will call back. Don't leave a message every time you call; maybe leave only one message per week (one message every five attempted calls).

In this phone-call stage make one or two attempts a day for the first few days. Then reduce calls to once a day for the next few days. After doing this for six or seven days, start backing off a little and call every two or three days.

Voice mail example:

Hi John, sorry I missed you. I will try you again soon. Bless you!

If you have been trying to call for two weeks and you're not getting a response, then you need to switch your approach. Use some other means of communication: another postcard of a different type, a text, Facebook, a short letter, or try to see them in person. If this isn't working, then leave another message acknowledging how busy they must be, your disappointment in not being able to reach them, and that you hope to talk with them in the future. Don't stop trying, but back off and use a more subtle approach; for example, a nice handwritten letter.

Don't take this as rejection! Many people are very busy, and many need to return dozens of calls a day. Sometimes they are traveling on business or family vacation. I have a friend on my team who is not going to respond no matter how often I call or email, but if I am in town he is happy to see me and wants to connect. He just doesn't email or talk on the phone often.

Practice your phone calls repeatedly following the outline, until it becomes natural. Role-play with friends before you start making calls, and ask for their feedback. I recommend that you do this a number of times, maybe twenty or more.

Practice by leaving a proactive message on a recording device; pay attention to wording, volume, speech speed, the positive way that you speak about your ministry, and the opportunity to share with them. Practice this; many freeze up when they hear a voice mail message request.

If you speak too fast, have a bad choice of words, use aggressive language, or leave out important details, you will end up sending the wrong message. Speak a little slower, choose your words well, and speak positively—then you will leave a good impression. We want them to actually be excited about speaking with you, and you have a better chance if you leave good, proactive messages.

If you are calling a business office, you may want to keep these things in mind:

> » Give careful attention to the receptionist or secretaries; they will play a major role in helping you connect with the boss. Give them reasons to like you.

> » If you call on a Monday, make it after lunch; Monday morning is often very busy.

> » Most workdays, a mid- to late-morning call would work well: 9:30–11: 30 a.m. If you call in the afternoon, make it well after lunch, 1:30 p.m. or later.

» If you call on a Friday, don't make it at the end of the workday. Fridays do provide a good opportunity to set appointments for the following week, but call earlier on Fridays.

Things to keep in mind when calling a church:

» Many churches close their office Mondays, and for many pastors this is a day off.

» Tuesdays and Thursdays are often lighter workload days for churches.

» Ask the secretary for the best time and way to contact the pastor.

» Ask if the church has a missions board or director. Find out who you need to talk to and the best way to contact them. Often, pastors are not the people you need to speak to.

» Working with churches is a much slower process, so don't get discouraged. It could take months to get your final answer.

This outline is a starting place to help you get going. It's a good tool for keeping you on track and will help you with some of the more challenging conversations. Being well prepared will pay off!

Handwritten appointment reminder

Once you have made contact and set an appointment, you might think about sending a confirmation email, text, or postcard. If you have time, the postcard would be the best. Take a minute to write your postcard right after the phone call, while it's still fresh in your mind and your excitement is high. It should include the time, date, and meeting place. Share your excitement and your gratitude. Another point of contact never hurts. Try to time it so that they receive the confirmation postcard a day or two before your appointment.

John and Jane, it was great to talk with you both the other day! Thank you so much for your willingness to meet with me. I am really excited about the work the Lord has called me to and I look forward to sharing with you. I will see you Tuesday at 7:00 p.m. at your house for dinner. Blessings to you both, (Sign your name).

When you are meeting with them just a couple of days after the phone call, the postcard would not work well. Use an email, text, or Facebook message for your appointment reminder.

Reminder

This is why it is so important to gather as much contact information as you can while you are building your contact list. Work at getting addresses, home and cell numbers, emails, and all other important information. Start inviting them to be friends on Facebook long before your campaign season. The more information you have, the better you can respond when you reach the point of phone calls. Being in the middle of your phone-call phase is no time to try and come up with email addresses; you must do as much information gathering as you can—it needs to be done in advance.

Summary

1. *Mark the date on your calendar, pray, and don't hesitate to make the call.*

2. *Dressing the part of your new career in ministry when making your phone calls will put you in the right frame of mind as you communicate with others.*

3. *Make sure you are in a quiet place with limited distractions as you make phone calls to your potential partners.*

4. *The goal of the phone call is to ask for a face-to-face appointment.*

5. *Consider sending a pre-call text.*

6. *Your phone call should include a greeting, (possibly small talk), transition, excitement about full-time ministry, invitation to meet, finalized details, and a phone-call wrap-up.*

7. *Work to keep your phone calls short. Don't share the whole story over the phone.*

8. *Use wisdom and good judgment when calling people. Take into account their lives with both kids and work schedules.*

Please complete the following homework assignments:

Homework #9b: Write Your Letter: Second Draft

Homework #10a: Written Phone Call: Yes

Homework #10b: Written Phone Call: No

Homework #10c: Written Phone Call: Have Not Read the Letter Yet

Homework #10d: Practice Phone Call: Yes

Homework #10e: Practice Phone Call: Various Responses

10.1 SUPPLEMENT

Phone-Call Flowchart

Can I share with you in person?

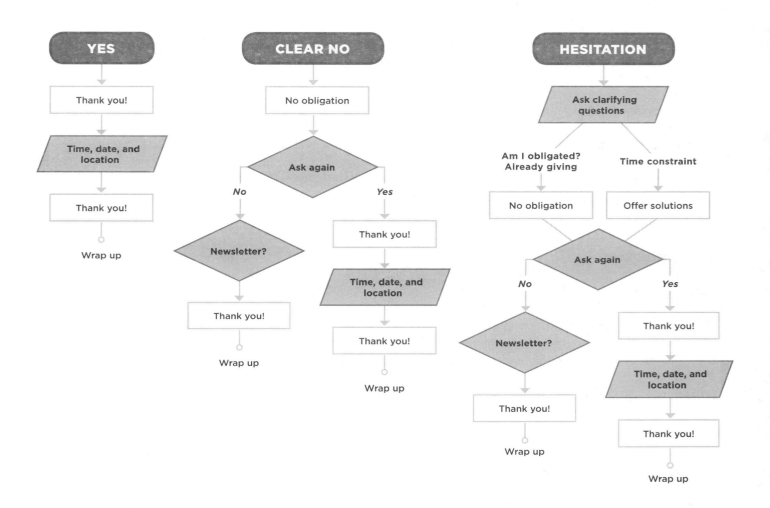

10.2 SUPPLEMENT

Mock Phone-Call Role-Play Checklist

The greeting	Yes	No	N/A
Did the person calling identify themselves?			
Did they make sure they had the right person?			
Did they make sure it was a good time to talk?			
Did they make small talk?			
Did they seem to listen well?			
Did they sound personable?			

The transition	Yes	No	N/A
Did they state the reason for the call?			
Did they refer to the letter? (not applicable for cold-call or possible referrals)			
If the person DID NOT read the letter, did they set a time to call back?			
If the person DID read it, did they "cast vision" and summarize?			

Asking for an appointment	Yes	No	N/A
Did they ask for an appointment?			
If person said yes to appointment			
Did they say thank you?			
Did they set the details of time and date?			
Did they repeat the details before ending the call?			

If person said yes to appointment, *with hesitation*			
Did they listen well and address concerns?			
Did they offer some meeting options?			
Did they stay flexible to meet the person on their timetable?			
Did they set the appointment?			
Did they say thank you?			
Did they repeat the meeting details?			
If person said no to appointment			
Did they acknowledge and address concerns?			
Did they clarify that there is no financial obligation?			
Did they ask for the appointment again?			
Did they "reach" for mailing list?			
Did they say thank you?			

Assessing the missionary (the caller)	Yes	No	N/A
Were they friendly and did they seem to listen well to details?			
Did they sound genuine?			
Did they seem excited?			
Did they sound scripted or a little rigid?			
Did they honor time well?			
Did they offer solutions to any problems/concerns?			
Regardless of outcome, was the missionary positive and upbeat, and did they seem excited?			

10.3 SUPPLEMENT

Sample Phone Scripts

Sample phone conversation, if you're *starting* ministry

1. **Greeting**

   Hi, This is _____. Is this _____? OR Is _____ there?

   Do you have just a minute? OR Is this a good time to talk? OR Did I catch you at a good time?

   Make small talk if it's there, for one or two minutes, depending.

   How are you?

   Ask about church, work, or family.

2. **Transition: did they read the letter?**

   _____, I don't want to keep you long. The reason that I am calling is that I recently sent you a letter sharing with you what the Lord has been doing in my life, and sharing with you that I am launching out into full-time ministry at ABC ministries. _____, have you had a chance to read my letter?

   If they *haven't* read it:

   I want to give you time to read the letter. How about I call back in four days. Would that give you time?

   If they say yes:

   OK, great, that would be Friday (state the date). Can I call you Friday (state the date) at four?

   If they *have* read it: share excitement about ministry, and cast a little vision about the ministry.

   I am launching out into full-time ministry with ABC Ministries. I'm really excited about what God is doing within me and through the ministry at ABC. We are looking forward to sharing the gospel on college campuses and raising up young adult leaders.

3. **Ask for an opportunity to share more with them**

   If you are taking a trip to their city, share with them the dates you will be there and work it into your ask.

_____, I would like to have an opportunity to meet with you and share a little more about all that the Lord is doing with us, how He has called us, and inform you about some ways that you could be involved. _____, could I have an opportunity to connect with you in the next few days or early next week? (or state the dates you will be in their city)._

Pause and silently wait for them to answer.

If they say yes: Say thank you, express gratitude, and move toward setting appointment.

If they say no: Acknowledge their response, assure them that there is absolutely no financial obligation at all, share excitement about ministry, and ask for the opportunity again.

4. **Set the appointment (have 4 to 5 times and locations to offer them)**

   _____, I have a few open times this week. Would Thursday afternoon or Friday work for you?_

   After a couple of attempts to try to get on their schedule:

   _____, what works best for you?_

   In some situations you may want to let them know about how long the meeting would be. Share length of meeting if:

   » They sound concerned about the time

   » You are meeting during the middle of the day

   » You know you are meeting on their lunch break

   » You have very little or no relationship

   _____, thank you for taking time on your lunch hour to meet with me; it won't take more than thirty minutes._

   Adjust your length of time based on the situation or their concern: thirty to forty minutes, or less than an hour. If you're meeting in a home, this won't be an issue.

5. **Confirm time, date, and location. Get detailed directions.**

   _____, I will be coming from the south part of town. What's the best way to your office?_

   » If you have already sent a letter this may not be necessary, but it never hurts to verify.

   » If it's an excited friend, be sure to get specific location, address, and directions.

   » Make it easy for them—offer a place near their home or work.

6. **Wrap up the phone call**

Wrap up the phone, thank them for the opportunity to share, and mention how much you are looking forward to it.

_____, *thank you again for the opportunity to share with you how the Lord is moving through ABC Ministries and impacting college students. I look forward to seeing you.*

Summary

Phone call to potential new partner:

» Take a minute to pray.

» Greet them.

» Identify yourself.

» Make sure you have the person you want to talk to.

» Ask if it is a good time to talk.

» Chat briefly (possibly one to two minutes.)

» Transition: did they read the letter?

» Express excitement about going into full-time ministry.

» Ask for an opportunity to share more with them.

» Set appointment.

» If needed, let them know how long it will take.

» Confirm date, time, and directions.

» Get directions to their house or meeting place.

» Thank them for the opportunity to share, and mention how much you are looking forward to it.

Sample phone conversation, if you're *already* in ministry

1. **Greeting**

Hi, This is _____. Is this _____? OR Is _____ there?

Do you have just a minute? OR Is this a good time to talk? OR Did I catch you at a good time?

Make small talk for a minute or two, if it's there.

How are you?

Ask about church, work, or family.

2. **Transition: did they read the letter?**

> _____, thank you for giving me a minute of your time. The reason I am calling is I recently sent you a letter sharing with you about the ministry that I have been involved with over the last five years at XYZ Ministries. _____, have you had a chance to read my letter?_

If they _haven't_ read it:

> _I want to give you time to read the letter. How about I call back in four days? Would that give you time?_

If they say yes:

> _OK, great, that would be Friday (state the date). Can I call you Friday (state the date) at four?_

If they _have_ read it: share excitement and cast a little more vision about the ministry.

> _I am really excited about serving the Lord at XYZ. I have been here for five years, and I have seen the Lord touch so many lives, and I am encouraged by the fruit He is bringing forth. The Lord has made it clear to me that I am called to _____, and I enjoy walking out my calling at XYZ._

3. **Ask for an opportunity to share more with them**

If you are taking a trip to their city, share with them the dates you will be there and work it into your ask.

> _____ I would like to have an opportunity to meet with you and share a little more about all that the Lord is doing with us, how He has called us, and inform you about some ways that you could be involved. _____, could I have an opportunity to connect with you in the next few days or early next week? (OR state the dates you will be in their city)._

Pause and silently wait for them to answer.

> If they say yes: say thank you, express gratitude, and move towards setting appointment.

> If they say no: acknowledge their response, assure them that there is absolutely no financial obligation at all, share excitement about ministry, and ask for the opportunity again.

4. **Set the appointment (have 4 to 5 times and locations to offer them)**

> _____, I have a few open times this week; would Thursday afternoon or Friday work for you?_

After a couple of attempts to try to get on their schedule:

> _____, what works best for you?_

In some situations you may want to let them know about how long the meeting would be. Share length of meeting if:

- » They sound concerned about the time.

- » You are meeting during the middle of the day.

- » You know you are meeting on their lunch break.

- » You have very little or no relationship.

    _____, *thank you for taking time on your lunch hour to meet with me. It won't take more than thirty minutes.*

Adjust your length of time based on the situation or their concern: thirty to forty minutes or less than an hour. If you're meeting in a home this won't be an issue.

5. Confirm time, date, locations: get detailed directions

_____, *I will be coming from the south part of town, what's the best way to your office?*

If you have already sent a letter this may not be necessary, but it never hurts to verify. If it's an excited friend be sure to get specific location, address, and directions. Make it easy for them—offer a place near their home or work.

6. Wrap up the phone call

Wrap up the phone, thank them for the opportunity to share, and mention how much you are looking forward to it.

_____, *thank you again for the opportunity to share with how the Lord is moving through XYZ Ministries and impacting college students. I look forward to seeing you.*

Summary

Phone call to potential new partner:

1. *Take a minute to pray.*

2. *Greet them.*

3. *Identify yourself.*

4. *Make sure you have the person you want to talk to.*

5. *Ask if it is a good time to talk.*

6. *Chat briefly (possibly one to two minutes).*

7. *Transition: did they read the letter?*

8. *Express excitement about going into full-time ministry.*

9. *Ask for an opportunity to share more with them.*

10. *Set appointment.*

11. *If needed, let them know how long it will take.*

12. *Confirm date, time, and directions.*

13. *Get directions to their house or meeting place.*

14. *Thank them for the opportunity to share and mention how much you are looking forward to it.*

Appointment: Prepare, Share, and Invite

Overview: Your appointment is an opportunity to share what God is doing in you and through your organization. There are a number of things you need to learn in order to be well prepared, build relationship, communicate clearly, and invite people into missions. In this session you will learn what actually goes into an appointment kit, some basic things to remember about your appointment, an appointment outline, and how to invite and start your new partnership. The aim of this session is to help build your personal confidence for meeting new people, sharing about your organization, and inviting these people to play an active role in the Great Commission.

Fourth point of contact: the appointment

Practice your appointment with a friend, and if you can, videotape the mock appointment. This will help you learn from your mistakes. You are going to make mistakes, but it would be better to make them while in practice with a friend than with your first three or four potential partners. Have your practice friend throw three or four different situations at you: the good appointment, the rough appointment, and the lots-of-questions appointment. Change the endings: support, no support, prayer support, special gift, and so on. Remember to practice, practice, and practice.

Take time to prepare an appointment kit. This kit would include:

1. Partnership response card, which should include contact information, the giving amount, and frequency

2. Budget sheet with monthly needs: both long-term and short-term needs

3. Giving instructions

4. Any materials about your ministry you want to share (optional)

5. Copy of a recommendation letter (sample)

6. Self-addressed, stamped envelope

7. Pen and thank you cards

8. Breath mints

9. Directions to the appointment

10. All of the above could be put into a nice padded folder or binder

Before you go to your appointment, make sure you are fully prepared. Dress the part: if you are going to meet a business person over a business lunch, cut-off shorts and flip-flops are not the best choice. Don't feel the need to over-dress, but looking neat, well-kept, and prepared will help communicate the right message.

Look nice, put some breath mints in your pocket, and get used to carrying them. Meeting and talking to new people is part of your assignment as a full-time missionary. We want to be ready at all times.

Remember the reason for your appointment! You are going to share with someone what the Lord is doing with you and through your organization, and you are going to extend to them an invitation to be a part of it. Therefore, stay focused and make the invitation.

Many of your appointments are going to be with friends and you should expect longer meetings of about one and a half or two hours to be fairly standard. On several occasions, a shorter meeting will be required; therefore, you must be prepared and organized. Be ready to share and invite in thirty minutes if necessary. The more you practice your appointments, the better you will get at sharing vision and extending an invitation to participate. Be sure to practice the thirty-minute mock appointment.

If you have been keeping a partner profile, then take time to review your notes before your appointment. In the event that you're using a computer, iPad, or a flipbook presentation, be sure to have all of this together in a neat package that is ready to go at all times. You don't want to be searching for materials minutes before an appointment, and you don't want to be in the middle of an appointment and discover that you forgot something. This would not make a good impression.

Think through your presentation and know what you want to say. Remember, this is the moment you have been working toward; you now have your face-to-face meeting and a chance to share the exciting ministry God has called you into.

The person you are sitting across from has had many chances to say no, but they haven't. You asked for an opportunity to share with them and they said yes. You have prepared for this, you know your vision, you know your calling, and you have confidence that God has brought you to this point—that He is going to provide for you.

Before you go, take a minute to pray and ask the Lord for clarity. Review any information you might have on the person you are meeting. Make sure you have all of your materials and information ready: pen, contact information, giving instructions, and ministry information.

Remember: you are not going to do sales—you are going to share and invite.

You can use your letter as an outline for your conversation, and this is your opportunity to unpack all that wasn't said in that letter. You could spend three, five, seven, or nine minutes on each one of your letter's paragraphs and you could spend ten minutes on each paragraph as well. *Make it conversational and keep it natural.*

Be ready to answer questions, and keep your answers short to help you stay on track. Try to make good eye contact and be confident, and try not to ramble. Don't be nervous. People are much more ready to give than you think, and besides, they are happy to see you!

When they say yes, that is the best time to say thank you. You also want to find out what their frequency and level of partnership is going to be.

> *John and Jane, thank you so much; I look forward to working with you! John and Jane, how much and how often would you like to give?*

This would be a good time for you to have them fill out a partnership commitment card that you will keep. Also share your giving instructions.

John and Jane, would you take a minute to fill out this partnership card for us? It's not a contract or anything; it's simply a way for us to keep track of our partnership as we are working toward our financial goal.

Have a copy that you can leave with them. Say thank you again, and then share fellowship with your new partners!

A few things to keep in mind about your appointment

1. Do not be late.

2. Dress the part.

3. Have all you materials ready: you don't want to be looking for a pen when they're ready to write you a check.

4. Stay on track and keep it short.

5. Make lots of eye contact.

6. Answer questions, but don't let them derail the conversation.

7. When it's time to ask, look them in the eye and ask, "John and Jane, will you partner with me in ministry?"

8. Wait for their answer.

9. Say thank you well and often.

Outline of your appointment

Your appointment outline could look a little like this; adjust it as needed, and be willing to improvise if you have to.

1. **Greeting and small talk**

   » Ask about them and their family, their interests, hobbies, and their heart for missions. Try to ask a couple of questions about each subject and listen well, taking mental notes. Or just do it on the fly and be natural.

   » If you have an hour or longer appointment, then ten minutes of small talk is enough, but no more than that. If you are having dinner with a friend, then all of the dinner time is small talk. Move toward sharing your vision after you eat. Be natural.

APPOINTMENT OUTLINE

1. Greeting
2. Transition
3. Catch-up
4. Calling to ministry
5. Share the vision
6. Vision and values of the organization
7. Questions
8. Invite
9. Respond accordingly
10. Wrap-up
11. Fellowship
12. Thank-you card

» If you are meeting with a person you have little relationship with take time to build rapport. Ask them about their family, work, and church life. Ask a few questions on each topic. Listen well; be engaging.

2. **Transition**

You can start your transition by saying,

John and Jane, thank you for meeting me here and giving me chance to share with you about how the Lord has called me into ministry and how He is impacting students at XYZ University.

3. **Bring them up to date**

» Tell them where you have been and what you have been doing. Maybe you have moved or already started in ministry. You are bringing them up to date since the last time you talked with them, or at least the last three months of ministry.

» You may share some old memories or talk about old friends. How is their church life, family and children, hobbies? This would be a great time to share a recent testimony.

4. **Talk about how you were called into full-time ministry**

» Relate when and how the Lord started speaking to you about this calling.

» How it developed and how you first responded. Feel free to share some of the struggle.

» Bring this part of the story up to the present and be sure to share how the Lord has led you to this point.

5. **Share the vision that God has given you**

» You need to be confident in your calling. Your confidence will give them confidence.

» Share your vision with excitement, conviction, clarity—and with a sincere heart. Be natural.

6. **Talk a little about the missions organization you are working for**

» Convey the overall vision of your missions organization.

» What they do and where they do it. Maybe mention unique things about your mission.

» If you are sharing a very short video, you may want to start it at this point.

» Be sure to mention that your mission requires all missionaries to raise their own support. Be ready to answer any questions as to why.

» Let them know when you will start full time, if applicable.

7. **Make room for questions**

   » You should be making room for their questions throughout the appointment. Remember: this is a conversation more than a presentation.

   » At this point, ask them, "Do you have any questions?"

   » You want the air to be clear before you invite them.

8. **Invite them to partner with you**

   » After you have shared your vision, it's time to ask them into partnership. Be confident, do not apologize, be sincere, and smile.

   » Then take a short pause and transition with a restating of your vision/call in a sentence.

   » Do not hem-n-haw around and don't look away. Look them right in the eye and say, "John and Jane, will you partner with me in ministry?" Continue to look them in the eye and wait for the answer. Don't speak for them—let them be the next ones to talk.

9. **Respond accordingly**

   » If they say yes, then say thank you and move toward wrapping up with the partnership card and the instructions for giving.

   » If they say no, try to discern the no. If it's a clear no, then move toward a special gift.

   » If they say a halfway yes, something like, "Well, I might . . . what would help you?" then share that you are asking the Lord to give you monthly partners.

   Do not ask for a specific amount. Ask them to partner with you in ministry. If they say, "Well, what would help you?" Say, *"I want you to feel like a part of our team; I encourage you to partner in a way that excites your heart."* Most people by the time of the appointment know the dollar amount of their partnership.

   If they express a desire to partner with you, but are not sure about monthly, listen closely and try to help them. Be ready to make a way for the quarterly, yearly, or occasional giver.

10. **The wrap-up**

    » Thank them, and maybe extend an invitation to be a prayer partner.

    » Give them a partnership card.

    » Give them the giving instructions.

11. **Fellowship**

Write a thank-you card

As soon as you leave the appointment, send them a thank-you card. Talk about your time together and how much you look forward to working with them. Cite the dollar amount they partnered for and comment on how much it will help. Let them know what their partnership will accomplish: outreach, salvations, training, intercession, mission trips, acts of justice, mercy deeds, etc.

Remember: practice, practice, practice

Practice your appointment with a friend and, if you can, videotape the mock appointment. This will help you learn from your mistakes. You are going to make mistakes, but it would be better to make them in your practice with a friend than with your first three or four potential partners. Have your practice friend throw three or four different situations at you: the good appointment, the rough appointment, and the lots-of-questions appointment. Change the endings: support, no support, prayer support, one-time gift, and so on. Remember to practice, practice, and practice.

Summary

1. *Practicing your appointment with friends to work out the kinks will help minimize lost opportunities during your actual appointments.*

2. *Your appointment kit should include: partnership response card, giving instructions, monthly budget, ministry materials, recommendation letter, a stamped, self-addressed envelope, pen, and a thank-you card.*

3. *Because you have worked hard for this appointment, make sure to dress the part. Be well-prepared and stay focused.*

4. *This face-to-face appointment is about biblical partnership—not sales—so keep it conversational and natural, not pushy and demanding.*

5. *Your appointment with a potential partner should include a greeting and small talk, transition, bringing them up to speed, the story of how God called you, your vision statement, information about your organization, room for questions, a clear invitation to partnership, and a wrap-up, including filling out appropriate forms and fellowshipping.*

6. *Within twenty-four hours of your appointment, regardless of whether they said yes or no to partnership, you need to put a thank you card in the mail, thanking them for the opportunity they gave you.*

Please complete the following homework assignments:

Homework #11a: Thinking It Through

Homework #11b: Appointment Script

Homework #11c: Appointment Script: Yes

Homework #12a: Practice Appointment #1

Homework #12b: Practice Appointment #2: Including Ask

11.1 SUPPLEMENT

Appointment Flowchart

Will you partner with me in ministry?

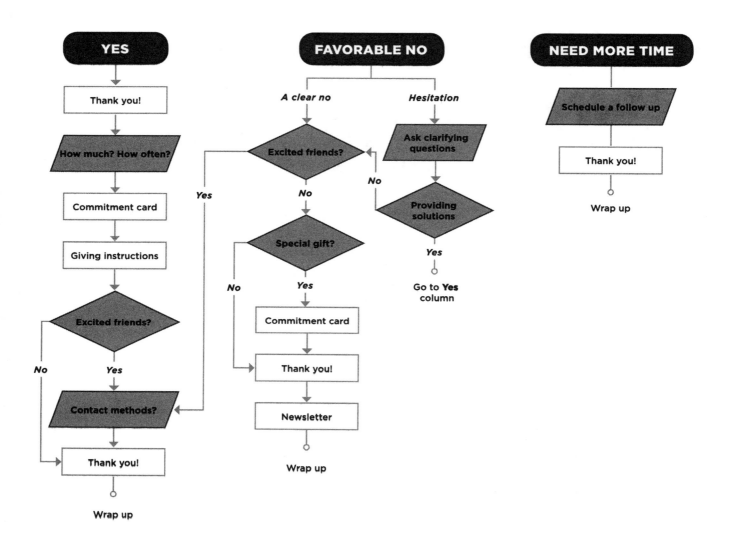

11.2 SUPPLEMENT

Mock Appointment Role-Play Checklist

The greeting	Yes	No	N/A
1. Did they greet them by name?			
2. Did they make lots of eye contact?			
3. Did they wait to be invited in?			
4. Did they smile and were they friendly?			

Build rapport	Yes	No	N/A
1. Did they engage in conversation well?			
2. Did they ask questions, family, work, church, personal interest, etc.?			
3. Did they remain conversational?			

Transition	Yes	No	N/A
1. Did they slow down and make a transition?			
2. Did they call them by name and thank them for the time?			
3. Did the transition have vision or assignment in it?			
4. Was the transition over 30 seconds and less than 90?			

The body of the appointment	Yes	No	N/A
1. Did they bring them up to date?			
a. Could you hear God at work in them?			
b. Did they sound happy and excited?			
c. Do you have a clear understanding of their last few months?			
d. Did they smile and were they friendly?			

The body of the appointment	Yes	No	N/A
2. Calling or ministry assignment			
a. Did they make a clear statement about calling or assignment?			
b. Did they share how God has led them to this decision?			
c. Does it sound like they are obeying the Lord?			
d. Do you know what their assignment is in general?			
e. Do you know their heart concerning it?			
3. How they plan to walk it out			
a. Did they share about the ministry organization?			
b. Did they communicate vision and values clearly?			
c. Did they share that all the organization's missionaries have the privilege of raising ministry team?			
d. Did they answer any questions?			
e. Did they share about their assignment within the ministry?			
f. Can you see how their calling dovetails with the ministry?			
g. Could you repeat their calling and assignment back to us?			
4. The invitation			
a. Did they state their calling or assignment?			
b. Did they make it clear that they cannot do it alone?			
c. Did they make a clear invitation?			
d. Did they maintain eye contact and wait for an answer?			
e. Did they respond appropriately?			
f. Did they present a partnership card?			
g. Did they ask about excited friends?			
h. Did they ask about a special gift?			

Appointment: Excited Friends

Overview: When God called you into full-time ministry, He simultaneously committed to move on people's hearts to partner with you. Many of the people that God has in mind for your ministry you currently do not know. In this session you will learn about the power of recommendations, how to ask for excited friends with clarity and confidence, and how to follow up with those excited friends. The aim of this session is to share both the importance of adding people to your team that you currently do not know as well as the "how to" of adding people to your team.

Introduction to excited friends

We are always recommending things to our friends. Have you been to a conference someone has recommended or a restaurant? Or bought a book, or watched movie, downloaded an app? A large portion of the things we love and enjoy in life we experience because a friend has recommended them to us.

People who say yes to partnership (both financial and prayer) are the ones most excited about your ministry. Undoubtedly, if more people knew about you and what you are doing, they too would be excited. There are literally thousands of people out there who would be excited about you and your ministry if they knew about it. I call these people *excited friends.*

The word *referral* has many negative thoughts and emotions connected to it, so I choose to use the term excited friend, which is a more accurate word that describes your situation.

Excited friends are similar to your existing friends: they need four or five points of contact before you can expect an answer. There is no way to quantify it exactly, but a personal recommendation from a close friend is worth about two or three points of contact.

Excited friends

Being introduced to excited friends is a key to building your complete partnership team. When you do your partnership campaign the way we have described in this training, thirty percent or more of your team will be people whom you currently do not know. It will be very difficult for you to reach your fully funded mark—as well as stay properly funded—apart from excited friends.

Connecting with many people outside of our own circles is key to long-term success in ministry, and it is good for the Body of Christ as a whole. Many would be happy to be a part of your work; they just don't know that you exist. Friends are a great way to meet interested, like-minded people.

Excited friends are not referrals, leads, contacts, or hot prospects, but brothers and sisters who share in our interest and concerns surrounding the Great Commission.

They want to see Jesus' name lifted high and His fame going throughout the earth. They would be happy to sow into you and your organization; they just need a chance to meet you and hear your story.

The more people you invite, the more will partner with you.

The best time to talk about excited friends is during your face-to-face appointments. Once you have talked about partnership, have had them fill out a partnership card, and have shared the giving instructions—then you want to address the topic of excited friends. I will also ask about excited friends when I receive a no to the partnership invitation if the person is nevertheless happy for me and excited about my ministry.

Some people want to use excited friends as "plan B" in the event that they don't meet their financial goal with their closest friends. *Please do not make this mistake.* In the appointment our excitement is high; there's momentum and interest. But trying to revisit the topic later is more challenging. The best time to talk about excited friends is in the first face-to-face meeting.

Outline for excited friends introduction:

Step one: Acknowledge and inform

» Acknowledge their willingness/excitement.

» "There's another way that you can play a vital part!"

Step two: Describe your situation

» "We have not yet met all the people necessary to reach our financial goal."

» "As we have shared, many have been excited by what the Lord is doing through ABC Ministries."

Step three: Ask for an introduction

» "Will you introduce me to your friends so that I might have a chance to share with them?"

Step four: Who are the people

» "Who are the people in your social sphere who would share in your excitement/concern?"

Step five: Who will do the contacting

» "Will you contact them, or could I?"

Step six: Gather contact information

» "What is the best way to contact them? By letter, email, or phone?"

» Gather all the contact information.

Step seven: Follow through

» Share/send them ministry materials.

» Call the potential excited friend and ask for an appointment.

» Meet the excited friend.

» Follow up with them if necessary.

Language is important

When we are asking to meet their potentially excited friends, we have to *choose our words carefully, in a way that our friend can hear our heart behind the request we are making. If we sound like we are only hunting for contacts, our friend may disconnect and shut down before we have a chance to be heard. Focus on the mission.*

As we work through our outline there are a few things that I want them to hear as I share and ask: I want them to hear gratitude. I want them to hear the opportunity for them to be involved. I want them to clearly hear my situation. I want them to hear that people are stirred and joining our team. I want them to clearly hear what I am asking them to do.

Step one: Acknowledge and inform

Jim and Jane, <u>thank you so much for your willingness</u> to be a financial partner with me in the work at ABC Ministries. <u>There is another vital way that you can be a part</u> of this financial partnership team.

If they have not said yes to partnership but are happy for you and excited by the ministry, then just inform them.

"here is another vital way that you can be involved.

Step two: Describe your situation

In this season I (or we) am working to build a ministry team of financial partners who will work with me in reaching teens for Christ through ABC Ministries. God has given me several opportunities to share about how He is moving through this exciting ministry and impacting teens with the gospel. As we have been meeting with friends, they have introduced us to their friends, and many have been stirred by God to become financial partners with us in ministry. Currently I have not yet met all the people needed to finish out our team.

In the language above, they:

>> clearly hear my situation,

>> hear that friends are introducing me to their friends,

>> hear that friends and friends of friends are stirred and becoming partners.

Step three: Ask for an introduction

Remember confidence is a key to being successful in developing financial partnership. Have confidence in your calling, that God is able, and that He has a team for you. Believe that God stirs hearts through sharing and that He wants others involved through this ministry.

Jim and Jane, while I'm here in Omaha for the next two weeks I plan to meet as many people as I can, sharing with them about how God is changing the lives of teenagers through ABC and inform them about ways they could be involved. Will you introduce me to your friends, by letter, email, or phone, that they might have a chance to hear how God is moving through this ministry?

The language above clearly communicates:

> » That you plan to share with as many people as you can

> » That you want them to have a chance to hear about the ministry

> » That you're asking them to introduce you

Be very clear in what you want the person to do for you.

When you use the right language and ask correctly they will say yes to introducing you. If you are hearing nos in your appointments, then talk with your coach, let them instruct you on how to ask correctly.

Step four: Who are the people

Maintaining a confident attitude, ask who the people are in their life that would be excited by this ministry or share in their concern for (ministry focus). Ask the question in the positive: "Who are the people in your church?" Don't ask it in the passive: "You don't happen to know anybody, do ya?" OR "Do you know anybody that might wanna give to our ministry?" Use action-oriented words and buzzwords for your organization that represent the ministry.

> » ". . . impacting college campuses through the love of Christ."

> » "Planting churches in Southeast Asia."

> » "Equipping young leaders through night-and-day prayer."

> » "Taking the love and truth of Jesus Christ to the nations."

> » "Bringing prayer and missions together for a greater harvest."

> » "Who shares in our concern for the fatherless?"

The person you are talking to has 200-300 friends at church, work, social settings, and in their family. Help them think of names by breaking down their life into smaller categories. With pen in hand and excited friends sheet out in front of you, ask for names.

> *Jim, who are the people at your church who share in your excitement for planting churches in Asia?*

As they share write the names down on your sheet. Try to get two or three names before moving on. Ask basically the same question again in a different context, with a different set of action words and buzz words.

> *Jim, how about your men's ministry? Who are the people there that share in your concern for reaching the lost?*

Again try to get a few names before moving on to the next context.

> *Jim, how about your work? Who are the people there that share in your excitement for taking the gospel to unreached regions?*

Different contexts to ask about people could include: home church, Bible study, men's or women's ministry, home group, workplace, neighbors, family, and social settings like hobby clubs or recreation groups.

Try to keep the person you are meeting with *thinking*. Work through the groups of friends one at a time—do not suggest more than one at a time. This will let them focus by staying in one category a little longer, producing more names.

After compiling a list of names, ask them for help in prioritizing your list, and you can say something like this:

> *If you were in my situation, raising a financial partnership team so that you could fully obey the Lord with ABC Ministries, who on this list would you talk to first?*

Step five: Who's doing the contacting

Now that you have gathered a number of names we need to find out who is going to do the contacting. We want to honor all existing relationships, not stress them. Assume that they would like to do the contacting and mention it first in your question. For example:

> *Jim, will you contact them, or do you think I could?*

If they would like to do the contacting then offer them:

> » A pre-written letter of recommendation

> » A pre-written email

> » Will they be calling their friend to introduce you and see if you have permission to contact them?

> » Will they arrange a personal introduction?

Have your partner contact their friend. A call would be great, and their communication should be something like

> *I would like you to have a chance to meet my friend, Chris. He is in full-time ministry at ABC. I think you would enjoy his ministry as much as I have. Can Chris have permission to contact you? Would that be okay with you?"*

Then, the excited friend gives the permission. Note:

> » Your partner may want to send a little communication in writing to their friend before you call (see example).

> » You may want to write a communication before you call (see example).

Step six: Gather contact information if needed

If your friend or new partner has decided to do the contacting then you don't need contact information yet. That can come in a few days once your friend has contacted the excited friend. In the situation where you are doing the contact, now is the time to gather that information and gather as much as your friend has. The contact information you have may determine the method of contact.

Step seven: Follow through

If you make the call first, consider the following outline:

1. Make sure you have the right person when you call.

2. Identify yourself and help them know who you are.

   Hello Mr. Smith: my name is Sally Singer we have a mutual friend, Mike Jones. I think he shared with you that I would be calling.

   » Make sure that it is a good time to call.

   » Take a minute or two to build rapport, maybe around your mutual friend.

3. Transition:

   » *Well, Mr. Smith, the reason that I am calling is that I was recently talking with our friend, Mike Jones. I was sharing with him about the work that the Lord is doing through our ministry at ABC. Mr. Smith have you heard about ABC?*

   » Respond accordingly. Give about a one-minute overview. "ABC is an evangelical . . ."

4. Ask for an opportunity to share:

   » *Mr. Smith, I would greatly appreciate an opportunity to share more with you about how the Lord is reaching (insert people)* OR . . . *how the Lord is working through ABC* OR . . . *how the Lord is raising up young leaders* OR combine all three.

   » *Mr. Smith, may I have an opportunity to meet with you and share some ways that you could be involved?*

5. Set the appointment details.

6. Consider sending a brief letter with a ministry overview, written materials about the ministry, and/ or possibly a video link. Try to send something with a photo and contact information.

7. Go to the appointment.

8. You may differ in the ways you invite them to partner. Feel it out with the Lord. You have two options here:

   » You could invite directly by saying, "Will you partner with me in ministry?"

   » You could invite them indirectly by saying, "Will you pray and ask God what part He might have you play in this ministry?" Then, follow up in a few days.

9. A large percentage of excited friends will have to be followed up with after the appointment no matter what you do.

Things to remember about excited friends:

   » God has called you and has a team for you. He's stirring hearts around you.

   » Many people would gladly partner with you if they knew about your ministry.

   » You will not reach your realistic financial goal apart from meeting new friends.

   » Thirty percent or more of your team will come from these excited friends.

» Be sure to ask about excited friends in your appointments—don't wait until later.

» Ask your partner/friend to introduce you to their friends.

» Gather names of those who share in your concern or your excitement; use buzz words.

» Suggest social spheres, churches, small groups, Sunday-school groups, co-workers, and family, both immediate and extended family members.

» Determine who in your group is doing the contacting; offer letter, email, or phone call.

» Verify the time that you will contact the excited friend, and do it soon.

» Contact the excited friend.

» Use the phone-call outline.

» Explain a little about your organization.

» Ask for an appointment.

» Ask for additional contact information.

» Send ministry materials.

» Go to the appointment.

» Follow up if needed.

Summary

1. *Most people who say yes to partnership or are excited about the ministry are happy to recommend you and the ministry to their friends.*

2. *Over thirty percent of your overall team will be made up of excited friends, which means it will be difficult to reach your properly-funded goal without excited friends.*

3. *Excited friends aren't referrals, leads, contacts, or hot prospects; they are brothers and sisters in Christ who share similar concerns about the Great Commission.*

4. *When asking for excited friends, we must make sure that our request carries our heart with it—we don't want to come across as just "hunting for contacts."*

5. *Having confidence in the Lord's willingness to provide a partnership team for you will enable you to ask clear questions that aren't weak, but action-oriented.*

6. *We aren't asking people to make an assessment of their friends' ability to give. We are simply stating that we plan to share with as many people as possible.*

7. *Offer solutions for your potential partner to help them think of people they know.*

8. *During the name-storming process, gather names first and contact information a little later.*

Please complete the following homework assignments:

Homework #11d: Appointment Script: Excited-Friends Ask

Homework #12c: Practice Appointment #3: Excited Friends

Homework #12d: Practice Phone Call: Excited Friends

12.1 SUPPLEMENT

Excited Friends Flow Chart

Who are the people in your (social sphere) that share our excitement/concern for (ministry/people)?

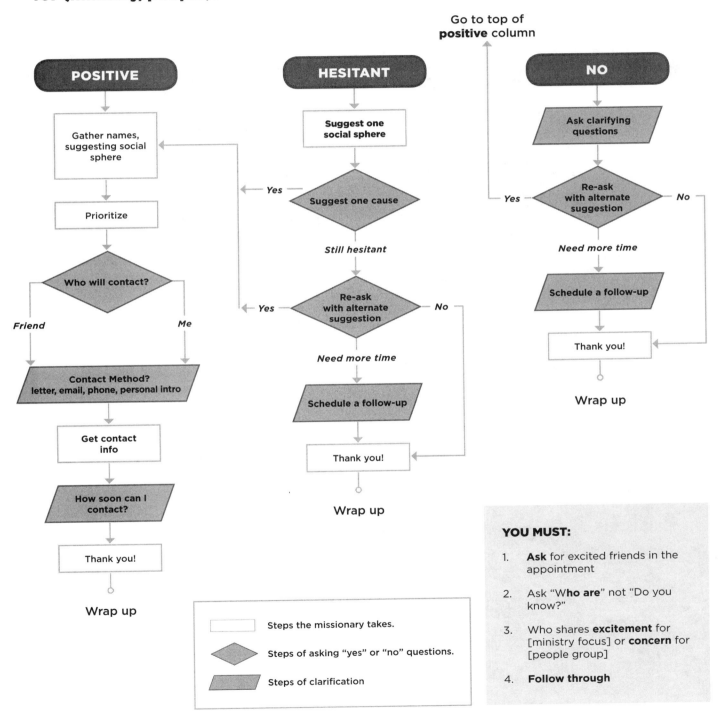

YOU MUST:

1. **Ask** for excited friends in the appointment

2. Ask "W**ho are**" not "Do you know?"

3. Who shares **excitement** for [ministry focus] or **concern** for [people group]

4. **Follow through**

12.2 SUPPLEMENTS

Example Letter: A partner sending a recommendation letter ahead of you and your phone call

Hi *(name of excited friend)*,

I want to introduce you to friends of ours, Rob and Rhonda Parker. We've known Rob and Rhonda personally for years, and we share a common heart and passion for Jesus.

Rob and Rhonda are full-time ministry workers with ABC Ministries. ABC Ministries is a missions base committed to intercession, worship, evangelism, training, equipping young adults, being mindful of the poor, and other acts of justice. All of the work revolves around and flows out of a night-and-day prayer meeting that began fifteen years ago and continues to this day.

We have been prayer and financial partners with Rob and Rhonda's ministry for over five years, and we have thoroughly enjoyed being connected with them. They are trustworthy, faithful, and encouraging to our lives in the Lord!

We want to personally recommend Rob and Rhonda's ministry to you. We think you would enjoy them and their ministry as much as we have. Rob will be contacting you by phone in a few days and would like to have an opportunity to meet with you and share further about their ministry.

I am excited about their work and I think you will be too.

Many blessings on you,

(name of your partner)

You could provide your partner some ministry materials they could insert in this letter.

Example Letter: Example of a written communication you could send to an excited friend before you call them

Hi *(name of excited friend)*,

Greetings in the name of Jesus!

Picture of yourself

My name is John Doe and we have a mutual friend, Sally Singer. My wife, Jane, and I have known Sally for about ten years now and first met her in a home group through our church. We, like Sally, have a heart and passion for Jesus and His coming kingdom. My wife and I were recently sharing with Sally about the ministry that we serve and she said that you would be excited to hear about how the Lord is (working; reaching the poor; and so on) at ABC Ministries in Kansas City.

We are full-time ministry staff at the ABC Ministries in Kansas City. ABC Ministries is a missions base committed to advancing the Kingdom of God through worship, evangelism, training, equipping young adults, mindfulness of the poor, and other acts of justice.

It is a great privilege to serve the Lord Jesus and prepare the earth for His coming. We, like the other staff members at ABC Ministries (and many other missions organizations as well), have this privilege and responsibility to develop a team of financial partners who make it possible for us do this work of the ministry. Sally and I are currently developing our team of partners. We would be grateful for an opportunity to share with you how the Lord is moving through ABC Ministries and the work we do. We will be calling you in a few days to ask you for an appointment.

We have also enclosed some information about our ministry and we look forward to speaking with you soon.

Many blessings to you,

(your name)

Letter could also include a ministry picture that is self-explanatory

Example Letter: Email from a familiar partner

Possible subject line: *Touching the poor, inner city, and youth with the love of Christ* OR *Equipping a generation of young leaders.*

Dear *(name of excited friend)*,

It was good to see you last week and catch up a bit. We love you and your family!

I want to introduce you to some friends of ours, Rob and Rhonda Parker. We've known Rob and Rhonda personally for years, and we share a common heart and passion for Jesus.

Rob and Rhonda are full-time gospel workers with ABC Ministries. ABC Ministries is a missions base committed to intercession, worship, evangelism, Christian education and training, equipping young adults, being mindful of the poor, and other acts of justice. All of the work revolves around and flows out of a prayer meeting that began fifteen years ago and continues to this day.

Like many other missions organizations, ABC staff members have the privilege and responsibility to develop a team of financial partners who make it possible for them do the work of the ministry. We have joined their team of prayer and financial partners and are grateful for the opportunity to invest in their work of (the Great Commission, equipping of young adults, etc.).

Rob and Rhonda are currently building their partnership team. We thought you would be encouraged to hear about their ministry, and we suggested they contact you. We are planning to share your contact information with them, unless you object, otherwise they will be contacting you soon.

If you have any questions, please do not hesitate to email or call.

Many blessings to you,

(name of partner sending email)

Example Letter: Email from a new ministry partner

Possible subject line: *A great opportunity for the kingdom of God* OR *Advancing the kingdom through prayer and missions.*

Dear *(name of excited friend)*,

It was good to see you at the basketball game last week; the kids are having a great season!

The other day we met with a dear family who are staff members with ABC Ministries—Rob and Rhonda Parker. ABC Ministries is a missions base committed to intercession, worship, evangelism, Christian education and training, equipping young adults, being mindful of the poor, and other acts of justice. All of the work revolves around and flows out of a prayer meeting that began fifteen years ago and continues to this day.

Like many other missions organizations, ABC staff members have the privilege and responsibility to develop a team of financial partners who make it possible for them to do the work of the ministry. We have joined their team of prayer and financial partners and are grateful for the opportunity to (sow into the kingdom, equip young adults, reach the lost, help fulfill the Great Commission, etc.).

Rob and Rhonda are currently building their partnership team. We thought you would be encouraged to hear about their ministry, and we suggested they contact you. We plan to share your contact information with them, unless you object, otherwise they will be contacting you soon.

If you have any questions, please feel free to contact me.

(name of new partner sending email)

Last paragraph could also read:

Rob and Rhonda are currently building their partnership team. We thought you would be encouraged to hear about their ministry. May we share your contact information with them so that you would have an opportunity to hear about this impactful ministry?

We look forward to your reply

Appointment: Multiple Strategies

Overview: Building a solid partnership team that will empower you to serve God in full-time ministry will require that you implement more than one strategy during your campaign. We use multiple strategies in order to reach the largest group of people on a personal level in a time-sensitive way. In this session we will cover four ways to develop partnership, how to create a plan for multiple locations, and how to implement the varied strategies. The goal of this session is for you to have the knowledge and skills necessary for a diversified strategy in your partnership development campaign.

Strategies for partnership development

As you develop a strategic plan for your partnership development, it must include diligence and faith. You will need to use a combination of the following strategies to raise your partnership team. One method done by itself does not guarantee success.

Four ways to develop partnership

1.   Individuals in face-to-face appointments

2.   Excited friends

3.   Cookouts and/or dessert gatherings (hosted by small groups)

4.   Churches

Have a strategy for every location

You probably have one to three areas where most of your contacts are located. Think through which strategies you may implement; sometimes you can implement all four strategies in each location. Reach, work hard, maximize your time.

»   Start dividing your contact list into groups based on geography. Each city or region should have its own list.

»   Divide each city or region list into groups of ten to fifteen contacts.

»   Be realistic about how long you should stay in each location to implement your partnership development strategy. Give yourself the time you need. Fight for the time if you have to. Most strategies will work best when you are at one location for an extended period of time.

»   In the Chicago area, if you had forty-five contacts, that would be three groups of fifteen. You would plan to be there no less than three weeks. Additionally, one to two days per week you are there should be designated for follow-up and transition. Therefore, you would need to be in Chicago for about three-and-a-half weeks.

Implementing strategies

The primary strategies that we suggest are: face-to-face one-on-one meetings, excited friends, hosted small groups/cookouts, church packets, and church visits/speaking engagements. We have seen hundreds of people utilize these various strategies during their campaign, resulting in consistent financial commitments as well as meaningful friendships.

Prayerfully consider which strategy you will use in each situation to develop your partnership team. You may use all of them in the same season, in the same city, and on the same trip.

Think through potential locations.

>> Your hometown; if married, your spouse's hometown

>> Where parents live

>> Where friends and relatives live

>> Cities you have worked in

>> Cities where good friends/partners have moved

>> Cities you have ministered in

>> You can do it!!

Individuals

We place a high value upon relational partnership development because the Bible places a high value upon relationships. Face-to-face appointments are a great way to build these relationships. It is a time-tested approach and works for everyone called as a full-time laborer. This has been God's way for about 3500 years.

We start with a letter, but it is not the typical missionary letter that you are considering. This letter only works because it is the first step in a four-step process. We follow up with a postcard, then a phone call to ask for the appointment, and then we go to the actual appointment. This gives the potential partner the time they need and removes the dynamic of a cold call. If you do this right and keep your schedule and momentum, they will actually be anticipating your call. A few people may even call you!

You will need to adjust your schedule for holidays, etc. I sent my letters out on the 1st of the month, then sent the postcard out on the 8th, then made the phone call around the 15th or 16th, and then had the opportunities for the appointments from around the 22nd to the 28th.

You will need to break this down into stages. Set these stages up so that you can be faithful to them every week. For me, this meant every Monday I would be ready to send something out. I had the letters stuffed, stamped, signed, and completely ready over the weekend. So, the first Monday morning, I had all my letters ready to mail. The next Monday morning, I had my postcards ready, and so forth. The following Monday, I started dialing the phone. This keeps you and the points of contact in a rhythm and momentum, also sustaining the initial effect of the invitation letter.

Cookouts & desserts

Hosted small groups, cookouts, or desserts are a great way to meet new friends. This is similar to asking for and meeting with an *excited friend*, except instead of being introduced to one person, your current partner or friend would introduce you to several people at once at a small gathering.

You would approach a good partner or friend about six or seven weeks in advance and ask them if they would host a cookout or dessert for you and invite a few of their friends. This is a great and effective way for a partner to help you build your team.

Personal recommendation process:

1. Contact #1—Personal recommendation letter

    You write the letter for your partner. They are the speaker in the letter, but you take all the work out of it by authoring/writing it for them. They send it to five, six, or seven households about three weeks prior to the event (see recommendation letter below).

2. Contact #2—Once the invitation has arrived and been in their home for three to five days, your partner/friend makes a call, invites the potential excited friends to come, and confirms their attendance.

3. Contact #3—Cookout! Meet and greet your host's friends, learn a little about their personal history with the Lord, and enjoy the cookout! When all the guests arrive:

    i.   Your partner gathers the people into their house, (about 4–12 people) and you go to meet them, with no big presentation or big ask. Just meet them, share, and inform.

    ii. Have the host introduce you. You will share about twenty minutes, maybe thirty if things are going good. Make it conversational. The host can ask questions if things are a little slow.

    iii. Have the host move you back into the kitchen after about thirty minutes.

    iv. Mingle, talk with everyone, ask questions, learn a lot more about them, have them talk *twice as much as* you do. Share a *little* about yourself.

    v.   Have ministry materials that your host can send them off with.

    vi. After the meeting, you and the host can determine who will do the contacting.

4. Contact #4—Follow-up

    The host can call twenty-four to forty-eight hours afterwards to see if you can contact the cookout guests, or the host could send an email asking/informing the guest that they would like to share their guest's contact information unless that guest objects.

5. Contact #5—Phone call: you call the guest to ask for an appointment.

6. Contact #6—Appointment: the same as for an excited friend; do the straight-up ask.

7. Do any follow-up if needed and start them on a newsletter.

For your partner who is helping you there will be a lot of steps. Coach them through the letter and through the call. This will be no problem if we do extensive planning on the front end. Do as much of the work as you can for your partner, and make it really easy for them. Provide them with an experience that would make them want to do this again!

Churches

When addressing a church many of the concepts are the same as approaching an individual but vary slightly because you will likely be speaking to a small group—like a missions committee or elder board.

» Things that motivate a group to say yes are different than for an individual. A group doesn't need a heart-connect in the same way that individuals do.

» Remember that the missions committee probably won't bring you before the entire board. Therefore, you will need to give them more information on the front end.

» It might take a couple of months for the topic of you and your ministry to come before the board or committee's table.

» You have to share with them enough material to make a decision, assuming they will probably make that decision in one meeting. Therefore make sure your packet has everything they need to make an informed decision.

The essential components of a church packet

The contents of a church packet consist of three primary things: a cover letter, modified invitation "ask" letter, and a spiritual resume. All three should be printed on resume-like paper. You could add to your packet material about the ministry organization (bi-fold, tri-fold, short booklet, etc.).

The cover letter

Your cover letter doesn't need to be long; it's serving only to greet your readers and explain the packet they are holding in their hands. I would suggest creating a header for this cover letter, a simple colored design. Additionally your cover should include a ministry logo. As you're creating this document keep in mind that you want it to appear professional and personable.

The total length of your cover letter should be two short paragraphs. We would suggest no more than two to three sentences per paragraph.

Open the cover letter with a greeting for the specific pastor, missions board, and eldership or church that you are addressing. It's best if this cover letter is addressed specifically to the group of people that make decisions related to missions giving. But if you don't know who that group is, we would suggest addressing the cover to either the missions board or the church name.

Here is an example of a cover letter:

Greeting
"Dear Grace Christian Fellowship Missions Board,"

First paragraph

"I am a full-time missionary with XYZ Ministries and currently in a season developing the financial partnership needed to carry out my assignment. I am submitting this packet that you would prayerfully consider partnering with me in ministry. My desire is that our ministries could work together to accomplish far more for His kingdom than either one of us can do working alone."

Second paragraph

"Enclosed is information that could help you in your leadership decisions. You will find: a personal ministry letter [this is your invitation, "ask letter"], a ministry resume, and ministry information. I will be contacting the church office in the near future and hope to have the opportunity to talk with you further."

Salutation

"Serving Him with you,"

Signature

Sign your name with blue ink. This is typically formatted four lines underneath your salutation.

Printed Name

"Tom Douglas." This is typically formatted two spaces underneath your signature.

Modified Invitation Letter

We suggest that you use the invitation letter that you have already created and are using for face-to-face appointments. Leave your headline/hook at the top; include a nice, high quality photo of yourself/family.

We need to make changes to the first section (opening paragraph) and the fourth section (closing paragraph). In the first section of your invitation letter you typically bring the people up to speed about your life over the past three to six months. But because this church packet and the modified invitation letter are going to churches that you have little or no relationship with, you need to talk about yourself a little more. Introduce yourself, your occupation, and the organization you work with.

In the fourth section our invitation will be sensitive to their time, relationship, method of operation, and budget restraints. Churches typically need more time to discuss the opportunity; there are many more factors to consider compared to a normal household. Therefore our invitation will be clear and direct but softer on the time element.

Here is an example of what the first section and the fourth section might look like:

Greeting

"Dear Grace Christian Church Missions Board," or "Dear Pastor Bill and the GCC Eldership,"

First section

"My name is Tom Douglas and I am a missionary at XYZ Ministries in Kansas City, Missouri. My wife, Susan, and I have recently celebrated ten years of marriage and we have three precious children, Ally, Bailey and Timothy. My family and I have been serving in full-time ministry for the past seven years. Both Susan and I have a deep commitment to the Body of Christ in the United States and throughout the world. It's our heart to serve God by serving the saints and equipping them to love Jesus wholeheartedly while also empowering them to serve in ministry to others."

Fourth section

"Our family is committed to growing in passion for Jesus and compassion for others, and like all missionaries at XYZ, we have both the privilege and responsibility of raising our own financial partnership team. Your financial partnership would empower us to give ourselves fully to the assignment God's given us. Susan and I respectively ask that you, Grace Christian Church, would prayerfully consider partnering with us.

"We will be contacting you in the coming days, once you have had time to pray. It is our sincere desire and hope that our ministries would work together. We look forward to speaking with you."

Spiritual resumé

Because you are aiming to develop long-term partnership with churches that you may not have relationship with, a spiritual resumé provides an opportunity for them to get to know you and your history of serving. Your resumé should communicate past ministry experience and training that is pertinent to your occupation in ministry.

Your spiritual resumé doesn't have to be long or done in great detail, but it does need some specific information. Adding a header or graphic at the top can make this document stand out, but remember that it should still be professional and personable. An organizational logo and name on your documents connects you to a ministry that is already established and helps give credibility to you and what you're doing.

Here are some things that you could include in your spiritual resumé:

Personal contact information
» Physical mailing address

» Current phone number

» Email address

» Website (if you have one)

Vision statement
This is a great place to put your one-sentence vision statement.

Experience
This should be primarily ministry-related but doesn't have to include full-time ministry positions. It can include places you have served within the local church, missions trips you have taken, outreaches you have served on, or other things you have done in ministry.

This could include any time you've led or helped with children's church or leading prayer meetings, programs you started, and any other additional service items. Here are some examples:

»	Served in vacation bible school	summer of '04, '05, '06
»	Usher/deacon at Grace Church	2007–2010
»	Prophecy team at Grace Church	all of 2011
»	Served on missions team to Guatemala	summer of 2012
»	Youth pastor at Grace Church	2012–2013

| » Missionary at XYZ Ministry | 2013–Present |

Education (this can be both spiritual and secular)

This should be an abbreviated bullet point list of what the education was and the year. They don't need any explanation as long as the words you use are descriptive enough. You don't want to list conferences that you have attended, unless they were lengthy intensives where you received specialized training. It's best if these are listed from the oldest to the most recent.

List all education that's either accredited or non-accredited. Here are some examples:

» Kansas City Community College, B.A. in political science	2010–2012
» Pastors' and leaders' empowerment training	2012
» Intro to ABC Ministry, six-month internship	2013
» ABC Ministry, Bible School	2014–Present

Personal reference

Provide the names and contact information of pastors, leaders, and lay people know you well. Offer two or three references.

| » Pastor Bill Shakespeare at Pumpkin Patch Church | (816) 555-4444 |
| » Pastor Greg Miller at Celebrate Recovery | (816) 555-4444 |

Packaging

When your church packet is finalized, you can put it into a large manila envelope with a clasp (with the church personally addressed on the outside), a clear presentation portfolio, or something similar. Whatever you choose, maintain the pattern of professionalism and personableness.

Something that will give this church packet a personal touch is to include one of your postcards with a hand written note on the back. Simply attach the postcard with a paper clip to the cover letter, positioning it in the middle or lower third of the cover letter.

The handwritten note in your postcard could simply say:

Dear Pastor Bill and Grace Christian Church, Thank you for taking a look at my ministry information. I am excited about what God is doing with my life in the global missions movement. I hope for an opportunity to share in person. Until He comes, Tom Douglas.

Selection of churches

Several sessions ago in this training you had a name-storming assignment, grouping people that you know based on relationship and region. We want to create a similar list for churches. Start by doing an Internet search using Google Maps. Do a search of churches in your area/region. Google Maps is extremely helpful, giving you church names, street addresses, office hours, sometimes a website, street view of the actual church, and phone numbers. When you have a website, log in and find out as much information as you can. Look for contact people for your packet. The person maybe listed under titles such as: missions board, missions committee, missions pastor, or missions director. Document this information for future use.

As in your previous assignment, group churches together in A, B, and C groups. A's would include churches you have relationship with, that close friends and family attend, or a church within your denomination. B's would include evangelical churches, churches that have a missional history, or churches you have limited relationship with. Group C would include all others. *(We do not recommend approaching churches that are known to be extremely liberal.)*

Churches that are most likely to partner with you are churches that have two hundred members or more. This doesn't mean that you should exclude smaller churches, but avoid spending most of your time with smaller churches. The majority of your list should be made up of churches with two hundred or more members.

Delivery

Many churches are closed on Mondays and it is often the pastor's day off; don't plan to visit on Mondays. Wednesdays can be really busy; try it but be sensitive. Church offices tend to get busier throughout the day; earlier in the day may be preferred. As always, go try it, and be sensitive.

Working with churches tends to be a slower process than working with individuals. The decision often times isn't something they can make right away. Typically churches have to look at their yearly budget, and factor in other giving responsibilities and timing. They may say yes to partnership but can't start for another six months. But there are times when you come at the right time and the partnership can began quickly.

Speaking with a church receptionist or church contact person

When you approach the receptionist, church leader, or contact person, make sure to greet them by sharing your name and asking for theirs. Then you could share for a minute or two about yourself and what you're doing.

When speaking to the receptionist, find out who it is that you need to direct the packet to, and try to get their contact information, which might just be a name and email. Often times the senior pastor is not the person who makes missional decisions; it may be with a board or team. Let the receptionist help you; they know who you need to speak with. Let them direct your packet. And be sure to ask if the church has a website.

Once this is accomplished, take a minute to ask about them, their relationship with the church, and so on. Listen well and build rapport. Be nice, represent your organization well, and know that good listening can go a long way.

It might sound something like this:

> *Hi, my name is Tom Douglas, and you are . . .? I'm a full-time minister. I work with an evangelical missions organization in Kansas City, Missouri, called XYZ Ministries. I'm making it a point to share with the Body of Christ about our organization and the role my wife and I play within it. I would love to have a chance to talk with your church about some of the ways we might be able to work together. I would love an opportunity to speak to your missions board, or elders board, about serving as one of your church's missionaries. What is the process here at Grace Christian Church for missionaries?*

It would be great to keep this conversation to about three to five minutes. First impressions are lasting, so make sure to connect well. Give this person a reason to like you. You want them working for you, making sure you're heard. Additionally they will be communicating the impression they have of you.

After you leave your church packet with them, we suggest that you follow up in person around ten days later. This ten-day time period will probably be enough time for them to review your packet but isn't long enough for you to fade from memory. If you are no longer in the same city, send a postcard.

When you return to follow up make sure to express your gratitude for this person helping you in the process of connecting with the proper people. Take another couple of minutes to build a little more rapport. Have a pre-written card ready, much like a postcard, and leave it with the receptionist.

Concluding thought

Committees are made up of people; therefore we still need to give them multiple points of contact, see them face-to-face, make direct asks, and be faithful with our follow-up.

Keep in mind that working with churches is similar to working with individuals. They need multiple points of contact, they need to hear vision, and they need to see your face. With most churches you will need to be faithful with your follow-up.

When approaching a church have a servant's heart. It's God's desire that His family works together. Always look to strengthen, build up, and encourage the local church. Help them do things in missions they might never have an opportunity to do on their own. Building partnership with churches takes time but will normally bear fruit in the long run, therefore be diligent. And it's important to keep in mind that this church's potential partnership with you will be a blessing to them as well as you.

When you get an appointment you already know what to do. Be prepared, be prompt, have an appointment kit and materials ready, be friendly, make good eye contact, engage the board in conversation, share, and invite. Following your meeting, make sure to send out your thank-you letter within twenty-four hours. In this situation we do not recommend a postcard. In this letter you could include something personal about the committee that you learned from your appointment, as well as their heart for missions. A one- or two-paragraph thank-you would be appropriate. Be sure to include your handwritten signature.

Sharing at a church

Some pastors and church members will want to help you and even invite you to speak at their church.

Go to the church service with good information about you and your ministry, and cast the vision for the Great Commission. Remember, your desire is to encourage the pastor and local congregation to move forward in their walk with Jesus and the Great Commission.

Your sharing will be twofold:

1.   Fuel their excitement for the Great Commission and the ways God is working through the ministry.

2.   Give them a vision for the type of ministry work you are involved with!

Your aim is to come away knowing three to five new people and getting the church excited about ministry and the Great Commission.

How to handle small groups

What if people invite you to talk at a small group?

The first thing you should think over is how you can serve them and excite their hearts about prayer, serving the poor, training young adults, and global missions. (Insert your type of ministry.)

If they give you more time to share, then take it:

1. Share about your assignment and the mission of your organization.

2. Bring a little ministry information to the meeting with you to be shared at the end of the meeting.

3. Make as much personal contact with people as you can by introducing yourself to people, having conversations, and asking people about their lives.

4. Do one-on-one follow-ups after the small group meeting.

5. You could take your own initiative with them.

6. Use the small group meeting as an introduction and a launching pad for one-on-one follow-up.

7. By the end of the night, you would like to have two or three personal contacts.

How does the multi-touch process work with a small group?

1. The leader of the small group has probably told them about you before the meeting.

2. You share at the small group.

3. You hang around and fellowship after the meeting and send them home with some material.

4. You contact them a few days later and ask for an appointment.

5. You have the appointment.

6. You have a possible follow-up.

Excited friends

Friends are always recommending different things to friends. Have you been to a conference someone has recommended? Or a restaurant? Or read a book? Or seen a movie? Bought a software program?

A large portion of the things you love and enjoy in life you are experiencing because a friend recommended it to you, and you are grateful.

When our appointments end in a yes, or at least a very excited no, you will ask them about their excited friends. They are the most excited about us and our ministry and will be the best word-of-mouth advertisement you could hope for. Undoubtedly, if more people knew about you and what you are doing, they would get excited also.

Literally thousands of people in our nation would be excited about you and your ministry if they knew about it.

The more people you invite, the more people will partner with you. More partners mean more ministry for longer periods of time.

Excited friends are similar to your existing friends in that they need four or five points of contact before we can expect an answer. We need to roll with each opportunity the best we can.

There is no way to quantify it exactly, but a personal recommendation from a close friend is equivalent to about two points of contact. Keep this in mind as you move forward.

You will have to follow up with a percentage of excited friends after the appointment. This is not a problem and is sometimes unavoidable no matter what you do.

We want to honor our existing relationships and not add stress to them. Do what is best for your existing friends, and do whatever makes them feel comfortable.

Excited-friend invitation process

1. After you have an appointment with your existing friend or partner, they would then call or email their friend. Your partner asks them, "Can Chris have permission to contact you, maybe first with a letter and then by phone? Would that be okay with you?" The excited friend then gives permission.

2. A specific letter to the excited friend:

   » "Mr. Smith, we have a mutual friend . . . He said you would be excited and encouraged by what I am doing . . . would love to meet with you." Tell them what you do and cast the vision in it.

   » Timing: the minute the friend says yes, send the letter.

   » It would be good to have developed written materials with photos that you can send with your letter. Tri-fold or bi-fold brochures or a larger postcard with additional information would work.

3. You call about three days later to arrange a meeting.

   » Take time to build some rapport on the phone.

   » Then, do a one- or two-minute overview of your organization and your ministry.

   » Next, ask for an appointment.

   » The letter helps you to not have to explain as much on the phone.

4. Appointment

   » Take time to build rapport. Get to know them and let them get to know you.

   » You may differentiate how you invite them to partner. Feel it out with the Lord. You have two options here:

      1. You could invite them the normal way by saying, "Will you partner with me in ministry?"

      2. Or, you could invite them by saying, "Will you pray about partnering with me in ministry and I follow up in three to four days?"

   » Be diligent with your follow-up if it's needed.

Summary

1. No one method will ensure that you reach your properly funded mark, which means you will have to use multiple strategies to accomplish your goal.

2. The four primary strategies that we see producing the greatest fruit in partnership are face-to-face appointments, excited friends, hosted small groups, and churches.

3. Most people have more than one location in which they are developing partnership, and this means you will have to create a strategy for each location.

4. Over seventy-give percent of your budget will come from individuals.

5. Having a close friend or current partner host a small group for you is an effective way to meet new friends and potential partners.

6. Churches are great potential partners in your ministry assignment, but they will need specific information, time, and a personal approach in order to make an informed decision.

7. Over thirty percent of your partnership team will be made up of excited friends, so learn how to ask clearly and with a heart to connect these others with their mission interest.

13.1 SUPPLEMENT

Sample recommendation letter for dessert or cookout

Dear *(name here)*,

I want to introduce you to a friend of mine, Sally Singer. I've known Sally for years—she grew up here in the Boston area and we share a common heart and passion for Jesus.

Sally is a missionary with ABC Ministries in Kansas City. ABC Ministries is a missions base committed to the Great Commission through worship, evangelism, Christian education, training, equipping young adults, being mindful of the poor, and other acts of justice. I've been a prayer and financial partner with Sally in ministry for over six years, and I have thoroughly enjoyed being connected with her. She is trustworthy, faithful, and encouraging to my life in the Lord!

I want to recommend Sally's ministry to you. I really think you would benefit from connecting with her as much as I have. Sally is going to be visiting Boston from October 26th through the 30th, and I'd love to introduce you to her. I will be hosting a cookout at my house on Saturday the 27th at 4:30 p.m. and I would love for you to come. It would give you a chance to meet Sally and get to know a little about her ministry.

I will be following up with you in a few days to verify your attendance. I look forward to speaking with you.

Blessings!

(your name)

Your Assignment Has a Budget

Overview: Jesus doesn't underpay His staff—He intends for you to be properly funded. Serving the Great Commission takes money and resources. Constant lack is unhealthy, unproductive, and causes us to question the call of God. Therefore we want to set a realistic financial goal that will allow us to obey the Scriptures and empower us to fully serve and obey God's call on our lives. Our goal is not to see how low we can go but rather to have a financial plan that allows us to serve the Lord long term.

Expect to raise 100% of your realistic budget

You need to be properly funded. That means you need to meet the budget necessary for you to accomplish your assignment as it is currently understood. Talk with the Lord, talk about your calling, and work through all the necessary dynamics. Determine what your calling is and what it will cost to accomplish it. Set the goal, and go for it.

Expect to raise the entire budget you set for yourself, but make sure you have a realistic budget. A realistic budget needs to meet all of your long-term needs including: giving, savings, retirement, car replacement, home repair, education, and all that pertains to life and ministry. The bare minimum is not realistic; it is simply putting off the inevitable. Don't settle for just getting by because in the end you really are not.

In the Midwest United States a small family could survive on $2,000 a month but not for very long. Within a year or two—or possibly sooner—this will catch up with you, and you will soon find yourself backed up against a wall. Making $2,000 may keep the creditors off of your back, but it will not keep your car running or replace it when it goes out and certainly won't let you save money to replace your car in the future. Set a realistic budget, and make this your new minimum.

Do not let up on your partnership development until you meet this new minimum. You must fight off the temptation to settle when it seems like you have enough; keep moving forward.

Don't excuse yourself from being fully funded

Being a missionary is not signing up for poverty. There is not a verse anywhere in the entire Bible that suggests we should be poor. When I say poor I mean always in need, living in a constant state of lack—living from one crisis to another.

> *You need to be fully funded to carry out your assignment long term. Do not let up on your partnership development until you meet your realistic budget. You must fight off the temptation to settle when it seems like you have enough; keep moving forward.*

Why is it that we almost expect missionaries to live at a lower standard? Where did this idea come from?

Any standard of living that is okay for the marketplace Christian is okay for the missionary Christian.

Do we expect Christian teachers to be poor, or Christian accountants, or Christian engineers, or pastors? Being broke is not part of the missionary job description. The Lord intends the same for the missionary as He does for the Christian businessman down the street.

Poverty is not a virtue!

Being in constant need is not being "more holy." Paul said that he lived through times of leanness and times of plenty, but his times of leanness were not his long-term lifestyle. What's okay for any Christian is okay for the missionary.

Do not make a subconscious vow of poverty. It's not what the Lord intends, it's not more holy, and it's not okay. Pray and ask the Lord to deliver you from a poverty mindset; refuse to participate in "poor talk" with yourself, spouse, or friends.

Your assignment has a budget

Determine what the assignment is that the Lord has given you, set the goal, and go raise the support needed to accomplish it. We do this in every area of life. If a young couple decides to build a house, they go visit builders, look at model homes, determine the options, and the builder says, "OK, it will cost this much." They will then go and get the money to complete the job. No one approaches a new house by saying, "Well, we are going to trust God for the money and pray, and whatever falls into our mailbox, we will build that much house with that much money." But this is the concept that is widely used to build missions!

We have to own the assignment and make plans for it to happen. We have to get delivered from this idea that we will just sit before an empty basket and do whatever ministry we can with whatever change trickles in. That is like saying, "I want to be wholehearted and established in the first commandment, and I will be as wholehearted and established as my six-minute devotional will allow me. Because that is all the time I can give and that my attention span will allow. Jesus, I want to burn for you on six minutes a day."

Not many people are living with a proper view of how God wants to fund His missionaries. Most of us settle and just get by however we can. So I want you to pray, get delivered from poor thinking, and fight to be fully funded. Do not stop your partnership development, and do not make excuses for yourself as to why you do not need to be fully funded. Set the number, be realistic, and keep working until you are there.

When we are *not* fully funded

When we are consistently underfunded, it brings *unnecessary* stress to our house and family. Sometimes this is far more stressful for the wife than it is for the husband. Often wives are left with trying to figure out how to feed a family of four on $50 or less.

When we are in a *prolonged* season of lack, it becomes easy to start questioning our call to ministry. "Did I really hear from the Lord?" This will also lead to questioning God. "God where are you? I thought You promised to provide." It can lead to resentment toward the missions organization, feeling they should have trained us better or even provided a salary.

> *Being a missionary is not signing up for poverty.*

> *Being in constant need is not being "more holy." What's okay for any Christian is okay for the missionary.*

You may even be tempted to live by credit cards. I actually know of an organization that taught its missionaries to use a credit card if necessary and then "believe God" for the money to pay the bill. There is no way that we could teach people to live this way. "The borrower is slave to the lender" (Prov. 22:7).

In prolonged seasons of lack our perspective can often become distorted, affecting the way we view our situation and thus affecting the way that we walk it out. This is when we start to adopt poor support-raising techniques like hard sells, pressure tactics, desperate appeals, and constantly talking about money needs by including it in every letter. This has a very negative impact on our contact base, and we cannot afford to do this.

We will often feel the pressure to return to secular work: even if only part-time. Pressure can come from our spouse, family, or culture. The twenty hours that you might work at a part-time job actually takes closer to thirty hours to fulfill, with prep time, travel, and breaks or lunch. Working a secular job and working in missions while trying to raise support can really bog us down mentally and physically. If secular work is the answer, you could have done that without going into full-time ministry. Working a secular job comes with a high price to the Christian called to full-time ministry (this would not include strategic marketplace missionaries, like a teacher in China).

> *In a prolonged season of lack, our perspective can often become distorted, affecting the way that we view our situation and thus affecting the way that we walk it out.*

Additionally, we have to make compromises in how we take care of and provide for our families. Living in a house that is falling down around us is not glorious and God is not honored by it. He actually speaks very clearly about the man who does not take care of his property. Mac and cheese or ramen noodles were never intended to be part of our long-term diet. Be healthy: eat, live, and act healthy.

A house that is in desperate need of repair, along with the weed-infested, foot-high grass in the yard, does not send the right message to our family and neighbors. When we can't meet the basic needs of being a property owner, not only do we send the wrong message but we also violate a few basic scriptures. In addition, maintenance is often far cheaper than repair.

When we are not fully funded, we are not fully available to walk out our assignment. If we are not fully available for the assignment, then part of the assignment is not being done. This means that some evangelism is not taking place, some discipleship is not taking place, or some intercession is not taking place. When you are not fully funded, it ultimately means the loss of some kingdom impact we could have had. An incomplete assignment will lead to standing before the Lord with some measure of regret.

What happens if you *are* fully funded?

In short, when you're fully funded, the results are the opposite of everything listed above, plus a whole lot more:

No stress

Being fully funded will reduce financial stress. Money, or the amount of it, can be a source of real stress to a marriage, and this has an impact on the missions work we are doing. The commitment, service, attitude, language, and overall heart posture of a fully funded missionary is far different than a consistently underfunded missionary.

Confidence

When you are fully funded, it gives you confidence about your ministry and your calling. It can also provide the confidence to step out into new projects.

No debt

Debt is not good for anyone and can be a ministry-killer for a missionary. I can't tell you how good it has felt to have zero debt since 2006 and how much it has helped us.

Healthy relationships

You will relate in a healthier way to your contact base when you are fully funded. The first benefit is that you won't be talking about money all the time. That gets old for everyone involved. Also, you can share a gift of appreciation or take someone to lunch.

Being fully funded means being fully available.

Fully available to serve

When you are fully funded, there is no need to leave your field of service for secular employment, and this means more time spent in your calling as a missionary. You can respond to any assignment the Lord may give you: short missions trips, relocate for a month, or flex with a sudden change of hours. You can move to Hong Kong for the summer if you need to, but if you are in constant lack and tied to a secular job, you can't move and you have little flexibility.

Full engagement

Not only will you be free to serve in whatever way the Lord would have, but your heart can also engage in a full way. I know far too many people who are bogged down in prayer because of underfunding. Constant lack makes your heart sick, and a sick heart doesn't pray well. I want to see prayer rooms filled with fully funded missionaries who are free to pray, and their only financial prayer is where to steward all the extra provision!

When you are fully funded, you can make long-term plans

Having a realistic budget that is met on a consistent basis will allow you to make long-term plans for your family. You can make plans for nice vacations, education for your kids, retirement for yourself, missions trips to a foreign field, planned giving, braces, the wedding, and college.

You can make ministry plans.

When you meet your budget on a regular basis, you can be prepared for a missions trip that pops up. How nice would it be to be able to pray about going and money not being the issue? Or how about when you hear that someone else is going on a trip and you can write a $1,000 check that doesn't empty your account? You can expand your own ministry, start new projects, minister to more people, bless more people, produce materials, or even form an operations budget.

You will take care of your family now and in the future.

It will allow you not to be an inconvenience or a burden to anyone. We need to be able to provide adequate housing for ourselves; living with another family or in your parents' basement might work for a short season, but it is no way to live long-term. We need to be prepared in retirement years as well, and that starts now. "A good man leaves an inheritance to his children's children" (Prov. 13:22).

Your team will be encouraged.

One of the things your team members originally needed to see in order to say yes to partnership was God at work in you and your calling. When we are in lack, not only does it make us ask questions, but it makes your team members ask questions as well. It's easy to get the impression that a person that is in constant need is not walking in the favor and blessing of God. This may not be true, but people can get that impression.

You will stay in the midst of your calling.

I have seen mature, well-meaning missionaries join the prayer movement and within a couple of years they are back home, discouraged and disillusioned, in secular work. Still called, still carrying an assignment from the Lord, but unable to continue due to a lack of funding. Being fully funded will make it possible for you to walk out your calling all the days of your life.

Your organization will be strengthened.

Global missions will only ever be as strong as their fully funded, fully available people. It is very hard to move forward in any work of the kingdom when you have to do it with part-time help or when you lose ten to fifteen percent of your staff each year.

Things to remember

Don't put a limit on your support; get rid of that bare-minimum number.

Set a realistic goal and don't stop until you reach it. I would even encourage you to go past your goal. Why? Because you can always grow as a ministry, and you always know people in need. *Make partnership development a lifestyle, not a project.* If you raise a million dollars, use what you need and give the rest away.

Big picture: you're raising support for the missions movement, so there is no limit!

You are raising money for the prayer movement and your household is part of the overhead for the prayer movement. This isn't for your comfort; this is for your time, that you might be free to give yourself fully to ministry, with longevity.

Partnership is a lifestyle; it never stops, regardless of the amount.

You are never done building your ministry team. The missions movement always needs support, so keep asking. If you reach a place where you really don't need any more, start supporting missions and missionaries, or expand your own ministry.

Summary

1. *It's important that when you start your partnership development, you expect to raise one hundred percent of the funds needed to be fully available to serve God and fulfill your assignment.*

2. *Setting a realistic budget should include: giving, savings, retirement, car replacement, home repair, and education, as well as your present needs.*

3. *Saying yes to full-time ministry isn't signing up for poverty. Whatever is permissible for a Christian is permissible for a full-time gospel worker.*

4. *When we determine our goal, we must create an action plan to reach that goal and then put that action plan into practice as we intentionally go after it.*

5. *When we are not properly funded, it can cause unnecessary stress on our household, create resentment toward both our organization and the Lord, and force poor practices with partners.*

6. *When we are properly funded, we reduce personal stress, receive confidence, experience life without debt, and enjoy healthy relationships with partners and the Body of Christ.*

7. *Reaching your fully funded goal shouldn't be as much about personal comfort as it is availability to God and your assignment.*

Please complete the following homework assignments:

Homework #13: Vision Of Being Properly Funded

Loving Your Team Well

Overview: When you get to the end of your partnership development campaign, you will have added people who are now co-laboring with you in full-time ministry. Learning how to communicate well and often with your partnership team must become a priority as you do the work of the ministry. In this session we will cover the DNA of a ministry lifestyle, how often you should say thanks, what good communication looks like, and how to write your monthly newsletter. The aim of this session is to provide you with concepts and some details that will strengthen the team of people you are running together with.

So you have a partnership team, now what?

You have just finished your face-to-face appointment and they actually partnered with you in ministry. You made it all the way through—and you didn't die!—and it was a lot more fun than you thought it would be.

Many who have done well this far stumble in the area of partner care. Why is that? It could be fear, lack of training, poor planning, ignorance, or a number of other reasons. But I think the main reason most people stumble in this area is due to the lack of a plan. As we have said many times in this training: every goal needs a plan. In this particular context, keeping your team is the goal.

I liken this to a parked car: it takes a lot of time, energy, effort, and hard work to get a parked car moving, but once it's moving, it is easy to keep it moving. The same can be said with our team. You are going to spend a good deal of time, labor, and energy team building in this heightened, focused season of your campaign. But now that you have a team, it is not hard to keep your team—but you do need a plan.

Let's determine the level of relationship we want with our team, let's determine what it takes to love well, then let's look at the amount of contact we need to have with our team—conversation, newsletter, and so forth. Let's look at the level of contact and communication we want, and then let's break it up into a daily, weekly, and monthly schedule. Then, let's write it down to have a detailed plan, outline, and a schedule worked into our calendar so that every day our calendar is already telling us what to do.

We want to love well. If you can get this one concept into your thinking as you approach your team, many problems will be taken care of in a very natural, organic way. Regardless of being a missionary called to full-time ministry, or that we profess the name of Jesus and we are believers, we have a lifestyle that *requires* that we love well.

They are our brothers and sisters. They are not just a financial means to an end and *not* an ATM machine. They are brothers and sisters whom we want to love accordingly.

Ministry is always about people, including the ones on your team. There is no ministry on earth that is so important that it doesn't involve people. Every ministry deals with people, and people are the focus. So here we have a real opportunity to love our team well.

It's really about walking in the second commandment. Regardless of your occupation, regardless of your time in the kingdom, you never graduate from this very basic need to walk in the second commandment. Our team is to be just as much the recipients of our ministry and love, kind words and encouragement, as the people you are occupationally ministering to.

The DNA of team relationship and our missionary lifestyle

These five values form the DNA of team relationship and our missionary lifestyle:

1. We want to acknowledge all giving.

2. We need to show appreciation.

3. We need to share achievement.

4. We want to cast vision.

5. We want to share future plans.

I have these values in front of me at all times. And these five things are what I am going to be stirring and cultivating all the time. It's a thread that runs through all my communications and face-to-face meetings.

Let's acknowledge all giving. Every gift we receive should be acknowledged in some way. There are a couple of reasons for this: one, most people just like the comfort and assurance that you received the gift they sent. If they don't hear anything, the check could have been lost in the mail or there could have been a glitch with electronic giving. So if we acknowledge the gift, minimally, that is comforting to them. Two, we want them to know we appreciate their gift. In a survey, people who had stopped giving were asked the question, "Why did you stop supporting your missionary?" And sixty-four percent of the time the people responded: "I stopped giving because I didn't believe they appreciated the gift," or "I don't believe they cared about me personally." Now when we take time to acknowledge all gifts:

1. It shows appreciation.

2. It can show gratitude.

3. It is a chance to love them.

4. It gives them the comfort of knowing you received their gift.

Have a plan

Let's have a plan or system. This is a little bit of what I do, but you will have to adjust it and work it out for yourself. As it comes to acknowledging all gifts, my wife and I have a system: all the gifts that come to our ministry are mailed to our house. Before we take them to the business office, we acknowledge all giving by first recording it in a ledger and then immediately responding to them with a thank-you. We have a little rotation that we use. We use emails, postcards, phone calls, or possibly what I call a personal message—either texting or Facebook. When that gift comes, we have a plan; we just stick to our plan, and we don't need to talk about it. It's just a normal part of what we do. We respond to it every time a gift comes in.

Now you might be thinking to yourself that this could be redundant. Well, it could be, but we mix up the medium that we use and also have a list of about eighty-three ways to say thank you. We pull from that list, and it helps us shape how we want to say thank you each time—an opportunity to say thank you in a different way. Some of the thank-yous are just a straight up thank-you. Some of them show appreciation, some of them cast vision, and some of them share achievement.

So, we have a plan! And as you just heard about the rotation, we have a pattern. Our pattern is basically two emails, then a postcard, then a phone call. Then we go back to emails. So, our support team will get a couple of emails, then a postcard, then a phone call. Then they will get a couple more emails, then a postcard, and then a phone call. So, by the end of the year our team has heard from us about every gift, and it isn't just redundant thank-yous, but it is expressed in different ways: with vision casting, appreciation, sharing achievements, and we do it with different mediums.

At the end of the year, everyone has been thanked and has heard from us outside of our regular newsletter. They have also received a couple of hand-written cards from us as well as a couple of calls from us. That is a good amount of contact, even if you just do it around the thank-you. That is a pretty good level of contact with your team.

Say thank you as quickly as you can

Try to acknowledge every gift as fast as you can. If you do not say thank you within twenty-four hours, then it's the same as not saying thank you. It's like a belated birthday; it loses its punch and specialness if we are saying thank you to a gift we received two weeks ago. So, if you have those gifts sent to the home office or a payroll system, usually there is a way you can see that online. Check that regularly and acknowledge all gifts as quickly as you can. These are guidelines and tips for acknowledging all giving.

All giving needs to be acknowledged with a thank-you

All increased giving, or extra giving, should also be acknowledged in writing with an email, a postcard, text, or phone call. If your $100-a-month partner sends you $150 one month, say thank you and acknowledge the extra $50. *Show them you saw it.*

Depending on the size of the gift and the person sending the gift, you may want to make a phone call. A call never hurts, and you should make a phone call every so often anyway to say thank you—regardless of the gift sizes. Depending on the person and depending on the size of the gift, you may want to make a phone call. In other words, if your very faithful $50-per-month partner suddenly sends you $400, you ought to get on the phone and say thank you. That's enough of a sizable increase over the normal giving that I wouldn't trust it to an email or a card. Although a card also would not be bad, it never hurts to dial the phone.

Your cell phone is a great tool. Don't go too cheaply on your monthly plan. It's a vital partner link and, now with smart phones, it's really a portable office—it can do so much for you. Learn how to use it well.

If a new partner sends their first gift, say thank you with a card. For example, during your campaign somebody promises $150 a month and they send their first gift. Respond to that gift with a card and get that official partnership off to a good start by acknowledging their gift with that card.

If a current partner sends an extra amount, say thank you with an email, a card, a text, or a call, depending on the amount of the gift.

If a current partner sends a regular monthly support gift, say thank you with an email, a postcard, a personal message—using the rotation plan I mentioned above.

If a current partner sends a gift significantly larger than the normal partnership level, then give them a call to say thank you. If it is just barely over the normal amount, then you might want to respond with a card, but then it never hurts to make a call.

When a new person sends a gift, call and say thank you right away. Maybe this is someone random that you didn't even talk to about partnership. Call them if at all possible. Maybe it's someone who has been on your mailing list for a year and suddenly they send you a gift; call them!

If a person gives infrequently, say once or twice a year or totally at random, call them to say thank you. This will allow you time to connect with them and build a little more relationship.

If you are speaking somewhere at a church or meeting of some sort and they are going to take an offering for you, be sure to say thank you on the spot, not only to the congregation, but if at all possible, get face to face with leadership, shake their hands, and say thank you. You can follow up a day later with a written letter to the church, say thank you, and send it to the church. Make sure you get contact and mailing information for the church before you leave.

If someone hosts you in their home on a ministry trip, etc., and they have given you a large gift, express gratitude by leaving the place neater than when you arrived. Be prepared to leave a small token gift such as a book, DVD, CD, or just a card. I make it a habit of stripping the bedding and leaving it folded up at the foot of the bed so they can launder it easily. You might want to leave a cash gift yourself, depending on who the person is. It's up to you, but be mindful of it, and think about it ahead of time so you will be prepared.

Show appreciation—similar to acknowledging every gift, but with some differences

Tell your partners how much you appreciate them, their friendship, and their partnership. Show them that you care about them as people, and you are grateful for the relationship and for the partnership. Now, one of the reasons I do this is because it's part of walking in the second commandment. Two, I want them to know I care about them and that it isn't just about the money. Three, if the financial partnership ends someday, you already have a great friend, and you can continue the friendship.

Show appreciation in writing, by phone, and by a personal message. I think it's a good idea to occasionally send a card out of the blue, telling them how much you appreciate them. You could phone them and just say, "*Hey, just wanted to call you to see how I could pray for you. I just really appreciate you!*" Speak encouragement and blessing, mention the gifts that you see in them, and prophesy to them. You want to show appreciation to them as people.

When you do your yearly visits—it might be more than once a year—but when you do your regular visits with your existing team, consider taking a small gift. If you do, then make it personal. You don't have to do this in order to show appreciation, but it is just one way that you can show appreciation. If you do take a gift, try to make it as personal as possible. In other words, if you have thirty-five people on your team and you are going to see all thirty-five during a two-week trip in the spring, don't take them all the same CD or the same book.

If you can, observe the individual and their lifestyle. Try to determine what kind of person they are, what they like, their habits, their taste, etc., and then share a gift that's appropriate for that person as much as possible. In sharing a gift, if I don't think I can do that or it's going to be too expensive by the time I buy everyone on my team a gift, then I choose to show appreciation in a different manner.

Birthdays and anniversaries are a great time to show appreciation and to speak a blessing, to encourage, and to prophesy. There are software programs that will alert you to things like that. Think about sending it so that it arrives the day before their birthday—or if you call them, consider calling the night before. The reason is that on their birthday they are going to get bombarded all at once by Facebook messages and other people calling. If you do it the day before, it will be unique and you will get solo time.

Another way you can show appreciation is to consider helping your partners in a practical way. Maybe they are moving, maybe when you are in town they are painting their house, maybe you host them in your city, maybe you can help them coordinate a short-term missions trip with your organization, or maybe you can arrange for them to receive prophetic ministry. Remember—sixty-four percent of the people that stopped partnering with their missionary said it was because they believed the person was not grateful or did not appreciate them as a person. Live in a way that you will *never be accused* of these two things.

Share achievements

It's important that we remind our team from time to time what their partnership accomplishes. Share with them the fruit that you are seeing as a result of their partnership. It's the reason they decided to partner with you in the first place—they wanted to make a difference. It's important that we share testimonies, stories, videos, letters, and phone calls. When you do this, it helps them connect their partnership to the fruit. *"Because of your partnership, I was able to go serve full-time today and two people heard the gospel. They thank you and I thank you."*

You have an opportunity to see the fruit of your ministry much more than they do. You have to be conscious of having a plan that shows them the difference they are making.

Don't make it a list of things you put at the bottom of your newsletters, but tell a story: put them on the scene, share the ministry with them, show them the impact that their giving is making, and remind them that apart from their partnership you would not be able to do it.

Consider a newsletter dedicated to sharing achievements once or twice a year. In other words, the whole letter itself isn't just current events of the previous month or what you plan to do next month, but you might think about writing one entire letter about what you achieved together in that year.

Consider possibly sharing achievements in the last paragraph of your newsletter. Now, I call it a sign-off of sorts. Maybe you wrote about the youth group or the outreach through the whole letter, but sometimes at the end, in a signing-off kind of way, I mention what we are accomplishing together and what we are achieving together. I thank them for it. I weave that into the thank-yous; I weave that into postcards; I weave that into letters; and sometimes I even weave it into phone calls. That's what I mean by that underlying current that runs through your ministry. It's the DNA. It's the lifestyle of your life as a missionary.

Cast vision

"Where there is no vision, the people perish" (Prov. 29:18, KJV). The more accurate ASV translates this verse as, "Where there is no vision, the people cast off restraint." God created us to respond to vision, but if we don't have a vision before us, if we are not reminded of where we are going and why we do what we do, we will forget it all and begin to cast off restraint. When we lose our vision, that constraint begins to loosen and we cast it off. So, when they begin to lose vision about you and your ministry and why they are involved, they will begin to not pray, and then not give.

As I mentioned before, God designed the human heart to partner with vision. We actually want to be a part of what God is doing; we want to be a part of something epic, and we want to know that we are making a difference. When you keep your vision in front of them, it's a great way to stimulate the heart.

Vision doesn't need to be large and grand, but it does need to be clear. Don't try to make it spectacular. Be clear, be honest, and be accurate. I promise you that if you are called to ministry and you are sharing the facts, it will be full of vision.

Any vision that you have should always be connected to God's global plan. I say this often, but it bears repeating: God is the original missionary. There is really only one mission at work in the earth and that is the restoration of all things; everything else is a supporting role. It is important that you have this understanding; it's important that you communicate this on occasion; and it's important that our people understand that all ministry is going in a particular direction, and it's all leading up to the restoration of all things. In other words, don't get so myopic in your own ministry that you (and they) lose connection with the bigger picture.

We want to be vision-driven not needs-driven. Needs come up every once in a while, but if they are the main focus and the thing that we talk about all the time, our hearts will grow dull and disconnected. We want to be driven by vision. God designed us to respond to vision, and when we keep that bigger picture—that thing that imparts life—when we keep that in front of us and others, it will help us stay engaged and focused, prayerful and committed.

Share future plans

You can share about upcoming events in a newsletter. At the end of the year when you write the "ask letter," you can talk about the future year that's coming and your plans. Again, we are talking about the DNA, the lifestyle of being a missionary working with a partnership team, and we are talking about acknowledgement, achievement, casting vision, and sharing future plans. You want to share plans with them a few times a year, keeping it out in front of them: where you are going, what's next, and what's on the horizon.

You can share about ministry trips, dates, deadlines that you are working toward, and any outreach events. Some of this you might need to raise additional funds for, and you could talk about it in a separate communication and so forth. Maybe you have a little text box in your newsletter titled, "Upcoming Events," and you can put little blurbs in there, little bullet points. Then, as the event approaches, you could talk about it in more detail. On your yearly visits you can sit down with them and tell them what you have planned for the coming year.

Communications

As we mentioned in the training, two really key components to successful partnership—both in building your team and in keeping your team—are communication and relationship. Always your communication is key, even if only in the process of building a team. It is extremely important. As we mentioned before, there are multiple means of communication and different mediums. Know which one works best for particular people and situations. Don't be fooled: not every medium always works because it is convenient. We want to use the right mediums for the right situations.

Have a communication plan. Consistency is vital. When I say have a communication plan, it's much like what I talked about with your partnership team (and this is *with* your partnership team), but also about expanding your team and cultivating contacts. Have a contact plan. Look at your contacts, break them down into categories, then into groups A, B, and C. The A group will be the greater relationships and the closer ones, and C will be more distant. Look at the type of communication you want to have with each of those groups by the end of the year, and then break that communication up into small segments and create a schedule. In this way, every week you can sit down and have, say, two hours of communication contact time. In those two hours, you look at your schedule, look at your plan, follow the steps, and do what your chart tells you to do.

By the end of the year, you will have stayed in good contact with your team and you will have stayed in good contact with your other contacts, your mailing list, and even your more distant friends. Have a plan and be consistent in it. I highly recommend that you break it up into small steps and do a couple little small things every day, or three or four times every week.

As I mentioned before, understand the limits of a particular medium. Email, for instance: we are looking at it less and less with more and more of it going to spam. I don't send an email unless I can afford for that information to not be seen. If it's extremely important or extremely critical, I don't send an email. Now, the exception to that is if I have been in a conversation and they are subsequently expecting an email. Or, if I am talking about my existing financial partnership team and from the very beginning I have established a pattern of brief emails around a thank-you or making plans, then I will use email as usual.

Also with emails, I try to limit each to just a couple of sentences. If I can't get the email done in a few sentences, then I find some other way to communicate. In fact, I am even getting to the point where I can communicate my point in the subject line and they can read it in their in-box without even opening it. Just be aware of the limits of each particular medium. Make quality your conviction, not convenience. Consider a couple of these things in your communication process:

Remain proactive

In other words, you be the one to call, you be the one to follow up, you be the one to start the conversation, you be the one to call on birthdays and holidays, anniversaries, and so forth. Don't sit around waiting for someone to call you. Also, when it comes to emails—anything for that matter—make things easy on them by removing as many hurdles as you possibly can. In other words, I am not going to write in a newsletter about a cool website that I have shared or that I have started, or here is a webpage, you ought to go check it out, or that there is something they would enjoy on YouTube, they should go check it out. What I will do, either on Facebook or email, is share, talk about what it is and will put a link right there to that page or site. When they open up their email, they will only get one or two sentences of introduction and then they can immediately click on a link. Don't make them have to search. Make things really easy for them.

Share photos

Consider sharing pictures with them through something like Picasa with a short email. One of the reasons I do this is to not clutter my newsletter with bunches of pictures. I would rather talk and share than use a lot of pictures. Pictures are fine, but most of the time I find they are overused in a newsletter. They are important, but sometimes you can send a short email, kind of an impromptu, spontaneous thing. Maybe something happened on an outreach or something like that. You can send a couple of sentences in an email and put a couple of pictures in it. You could open a Picasa account or something similar, and upload your pictures there. Then you can write an email or Facebook message telling them about it with a link to the pictures right there.

Share videos

Also consider sharing short videos from time to time. I think this is a great thing to do. Make it a decent, quality one. It doesn't have to be high definition taken with a $9,000 camera. If you are going to use just a cell phone, try putting it on a tripod to hold it steady. If you are doing it outside, think about putting something over the microphone that cuts down wind noise. Put some time into it, rehearse it, have an outline, and know what you are going to say before you do it. Make a good, quality video with good sound. A video can be a great way to communicate with your team that's quick, fast, and easy. Then you can share that link on Facebook or email.

You might want to think about opening up a Vimeo account and creating a video blog. Those types of things are really doable. Maybe you want to share just an update video—not a replacement for your newsletter—but something new and exciting, and they get to see you and hear your voice. It is far better than just writing.

Maybe you are going on a missions trip, and you can gather the team together. You are in the van headed to the airport, and you can put everyone in front of the camera and give a short little explanation of where you are heading. Let them know you couldn't do it apart from their partnership. Ask them to pray for you, and share with them two or three ways that they can pray for you. You might think about how to continue sharing with them throughout the trip. Little short videos are a great way to stay connected with your team and a great communication tool.

Lastly, as I have seen on Facebook, someone says, "Hey, you are going to love this video; check it out!" Well, I almost never check it out. But if you would talk to me about partnership, give me a little update about what is going on in your ministry, and give me a hint about what I am going to see in the video, I am much more likely to watch it.

Also, if I click on the video or that link, open that video up and see that it is over three minutes long, I am much less likely to view it. If it's less than three minutes, I am much more likely to watch it. If it is less than two or two and a half minutes, it is almost guaranteed that I will watch it. If you have a plan and you know what you are going to say, you can say a ton to your team in just a two-minute video.

Newsletters

I know it sounds rather cliché, but the number one goal of writing a newsletter is to get it read. We want to do everything we can to help this letter get read. We want it to be short; we want it to be clear; we want it to be encouraging; we want it to be real news and not a bunch of fluff and space filled up with pictures. We actually want to communicate with our team.

Your monthly newsletter is the most important part of your partnership team. It's the main place you are going to connect and talk. It is going to be your most vital tool in this relationship. It's your main point of contact, and therefore we don't want to skip it and we don't want to rush through it. We want to take the time to make it a good letter. In other words, because of the importance of this communication tool, we want it to be good communication that they look forward to, that they are happy to open up and read, and that actually says something to them when they open it.

There is a practice I have that helps me to be faithful in writing the newsletter, as well as helping the letter get read. You want one page, one side, one topic, and one person. What I mean by that is that when I write my newsletter, it is going to be on one piece of paper. I am going to communicate on one side of that piece of paper. I am going to cover only one topic. I am going to speak and write the letter as though I am only speaking to one person. One page, one side, one topic, one person.

If I have to write a two- or three-page letter that looks like a magazine spread every month, it won't get done. The shorter, concise letter is something I can be faithful to.

If it's *one page, one side*, they are more likely to open it up and read it. If they get overwhelmed with a volume of text and a multitude of different things going on at once when they open the letter, they are going to push it aside and not read it. So I make it short and easy on the eye.

I only address one topic. I often hear this from missionaries: "*I don't know how to find the balance of ministry, personal, and fun.*" I pick one topic and I write about that one thing—sometimes I don't even use a picture. If you are using one page, one side—but let's just say it's one page, one side, and one photo—that is going to put you somewhere around 380 to 420 words. If you're writing about one topic, it's amazing what you can get said in just that small number of words.

One person: I pretend, as I am writing, that there is only one recipient of the letter. I don't call them out by name, though. In other words, I don't talk to Jim all throughout the letter. But what I will do is pretend that there is one recipient. I will use phrases like "you" instead of "as you all know" or "as many of you know." That is automatically putting them in a group and putting them on a list, and I don't want to do that. I pretend there is one recipient, and the language becomes much more personal.

A couple of things about your newsletter

Take time to make it interesting. I see two extremes in this area. Most missionaries don't know what to write about, or they do but they overstate it or overwrite and give too much information. The other thing that I see happen is that we really don't have anything to say, and we try to say something anyway to validate our existence as a missionary. We try to show how much of an impact we are making and how awesome our ministry is when really, that month, there just wasn't a whole lot of new stuff going on.

Look for ways to emphasize their contribution to the ministry and involvement in it. Help them see the difference they are making. Connect them to it through their encouragement, their gift, the timeliness of their special gift, or their prayer. Take time to show them the fruit they are bearing through your ministry.

Be consistent. Mail your letter out approximately the same time each month, whether it's the 1st, 15th, or end of the month. You decide, but do that regularly and be consistent in it. This is good for you, and it is good for them. Get them anticipating your letter showing up at the same time each month.

One of the biggest mistakes we can make as missionaries is to be out of sight, out of mind. So don't be out of sight! Your newsletter is a great way to stay connected with people. In it, be sure to include a thoughtful, good, and sincere thank-you.

You are going to hear me say this repeatedly. Do not include financial needs in your monthly newsletter. Your monthly newsletter should be exciting, encouraging, and fun. Don't share financial needs in your newsletter, don't ask for funds, and don't drop hints, hoping they will understand your need and send extra. If you actually need financial help we will ask, but we will do it in a separate communication followed up by a phone call, then followed up by a face-to-face ask.

Be sure to personally address each letter to each team member. You can use mail merge to accomplish this.

We want to show real excellence and professionalism without losing the personal touch. Have a professionally laid-out letter that can be personal as well. Use good grammar, good punctuation, and good use of fonts. Don't make the letter look silly. Make it professional but without losing the personal touch.

Edit your own letter. Write, rewrite, and rewrite it again. Proofread it several times. I make this my practice: I write it, then I will rewrite it, then I'll go through with an edit, then check spelling and punctuation. I'll do this two or three times, and when I'm sure I'm done, I will hand it to my wife and she will find two or three additional mistakes.

Then we will walk away from it and let it sit for half a day or so, then come back and read it again. Finally, as a test we will print one hard copy. When we have it in hard-copy form, we almost always find one or two more mistakes on that hard copy.

Include contact information in every letter. You can do this at the top, at the bottom, as a banner on the side, or you can use a text box. Just be sure you get your contact information in front of them in each newsletter. I personally use a thin, straight, horizontal line at the bottom like a footer.

As I mentioned before, don't say things like, "As many of you know." Strike that from your vocabulary! Don't say things like, "As you know" or "You may have known." I'm surprised how many times I read statements like that in a letter, and they are saying something matter of fact as if I already knew it. Well, it turns out that I didn't know it. It's just an awkward thing in writing. It's better to not use it at all.

In some way, whether it's just one simple sentence or a PS, always express appreciation to your partners in every letter. Again, we are looking for ways to reemphasize their involvement.

As much as you can, put them on the mission field with you to make them part of the team. I do this sometimes by painting a verbal picture of the scene: what's going on, who we are going to, and I try to get a little bit descriptive about what happened when we got there, our emotions, and so forth. I try in my writing and in my communication phone calls to put them on this scene with me as much as possible.

Seek to avoid using language like I, me, or we too much wherever you're talking a lot about yourself and the ministry. Try to say things in a way that includes your partner, conveying to them that it's together we have managed to do this—that kind of language.

Remember, it's always helpful to emphasize your faith in God for this assignment: faith that He's given you, ability for the work you are doing, and the progress of your ministry. In other words, remind them that you are trying to obey: God has called you to do something; God has put you with this particular people group; and you are working together to see A, B, and C achieved among them. You know that God is going to do it and you are to stay on the course. Be sure to include that kind of communication from time to time.

Cast vision. Keep the purpose of the ministry before them, and restate this vision to them a few times a year. This is a kind of straight up, bold way of recasting the vision with an emphasis, saying, "This is why we do what we do." I would encourage you to do this at least three times a year in a very direct way. Now you might already have a vision-casting letter; that would be good once a year. Maybe you do the vision casting in a face-to-face meeting, so then you might do an abbreviated vision cast three or four times a year at the tail end of a letter or a postcard. Either way, it keeps the missions emphasis in front of them. We all need this.

Don't worry about being a super-saint because you're a missionary. Some people have the wrong expectation of us because we are missionaries. I don't worry about keeping up that front. I am very honest, open, clear, and willing to be a bit transparent in my communication with them—but I do restrain it. If I am having a tough time and I need prayer, I ask them for it. If I have gone through a season that has been very hard and discouraging, I don't mind talking to them about that. But I do limit it and I don't talk about it with my team as much as it happens. Because some of it is just hard, it isn't encouraging, and it can be a little bit depressing. I don't want my newsletter to be a depressing downer to them. I am not trying to hide anything, but I want that letter to be fun and encouraging, and I want them to look forward to it. If they are just getting a regular diet of how hard it is, how underappreciated I am, how much warfare I am going through, it just becomes a drag.

Make your missionary work real to your partners by including personal testimonies and pictures of people you have had an impact on with the gospel, and then give credit to your team for the breakthrough and the growth. In other words, if you have been ministering on a college campus and you led some young man to the Lord that you have been praying for, share a photo of that young man with you next to him. Tell a story about him and call him by name. Then at the end of that letter, hold your team responsible and give them credit for being able to reach that young man with the gospel.

A few things that a good newsletter contains—my summary:

A personal address: "Dear John and Jane." Use the address that is appropriate to the relationship you have. If they are on your team, you can probably address it, "Dear John and Jane." Maybe they are on your mailing list but not yet a team member in terms of financial support; they are a little more distant. Maybe you should address them, "Dear Mr. and Mrs. Smith," "Dear John Doe." Sometimes it may be just, "Dear John." You choose the address, but always make it personal. Again, use mail merge for this.

A handwritten note A handwritten note at the bottom of your letter from time to time is good. This PS is optional, but I do recommend that you write a PS two to four times a year. Write a few each month. Maybe if you have fifty newsletters you send, pull out ten newsletters each month and write a message at the end of it. By the time the end of the year rolls around, everyone would have gotten a couple of handwritten messages. Now, that isn't quite enough, but if you are coupling that with an occasional postcard, then they should be getting four to six handwritten messages a year. I always use blue ink to sign my letters. Because it is different from the black-type text, it has more of a natural handwriting feel to it. I feel strongly about that, and I want to encourage you to do so.

Make short paragraphs of various lengths, not exceeding seven or eight lines of text each. We don't want paragraphs that are ten, eleven, or twelve lines of text. It is too daunting on the eye and gobbles up too much white space on the letter. Keep your paragraphs a little shorter.

Use a balance of ministry and personal communication throughout the year. Try a ratio of 2:1 or 3:1 between ministry and personal. This means you are going to write two or three ministry letters and then a personal letter. I think this gives them a good balance. They want to hear about you and your family but they do care about the ministry— it's the primary reason they partnered with you. That is what they are sowing into, and they do want to see fruit. I would recommend that you write more about ministry than personal. I personally like 3:1.

Have an interesting lead sentence or headline that captures the reader's attention. The headline, much like a newspaper or magazine article, gives them a hint of what they are going to encounter if they choose to read the article. It is meant to draw them in. I choose to do that at the top of my letters. They don't have to be flashy, poetic, rhyme— or even be clever—but they do have to be clear. Consider using a headline or a hook or minimally a strong lead-in sentence with your first paragraph.

Simple, direct sentences with short, accurate words really help communicate.

If you have a name of your ministry, put it at the top; this is optional. I do encourage that you have a header or headline of some sort at the top. This doesn't need to be a great big banner that takes up one-fifth of your page; just a simple headline or small banner would be fine.

Absolutely *no* request for additional support of any kind is to be implied or otherwise! If you are in need of additional support, you can address it at a different time in a different letter, followed up with a face-to-face and ask, if it is possible. Don't drop hints, and don't ask for extra funds in your newsletter.

Some administrative tips about your newsletter

Send newsletters to your partners consistently

I recommend the first week of each month. Maybe they land in their home the 1st, 2nd, or 3rd day of the month. The day isn't as important as you just being consistent. What I found helps is that I will start my newsletter around the 24th and have a rough draft. I will usually have a final copy done by the 25th. It will be edited and corrected by the 27th. Then, on the 28th I might print it, stuff it, and stamp it to get it in the mail. Then they should receive it by the 1st, 2nd, or 3rd—something like that. I have it scheduled; it's in my calendar as an appointment, so I start writing on the 24th. To prepare, I leave small window appointments in my schedule for focused times that I can write my newsletter. This helps me to be consistent and faithful.

Sending a regular newsletter is a very important part of your ministry assignment. It's so important to take it seriously and do it well. In fact, Paul wrote newsletters and we are all very grateful for that!

Avoid scheduling commitments around that time of the month

Leave yourself time to get a good letter done. Obviously we can't put a hold on all ministry, but there are some things that you could do a week earlier or push back a week. Don't over schedule yourself those three or four days in the month that you are going to be writing your letter and getting it out. Ministry always seems to come at that time and it can overwhelm us, but we have to be faithful to this letter. We have to treat it as the vital, good communication tool that it is. We have to resolve to fight for the time to do it.

You may want to plan out your letter two or three months in advance; this is optional. You can actually pick the topics, outline them, and you may even start writing them. I have a friend who has two or three months of newsletters already written, printed, stuffed, stamped, and so forth. That is just something that works for him. If you do that, I think there is the potential to lose a little bit of that personal feel and a little bit of the excited feel when writing that far in advance. Find the system that works well for you.

Don't wait until the last minute to start preparing

Keep all your materials on hand. I suggest you have a box, folder, or file in your office or home that's full of envelopes, stamps, paper, and ink cartridges—everything you need to send your newsletter. Have a little supply box that you put thank-you cards in, blue pens, stamps, everything that you need. You don't want to get in a situation where you have run out of time and you have to crank out a newsletter today. Maybe you start typing it, go to print it, and you run out of ink—or you go to stuff and stamp it and you find you don't have any envelopes or return envelopes, things like that. Keep your stock and supply on hand.

Try to develop a habit of taking a few pictures

Whether it's a digital camera or your phone, develop this lifestyle of looking around for opportunities of things to write about. All these opportunities could be great testimonies—healings, that sort of thing. Perhaps you just prayed for someone and they had a significant amount of healing; you have your phone right there, hit record and take a sixty-second testimony, and then take a picture. Whether that makes it into your newsletter or not isn't the point, but have something you could put in the newsletter. Maybe it's something you just put into a file and share with them in an email.

Put an actual date on your newsletter

Don't just put June. If it's June 2nd at the time of writing, then write June 2, 2014.

Have a consistent layout

Have a standard layout for your newsletter; call it a template it you like. This will help keep your process short each month. You don't need to go through a creative battle every month, use a basic template. You can change the picture, content, and the way you say things, but I encourage you to get a basic template and run with that for about a year or so. Then, about once a year consider changing the layout.

Use easy labels

You can buy envelopes with the return address printed right on them. You could have that done at a print shop or you could do that on your printer. I do it with a little label that has our return address printed on it already and we peel and stick them right on both the return and address envelopes.

Keep up-to-date information

Be sure you are keeping all your contact information current. It never hurts, such as in a face-to-face visit, to run through that information or talk to them every once in a while to update everything and keep it fresh.

Your consistent, quality newsletter is the most important connection tool you have. Take the time and do a good job.

The yearly visit: why the regular face-to-face meeting?

I encourage you to meet with your partners face-to-face at least once a year. Some of us are in the position where we could do this two or three times a year when we are back home visiting, or maybe they come to your ministry for a conference or outreach. Minimally, do it once a year. In the event you have partners scattered from Kansas City to Florida to California, or even some in Canada, then it is more difficult to see every one of those partners each year. In this situation you could make it a goal to see as many of them as you can in a year, but you might have to accept seeing them every 2nd or 3rd year. In between, you can strengthen the communication with Facetime, Skype, video, and those types of things. Otherwise, plan yearly visits as often as possible.

This visit provides you an excellent opportunity to walk in the second commandment: love on them, encourage them, minister to them, and prophesy over them. This is your opportunity to share the stories and achievements— the details of a past event you already shared with them or even recent events. This meeting also provides a great way to say thank you, share stories, and share accomplishments. You can make it very personal.

Your meeting is part of a team briefing over the past year and looking forward to the next year. They are your team. How do you function together as a team if you don't have a briefing time? Like a football team, they get together in a huddle. You can look at these face-to-face meetings as a briefing time with your team.

This also provides an excellent setting to increase your involvement and expand your team. It's a perfect time to cast vision, share about the future, and invite them into increased involvement. I will talk about this more later, but one of the things we are going to do in our yearly visits is give people an opportunity to increase their giving, to share a special gift for a project, even to host a special event for us or introduce us to their friends.

It's possible ministry time for your team member and for you to take prayer requests. I can't tell you how many times these types of meetings turned into ministry times. You might be one of the most significant spiritual connections your partner has, and they can be greatly encouraged by you and the work you are doing. Be aware of that; take time to pray for them and minister to them.

Where there is no vision, the people cast off restraint—or they perish (Prov. 29:18). Remember, always keep the vision in front of them and call them higher. Remind them of what they are doing as partakers in the ministry, and always point to the future.

Always be prepared before you go to a meeting

Review information about your team member. I recommend that you keep a journal or notebook of information about the people that you meet: names, children's names, how long they have been believers, their church background, where they work, family history, and so on. Keep notes on the people you meet, and review this information right before you go to a meeting with them. I also would encourage you to use this information before you make phone calls as well.

Before you go into your meeting to share with your partner at your yearly visit, know what you are going to ask. I make it a point to ask something every time I am there. It's going to be about special gifts, excited friends, prayer commitments, something of that nature. Be prepared to respond and follow through on your request. If it's a prayer assignment, have it typed out on a card. Have a notebook and pen ready to take down the contact information of excited friends. Think it through before you go, and have a plan. Know what you are going to ask of your partner—what you are going to ask them to do—and be prepared to follow through on it.

Have all your materials and gifts in order and ready to share. Be sure to have everything up to date before you leave on your trip. Photos for example: if you are using photos and brochures, be sure to get them updated at least every other year. We don't want to use photos on brochures that are six or seven years old. Be sure to share on occasion some materials and resources that cast vision for your work. Whether it's a CD, book, or pamphlet, be ready to share things that actually help them gain a heart and appreciation for the type of work you do and/or the people that you minister to.

Think through your whole appointment—greeting, sharing, stories, testimony, vision casting, invitations. Have a plan and an outline for your meeting. Consider practicing this a couple of times before you go. Sometimes you will get a great plan, you will go into that meeting, and then the Holy Spirit just throws it right out the window! So to get the most said and done and the most vision casting with encouragement, think it through. Have a plan, have an outline, and roll with it.

Before you go, pull their giving report from your records or the partner software you may share. Maybe the organization you are with has a staff website. Have this up-to-date, accurate information before you as you go into the meeting. This can be a really valuable tool of encouragement. In other words, you can say, "Mr. Johnson, do you realize that in this past year of our partnership you have sown $2,200 into our ministry? Thank you very much!" That record should be available to you, so have that information at your fingertips. Know how you are going to share it and how you are going to use it.

Make sure you have a clear meeting time and location. You may want to send a reminder or appointment confirmation a couple of days before—or possibly a text. Remember, failing to plan is a plan for failure.

When meeting with a partner, at least seven things should happen

1. **Think about your greeting.**

   Know how you are going to say, "Hi." Know what you are going to say those first couple of minutes right inside the door. They might be ten-year friends and that is a lot easier and organic, or it could be someone you just met six weeks ago. Have a plan and think it through. Don't just figure it out on the fly.

   Be sure that during the meeting you acknowledge their giving. That's why gathering that information prior to the meeting is helpful. This is the time you can share those accomplishments we mentioned earlier in this session. Have a couple of them written down on whatever means you use to remind you of it. Have a couple of accomplishments ready to share.

   Before the meeting is over, cast vision for the future. Talk about what your future plans are or what's coming up, what you hope to achieve in ministry over the next twelve to eighteen months.

   There is going to be a place for asking. You are going to ask for increased involvement, prayer requests, etc., but there is going to be a point where you ask.

   There is going to be a time of praying. Even if there is no problem and everything is going great, don't end the meeting without praying for your partner.

   Leave some time for fellowship. If they are on a tight schedule and only have an hour, then save a few minutes of that hour so you can relax and fellowship. Do whatever is natural for good, healthy fellowship.

   Let's break these down a little bit.

   Review any notes you have on your partner from the last few conversations you had. Maybe pick up a conversation where you had left it off a few months ago.

   Consider having a short list of questions ready to help conversation. For example, if I don't have that much natural relationship with them yet, then I might have four or five go-to questions that I might ask them throughout the meeting. This helps conversation to move along, and you don't get caught in that awkward air time.

   If you are going to their house, don't be early and don't be late. If they have invited you over for dinner at 6:30 then show up right at 6:30 and knock on the door about 6:31. Don't be early, don't be late.

   Make the first ten minutes or so all about them. Ask them about their family, their work, what's going on at church, or their hobbies. Pull that out and use it. In the first ten minutes, make it all about them, and steer the conversation that way.

   All of the above is part of walking in the second commandment. It should also help set a comfortable tone for the meeting as well. If we are really walking the second commandment in love, then we are going to listen, and we are going to ask questions. We are going to pray, and we are going to be interested in what's going on with them. Also, just having this plan and some practical steps helps set a positive tone for that meeting.

2.   Acknowledge their partnership in the context of the yearly visit.

Say thank you. Mention their willingness to give and how encouraged you are. They have ten thousand other places they could be giving to. They have chosen to give to you and your ministry. Say thank you. Your thank-you should include how their giving touches you personally. It's encouraging and you feel blessed. Make them feel like a part of the team.

Your thank-you should also include some of the practicals: "I could not do this without your partnership." Let's learn how to say thank you well and say it often. You can say a thank-you well that really encourages them and calls them higher. You can also say thank you in a way that makes them feel uncomfortable. Learn how to say it well. If you do it with sincerity, vision casting, accomplishment, and achievement you will do well.

Tell them a ministry story of an impact you have made through their partnership, how you were thinking of them, and how grateful you were for their partnership. Have a couple of go-to stories: significant things like testimonies, healings, breakthroughs, etc. For example: how the Holy Spirit swept through a campus. In your yearly visit, have a couple of really exciting stories that you can go to. In those, share the people's names and places; give the details.

3.   Share accomplishments.

They partner with you because of vision. This is your chance to give that to them and update them. Vision will evolve as time goes on, so include them in that.

Give them a review of the past year. Share testimonies and tell stories. You can't get all the communication in your newsletters and the occasional postcard or phone call. Share more with them here about what was accomplished this last year.

Draw them into the story. Show them how their partnership has made the story possible.

Tell them in detail what their giving is accomplishing, and make it personal.

4.   Cast vision for the future.

Share with them what God has given you for the coming year. Be willing to share a little of the journey and how you arrived there; how the Lord has led you.

Break down your plans into two or three steps or into seasons or calendar quarters. This will help them see that you have thought it through, that you are following the Lord's direction, and you are being a good steward of the calling. In other words, don't say, "Ah, yeah . . . this year we want to do a, b, and c"—and just leave it at that. You may want to say, "This year we feel like the Lord has said a, b, and c to us and we want to get it done; so our plan to get there in this first quarter is to focus on a and b. In the second quarter we are going to focus on c. Then in the third quarter we are going to focus on d and e." In other words, don't say it so generically that you or they might question whether it's ever going to get done. Break it down a little, and explain it to them. Show them that you have thought it through, that you have a plan, and that you are going to execute it.

Invite them to join you in the journey through prayer. Have a prayer card with you to share with them that covers the next three months. Your prayer card should have points concerning the vision you just cast. It should not be overly general but specific to the vision you just cast. Write it down, make a specific request, put it on the card, and then update that card about every quarter. It's really difficult for someone to carry a prayer assignment every day for five, six, or seven months at a time. If you update it each quarter, talk with them, rewrite, make some more requests, and share the progress with them, then they can engage with the next step of the assignment.

If the vision you have just cast requires a specific dollar amount or a possible planned missions trip, new outreach, or what have you, then ask them to join you with a special gift.

5. **The asking part of your yearly meetings.**

Every meeting with a partner should include some kind of an ask. Don't draw back from the ask. Use it to draw them further into your ministry. Develop them into a more involved partner. We all grow in our giving just as we all grow in our Christianity. Here is a way to help them grow as one who has sent you into the missions field.

Regular asks help keep the partnership from getting stale. They provide an opportunity for stewardship and greater involvement. Here are a few things to consider in your asking:

Consider an increase in giving. In most households, the economics change about every two and a half years or so. There is a pay raise, a car is paid off, the kids are out of school, kids are out of braces, and one of the missionaries they support is no longer in missions, etc. Many are happy to give more when they can. Now that they have a little bit more money to work with, they are happy to increase their giving. Additionally, the American cost of living goes up about 3 percent every year. It costs more to live and it costs more to do ministry than it did a year ago. Marketplace people receive regular cost-of-living raises. For this reason, invite them to consider this in prayer for the coming year.

Your ministry is also growing and the economy is changing. There is always a need to increase your salary. Many of them will respond happily if you ask them to do so. I do it at the end of a meeting as a sort of take-away point. I say, "Hey Jim, Janice, I want to invite you to consider increasing your giving this year. We are growing the ministry, and we are doing a, b, and c, and we are going to need an increased salary. We are inviting team members to increase their giving by ten to fifteen percent in this coming year to help us reach our goals. Would you take a couple of weeks to pray about that, and I will follow up with you and see what you have decided?" It's that kind of invitation.

Also, ask for a special gift. As you have heard me say in this training before, I don't say "one-time gift," I refer to it as a special gift. This type of ask should only be done if the vision cast has been done first. Be sure to share the amounts, timelines, and dates. In other words, if I am going to ask for a special gift, it is toward a project. So I am going to share about the project; I am going to cast vision about the project; I am going to share the desires, goals, and how God has led me concerning this project; and I am going to share what the project is going to cost. Then I will ask them to share a special gift.

Maybe it is just something practical like a car or other transportation. I can share with them why I need a car and how it's going to help the ministry. Who can we reach, how many can we disciple? Here is the cost; will you join me through a special gift? Don't ask for the special gift unless you have properly cast the vision.

Another thing I will ask for from time to time is excited friends. This is really a personal recommendation from one friend to another. The marketplace calls this dynamic a referral, but that hardly describes what is happening. We make personal recommendations to our friends all the time: restaurants, doctors, mechanics, books, movies. We do things in life, we enjoy them, and we have friends we think would enjoy them also; so we happily recommend them to our friends. The issue with ministry is no different. I can't tell you how many books and CDs I have been blessed by because a friend recommended them to me. This is much of what we are doing—I will take the time to ask my partners about meeting their friends.

Host a recommendation meeting. In other words, ask your partner if they would host a small event in their home where you could share your ministry with eight to ten of their friends. We explained this in another part of the teaching and training, but right here we are talking about what we do on this yearly visit. This is one of the things I might do in a yearly visit.

We can ask about speaking opportunities. They could help set up a speaking situation with their own house church group or their Sunday school or maybe even with their pastor. Ask them about speaking opportunities.

6. **Let's pray for them. Every meeting should include prayer at some point.**

The right time to pray may be at the beginning. Small talk might present that opportunity. Usually it would be at the end, but be open to the Holy Spirit and follow His leading.

At any point in the conversation, as the Holy Spirit highlights something, take a moment to pray.

Maybe at the end you could take prayer requests. Write that prayer request down, and then take a moment to pray for them.

It may happen just for the fun of it. There may not be a request or an urgent need, but just in a good, fun, happy kind of celebrative way you could end that meeting with prayer.

Don't end a meeting without praying for them. Either by request, leading of the Holy Spirit, or pastoral reasons—be sure to pray for them before you leave.

7. **Make room for good Christian fellowship.**

Do this at the beginning or during an extended small-talk time or toward the end. Be sure to make room for it. Don't get locked into your outline so tightly that you forget to be a friend. Being a friend is important! This helps bring an organic nature to your meeting. Have time to fellowship, to hang out, and make small talk in a healthy way.

Make it as natural as possible. Let it fit in where it wants to fit in. You do this every day with your friends, and you know how to do it. Just be a friend; be natural.

If you are a dinner guest in their home, be sure to ask them what you can bring. If it's a more casual meeting, think about taking a little treat of some kind you could share. Maybe coffee, tea, bread, cheese, or a dessert. Maybe share a gift that would create a point of fellowship: a teaching series, a book, or some pictures from the ministry, something like that.

Be sensitive to their time. Fellowship well but don't overstay; depart gracefully.

Lapse in partnership

A lapse in giving is something that does happen on occasion. You may have a partner who forgets to send a gift. What do we do when this happens?

First, keep track of everyone's giving, and when you see they have missed a month, make a note of it. I just use a hard-copy spreadsheet with everyone's name and amounts. It is spread out over the course of a month. We have a different sheet for each month in a three-ring binder. When the gift comes in we highlight it. Then at the end of the month if there is a blank spot that hasn't been highlighted, I can clearly see anyone who didn't send their gift. Then, when I flip over to the next page and start another month, I will fill it out the same. Then, at the end of that second month if that spot is still not filled, in other words, if that particular partner has not given in the past two months, then I am going to call them.

When I do this I am assuming that something has kept them from sending their gift. I assume that there are problems with their job, health issues, a traumatic situation within the family, or something of that nature. I am assuming something has kept them from sending that gift. I go low, assuming that there has been a problem, and I am seeking to be pastoral.

When I get on the phone with them, say hello and everything, I ask them if everything is alright, if everything is okay with job, family, health, etc. They might say, "Hey, why do you ask?" Then I will move on into saying, "You have been such a great partner, so consistent in your giving, and when I noticed you had missed the last two months, I just assumed something had kept you from it. Maybe there was a problem at home or financially and I just wanted to catch up with you and see if there was any way I could pray for you."

Now, when this happens, most of the time I find out they just forgot and they are just a little embarrassed. But because we went low and did it in humility, it makes fixing the situation easy. Also on occasion you will find out there really is a problem: financial, health, or marital. Because you went low in humility, you have a great opportunity to minister to that person now. So go low, assume that something has kept them from giving. Remember that the key to all this is keeping good records.

I don't do it if they have just missed one month; anyone can miss one month. Once I see they have missed the second month, I will immediately get on the phone. Don't wait until three or four months have passed because that actually makes it more awkward. Get on the phone very quickly and catch it. Also if they have had some sort of trouble—because you went low—you have the opportunity to minister to them. Pray for them, minister to them, and love them well.

If it is strictly a financial situation, you might suggest a lower partnership amount for a season. If they did lose a job and take a dramatic cut in pay, offer a reduced amount as a possible solution. You will just have to play this situation by ear and be sensitive to the Holy Spirit. I would rather keep them engaged at a lesser amount than just drop it altogether. Stay connected with them.

The situation might actually produce the need for them to stop their partnership altogether. If so, acknowledge what they have done in the past, share accomplishments and achievements, and encourage and bless them. Reach for continued communication with the newsletter, and then open the door toward the future. In other words, you might have to postpone that partnership momentarily, but you end it on a good note with a great relationship, and they stay connected through the newsletter. You might be able to revisit that partnership at a later date.

All of that is fine, and all of that is healthy. In the event you do have to deal with lapsed giving, there is an easy way to navigate it and a healthy way that isn't weird and goofy. It starts with keeping good records. Don't do anything on the one-month mark, but wait and see if they have missed the second month. Respond immediately. Go low, assuming that something has prohibited them from giving. When you get on the phone, listen well, be pastoral, and love well.

Help them. If it's simply that they forgot, just encourage them that it is no problem and they could catch up in the next month. If they consistently have trouble getting that gift to you every month, encourage them to use electronic giving that would help in their consistency. Ask what you can do to help them carry out their giving intentions. If you go low and you go in humility, it will go well.

Summary

1. *In order to serve God long-term in full-time ministry, we will not only need to build a partnership team, but pastor well those people who are now running together with us.*

2. *The DNA of team relationships should include an acknowledgment of all giving, consistent appreciation, shared achievements, and regular vision casting and sharing future plans.*

3. *Loving our team well means that we have a communication plan where we are consistently sharing with them through the most effective mediums.*

4. *The most powerful tool in your communication tool belt is your monthly paper newsletter.*

5. *Your newsletter shouldn't read like multiple news clippings with frequent financial asks, cluttered with pictures. We want it to be a personal correspondence with a ministry partner.*

6. *The big-picture guideline for your newsletter is one page, one side, one-inch margins, one topic, and written to one person.*

7. *In your plan of consistent communication with your partnership team, you should include a yearly visit in which you say thanks, acknowledge their partnership, cast vision, and present a clear ask.*

Homework Assignments

HOMEWORK ASSIGNMENT #1
Meditation Questions

Your vision for ministry

The Lord has always had laborers; from the very beginning, He has had men and women serve in a full-time way. In saying yes to the Lord, you have joined a long line of servants who, through the years, have given their lives in full-time service. What an honor!

There is a tremendous confidence that comes from knowing that the Lord has called you into full-time, occupational ministry. Knowing that the Lord has called you, and what He has called you to, will help provide the confidence necessary to labor through the preparation and team-building time. This confidence will also provide considerable stability in the years to come.

What is your assignment?

As a servant commissioned to full-time, occupational service, you must know that the Lord has called you and what He has called you to. Knowing your assignment will not only benefit you, but will also help your future partnership team. You need to be able to communicate the assignment the Lord has given you clearly, accurately, and effectively. When it is clear in your own thinking, you will be able to communicate it confidently. Clarity is confidence! This clarity is what we mean by "vision."

Instructions

Read through the following questions and take them to the Lord in prayer. Meditate, ask questions, and allow time to hear the Lord's response. If you ask, He will answer.

> » Spend 30–40 minutes a day (minimum) talking with the Lord about each question.

> » Take time to journal your thoughts and feelings (at least a half page), paying attention to how your heart responds (e.g., panic, excitement, fear, anticipation, anxiety, hesitation) and what you think the Lord is saying.

> » Be prepared to show your work.

1. **Day 1 meditation.** If money and circumstances were not a problem, how would I serve the Lord?

2. **Day 2 meditation**. I am willing to be spent for You. How do You want to spend my life, and what do You want to purchase for Yourself?

3. **Day 3 meditation**. Lord, what must I do to stand before You without regret? (In terms of service assignment.)

4. **Day 4 meditation.** Lord, what are You asking me to do in this current season as Your servant? What must I do to obey?

_____

_____

_____

_____

_____

_____

_____

_____

_____

HOMEWORK ASSIGNMENT #2

Your Testimony

Checklist

☐ Yes, I wrote the long version of my testimony.

☐ Yes, I wrote the 1-page condensed version of my testimony.

☐ Yes, I shared my 5-minute testimony with a friend.

☐ Yes, I shared my 2-minute testimony with a friend.

☐ Yes, I shared my 30-second testimony with a friend.

☐ Yes, I read through the class notes.

Complete the following:

1. Write out your testimony in 2–3 handwritten pages (on the attached pages), including when you were born again, your early Christian walk, major points along the way, how you were called into full-time, occupational ministry, and how you ended up at the ministry where you currently serve.

2. After you have written your testimony, go back and look at the highlights and major points. Re-write a condensed version so it fits onto 1 page (attached). You will turn in both of these versions.

3. Share your story with three different friends (not your spouse) in the following time limits. Start from when you were born again up to your call to occupational ministry and then to the ministry where you currently serve. Have each friend time you and let you know when you go over.

   a. 5-minute version

   b. 2-minute version

   c. 30-second version

4. Read through the notes covered in class.

5. Be prepared, as you will share your 30-second testimony in front of the class.

Your testimony (long version) – Page 1 of 3

Your testimony (long version) – Page 2 of 3

Your testimony (long version) – Page 3 of 3

Your testimony (condensed version)

HOMEWORK ASSIGNMENT #3
Stewardship

Checklist

☐ Did you read through both sets of Stewardship notes?

☐ Did you answer all of the questions on the homework?

☐ Did you write the one-paragraph summary (Part 2)?

☐ Did you answer the last question about your own stewardship?

Part 1

Read through the following Bible passages and answer the corresponding questions.

> ⁵Thus says God the LORD, who created the heavens and stretched them out, who spread forth the earth and that which comes from it, who gives breath to the people on it and spirit to those who walk on it. (Isa. 42:5)

1. What do you think "who spread forth the earth and that which comes from it" means?

     _____

     _____

     _____

2. What do you think "who gives breath to the people on it" means?

     _____

     _____

3. What do you think "and spirit to those who walk on it" means?

     _____

     _____

4.   What happens to the heavens, the earth, breath, and spirit, if God is not acting on His own?

_____

_____

_____

¹The word which came to Jeremiah from the LORD, saying: ²"Arise and go down to the potter's house, and there I will cause you to hear My words." ³Then I went down to the potter's house, and there he was, making something at the wheel. ⁴And the vessel that he made of clay was marred in the hand of the potter; so he made it again into another vessel, as it seemed good to the potter to make. ⁵Then the word of the LORD came to me, saying: ⁶"O house of Israel, can I not do with you as this potter?" says the LORD. "Look, as the clay is in the potter's hand, so are you in My hand, O house of Israel!" (Jer. 18:1–6)

5.   What do you think the Lord is trying to say to Israel?

_____

_____

_____

6.   How would you describe the relationship between potter and clay?

_____

_____

_____

7.   How would you describe the relationship between God and Israel?

_____

_____

_____

8.   How much importance would you place on "the will" of the clay?

_____

_____

_____

[12]Blessed is the nation whose God is the LORD, the people He has chosen as His own inheritance. (Ps. 33:12)

[4]For the LORD has chosen Jacob for Himself, Israel for His special treasure. (Ps. 135:4)

[6]"For you are a holy people to the LORD your God; the LORD your God has chosen you to be a people for Himself, a special treasure above all the peoples on the face of the earth." (Deut. 7:6)

[2]For you are a holy people to the LORD your God, and the LORD has chosen you to be a people for Himself, a special treasure above all the peoples who are on the face of the earth. (Deut. 14:2)

9. The word *chosen*, which appears in the four verses above, reflects the will of God. How should that word shape your thinking about the Lord and your own relationship with Him?

_____

_____

_____

10. Make other observations from the four verses listed above and list your findings.

_____

_____

_____

_____

[17]"They shall be Mine," says the LORD of hosts, "on the day that I make them My jewels. And I will spare them as a man spares his own son who serves him." (Mal. 3:17)

11. There are a few parts of this verse that speak of the Lord's ownership. List them and explain.

_____

_____

[1]The earth is the LORD's, and all its fullness, the world and those who dwell therein. (Ps. 24:1)

12. Write your own 3–5 sentence commentary on the above verse; your statement should reflect God's comprehensive ownership.

_____

_____

_____
_____
_____

13. How should this verse shape our thinking as servants?

_____
_____

14. How should this verse impact our stewardship?

_____
_____

Part 2

After answering all the questions above, read through all of your Stewardship notes (both Old Testament and New Testament) and then write a one-paragraph summary of what the Bible says about stewardship. Be sure to include our responsibility and the privilege of stewardship.

_____
_____
_____
_____
_____
_____
_____
_____
_____

_____

_____

_____

_____

_____

Now that you have summarized your Bible study, what do you think the Lord is requiring of you? Answer the following question. Your answer should be no less than 4 or 5 sentences.

How must I steward (manage) my life in order to hear the Lord say, "Well done, good and faithful servant" (in terms of my service to Him)?

_____

_____

_____

_____

_____

_____

_____

_____

HOMEWORK ASSIGNMENT #4
Old Testament Study

Checklist

☐ Did you read through your notes?

☐ Did you read through the verses and answer the questions?

☐ Did you write your summary?

Read through the following Bible passages and answer the corresponding questions.

> [21]"Behold, I have given the children of Levi all the tithes in Israel as an inheritance in return for the work which they perform, the work of the tabernacle of meeting. [22]Hereafter the children of Israel shall not come near the tabernacle of meeting, lest they bear sin and die. [23]But the Levites shall perform the work of the tabernacle of meeting, and they shall bear their iniquity; it shall be a statute forever, throughout your generations, that among the children of Israel they shall have no inheritance. [24]For the tithes of the children of Israel, which they offer up as a heave offering to the LORD, I have given to the Levites as an inheritance; therefore I have said to them, 'Among the children of Israel they shall have no inheritance.'" (Num. 18:21–24)

1. Why was the tithe given to the Levites?

   _____

   _____

2. Where did the tithe come from?

   _____

   _____

3. Did the Levites have a "real job"?

   _____

   _____

4. Reflection: Why do you think the Levites did not have secular jobs?

_____

_____

There was provision even for the "non-Levite"

> *⁶And he said to him, "Look now, there is in this city a man of God, and he is an honorable man; all that he says surely comes to pass. So let us go there; perhaps he can show us the way that we should go." ⁷Then Saul said to his servant, "But look, if we go, what shall we bring the man? For the bread in our vessels is all gone, and there is no present to bring to the man of God. What do we have?" (1 Sam. 9:6–7)*

5. What made them think they had to take a gift when it wasn't part of the Law? There seems to be a cultural etiquette to give in this way; how do you think this developed?

_____

_____

> *⁸And the servant answered Saul again and said, "Look, I have here at hand one-fourth of a shekel of silver. I will give that to the man of God, to tell us our way." ⁹(Formerly in Israel, when a man went to inquire of God, he spoke thus: "Come, let us go to the seer"; for he who is now called a prophet was formerly called a seer.) ¹⁰Then Saul said to his servant, "Well said; come, let us go." So they went to the city where the man of God was. (1 Sam. 9:8–10)*

6. Do you think they were purchasing prophetic ministry? Please explain.

_____

_____

7. Do you think this culture valued prophetic ministry and wanted to see it go forth?

_____

_____

> *⁸Now it happened one day that Elisha went to Shunem, where there was a notable woman, and she persuaded him to eat some food. So it was, as often as he passed by, he would turn in there to eat some food. ⁹And she said to her husband, "Look now, I know that this is a holy man of God, who passes by us regularly. ¹⁰Please, let us make a small upper room on the wall; and let us put a bed for him there, and a table and a chair and a lampstand; so it will be, whenever he comes to us, he can turn in there." ¹¹And it happened one day that he came there, and he turned in to the upper room and lay down there. (2 Kgs. 4:8–11)*

8.   Why do you think she wanted to provide for the prophet?

_____

_____

9.   Do you feel like she does any type of evaluation before she gives?

_____

_____

_____

10.   Do you think this couple managed their resources for the advancement of the kingdom?

_____

_____

_____

1 Chronicles 28–29

Read through 1 Chronicles 28 and 29. Listed below are just the highlights.

> [1]*Now David assembled at Jerusalem all the leaders of Israel: the officers ... captains over thousands and ... over hundreds, and the stewards over all the substance and possessions ... with the officials, the valiant men, and all the mighty men of valor. (1 Chr. 28:1)*

David has something he wants to share, and he gathers all his leaders together to share it with them.

> [2]*Then King David rose to his feet and said, "Hear me, my brethren and my people: I had it in my heart to build a house of rest for the ark of the covenant of the LORD, and for the footstool of our God, and had made preparations to build it." (1 Chr. 28:2)*

David is sharing with them what he has in his heart.

> [11]*Then David gave his son Solomon the plans for the vestibule, its houses, its treasuries, its upper chambers, its inner chambers, and the place of the mercy seat;* [12]*and the plans for all that he had by the Spirit, of the courts of the house of the LORD, of all the chambers all around, of the treasuries of the house of God, and of the treasuries for the dedicated things;* [13]*also for the division of the priests and the Levites, for all the work of the service of the house of the LORD, and for all the articles of service in the house of the LORD. (1 Chr. 28:11–13)*

David had done considerable prep work before he ever shared the vision.

11.   Why does David gather all these leaders together?

_____

_____

12. Reflection: Why did David gather these particular men instead of all the men of Israel or all of the people of Israel?

_____

_____

_____

13. What is it that David had in his heart to do?

_____

_____

14. What were David's plans?

_____

_____

15. How did these plans come to David?

_____

_____

16. David had something in his heart to do. List the ways that David worked to make it happen.

_____

_____

_____

Furthermore King David said to all the assembly: "My son Solomon, whom alone God has chosen, is young and inexperienced; and the work is great, because the temple is not for man but for the LORD God. ²Now for the house of my God I have prepared with all my might: gold for things to be made of gold, silver for things of silver, bronze for things of bronze, iron for things of iron, wood for things of wood, onyx stones, stones to be set, glistening stones of various colors, all kinds of precious stones, and marble slabs in abundance. ³Moreover, because I have set my affection on the house of my God, I have given to the house of my God, over and above all that I have prepared for the holy house, my own special treasure of gold and silver: ⁴three thousand talents of gold, of the gold of Ophir, and seven thousand talents of refined silver, to overlay the walls of the houses; ⁵the gold for things of gold and the silver for things of silver, and for all kinds of work to be done by the hands of craftsmen. Who then is willing to consecrate himself this day to the LORD?" ⁶Then the leaders of the fathers' houses, leaders of the tribes of Israel, the captains of thousands and of hundreds, with the officers over the king's work, offered willingly. ⁷They gave for the work of the house of God five thousand talents and *ten thousand darics of gold, ten thousand talents of silver, eighteen thousand talents of bronze, and one hundred thousand talents of iron. ⁸And whoever had precious stones gave them to the treasury of the house of the Lord, into the hand of Jehiel the Gershonite. ⁹Then the people rejoiced, for they had offered willingly, because with a loyal heart they had offered willingly to the Lord; and King David also rejoiced greatly. (1 Chr. 29:1–9)*

David is inviting the men to his vision and asks them to help, and they all do so willingly.

17. Reflection: What do you think David meant when he said he prepared with all his might?

_____

_____

_____

18. David gave out of his own special treasure. What made David do this?

_____

_____

_____

19. David asked the men a question. What is it and is it clear?

_____

_____

_____

20. Why did the men give? What was the nature of their response?

_____

_____

_____

21. What was the corporate response to their giving and why?

_____

_____

_____

22. Was David rejoicing over the willingness to give or over the fact that the temple was going to get built?

_____

_____

¹²"Both riches and honor come from You, and You reign over all. In Your hand is power and might; in Your hand it is to make great and to give strength to all." (1 Chr. 29:12)

¹⁴"But who am I, and who are my people, that we should be able to offer so willingly as this? For all things come from You, and of Your own we have given You."(1 Chr. 29:14)

¹⁶"O LORD our God, all this abundance that we have prepared to build You a house for Your holy name is from Your hand, and is all Your own." (1 Chr. 29:16)

¹⁷"I know also, my God, that You test the heart and have pleasure in uprightness. As for me, in the uprightness of my heart I have willingly offered all these things; and now with joy I have seen Your people, who are present here to offer willingly to You." (1 Chr. 29:17)

23. What is the source of all riches?

_____

24. Reflection: Why do you think David was so moved by their willingness to give?

_____

_____

25. Was asking a necessary evil for David, or did he do it with gladness?

_____

_____

26. Faith requires work. What was David's work?

_____

_____

27. How would this situation be different if David had not prepared?

_____

_____

28. How would this situation be different if David had not asked?

_____

_____

¹A certain woman of the wives of the sons of the prophets cried out to Elisha, saying, "Your servant my husband is dead, and you know that your servant feared the LORD. And the creditor is coming to take my two sons to be his slaves." ²So Elisha said to her, "What shall I do for you? Tell me, what do you have in the house?" And she said, "Your maidservant has nothing in the house but a jar of oil." ³Then he said, "Go, borrow vessels from everywhere, from all your neighbors—empty vessels; do not gather just a few. ⁴And when you have come in, you shall shut the door behind you and your sons; then pour it into all those vessels, and set aside the full ones." ⁵So she went from him and shut the door behind her and her sons, who brought the vessels to her; and she poured it out. ⁶Now it came to pass, when the vessels were full, that she said to her son, "Bring me another vessel." And he said to her, "There is not another vessel." So the oil ceased. ⁷Then she came and told the man of God. And he said, "Go, sell the oil and pay your debt; and you and your sons live on the rest." (2 Kgs. 4:1–7)

29. How did the Lord provide for the woman and her sons?

_____

_____

30. Who all was involved in meeting the needs of the woman?

_____

_____

31. What does it mean in verse 1 that she cried out to Elisha?

_____

_____

32. What role did the woman play in verse 3?

_____

_____

33. Look at verse 6: what would have happened if she had gathered more vessels?

_____

_____

34. What was the money used for first?

_____

35. What else do you see in this verse?

_____

_____

_____

_____

Homework Assignment

Read through this session again. Take time to read and meditate on the verses, walk through the questions and the comments after each set of verses as well as your answers, and make observations.

Take your answers and observations and form them into a summary, including the points from the verses. From our Bible study so far, what can we say for sure related to what the Word says about provision, support, giving, what part we play, and so on?

Summary.

_____

_____

_____

_____

_____

_____

_____

_____

_____

HOMEWORK ASSIGNMENT #5
New Testament Study

Checklist

☐ Did you read through your notes?

☐ Did you read through the verses and answer the questions?

☐ Did you write your summary?

Read through the following Bible passages and answer the corresponding questions.

> ¹*Soon afterward he went on through cities and villages, proclaiming and bringing the good news of the kingdom of God. And the twelve were with him, ²and also some women who had been healed of evil spirits and infirmities: Mary, called Magdalene, from whom seven demons had gone out, ³and Joanna, the wife of Chuza, Herod's household manager, and Susanna, and many others, who provided for them out of their means. (Lk. 8:1–3, ESV)*

1. Notice that Jesus (God in the flesh) put Himself in a position of being dependent on others. Why do you think He did this?

_____

_____

_____

2. Why didn't Jesus just continue working at the carpenter shop? Why didn't He "make tents"?

_____

_____

_____

3. Why didn't He just make bread when He needed it?

_____

_____

4. How many people supported Jesus and His team?

    _____

    _____

5. How much support did Jesus receive? Are there other scriptures that reflect the amount of money Jesus may have received? Think about this one and do a little searching.

    _____

    _____

    _____

⁵Jesus sent out these twelve, instructing them [commanding them, NKJV] as follows: "Do not go to Gentile regions and do not enter any Samaritan town. ⁶Go instead to the lost sheep of the house of Israel. ⁷As you go, preach this message: 'The kingdom of heaven is near!' ⁸Heal the sick, raise the dead, cleanse lepers, cast out demons. Freely you received, freely give. ⁹Do not take gold, silver, or copper in your belts, ¹⁰no bag for the journey, or an extra tunic, or sandals or staff, for the worker deserves his provisions. ¹¹Whenever you enter a town or village, find out who is worthy there and stay with them until you leave." (Mt. 10:5–11, NET)

Jesus gives a clear ministry assignment. Verses 9–11 are part of that assignment.

6. Why did Jesus give the command in verses 9 and 10 (the answer is in the last part of v. 10)? Why do you think Jesus did it this way?

    _____

    _____

    _____

Jesus was saying to them, "I don't want you funding your assignment; you're working and I will make sure you're paid." The reason for not taking money wasn't some kind of "super faith-building" mission, although I'm sure their faith was built by the provision.

Part of their assignment was securing provision. This was an order just the same as preaching the gospel of the kingdom or healing the sick (v. 11).

7. Notice in verse 11 they are to find out where the housing is, but they have to ask. Verse 11 is part of the commission. What does this mean for you?

    _____

    _____

The provision was already there before they even left. If you are called and serving the Lord, the provision is there. We must to do our part and ask; finding the provision that is already there is part of the assignment.

8. Who was the provider and by what means?

_____

_____

9. What part did the disciples play? What did they have to do?

_____

_____

> *3"Go! I am sending you out like lambs surrounded by wolves. 4Do not carry a money bag, a traveler's bag, or sandals, and greet no one on the road. 5Whenever you enter a house, first say, 'May peace be on this house!' 6And if a peace-loving person is there, your peace will remain on him, but if not, it will return to you. 7Stay in that same house, eating and drinking what they give you, for the worker deserves his pay. Do not move around from house to house. 8Whenever you enter a town and the people welcome you, eat what is set before you." (Lk. 10:3–8, NET)*

This is the sending of the seventy, yet the instructions are the same.

> *35And He said to them, "When I sent you without money bag, knapsack, and sandals, did you lack anything?" So they said, "Nothing." 36Then He said to them, "But now, he who has a money bag, let him take it, and likewise a knapsack; and he who has no sword, let him sell his garment and buy one. 37For I say to you that this which is written must still be accomplished in Me: 'And he was numbered with the transgressors.' For the things concerning Me have an end." 38So they said, "Lord, look, here are two swords." And He said to them, "It is enough." (Lk. 22:35–38)*

Notice the contrast with the first assignment from Matthew 10. Jesus is contrasting the difference between the short missions with the way life is going to be after His departure.

Jesus is not telling them they now have the responsibility of self-support, but rather they need a shift in their thinking. He is instructing them to think long term—to make provision for a longer, more dangerous mission. He is preparing them for the danger and hardship they are about to face.

10. Jesus is comparing two events, the previous event of Matthew 10 and the current situation here in Luke 22. Why do you think Jesus is comparing, and what point do you think He is trying to make?

_____

_____

_____

_____

_____

11. Reflection: Why was a sword so important that Jesus instructed them to sell a change of clothes to buy a sword?

_____

_____

_____

Jesus is not changing His position on a worker being worthy of a wage. Paul affirms Jesus' teaching:

> [22]I also have been much hindered from coming to you. [23]But now no longer having a place in these parts, and having a great desire these many years to come to you, [24]whenever I journey to Spain, I shall come to you. For I hope to see you on my journey, and to be helped on my way there by you, if first I may enjoy your company for a while. (Rom. 15:22–24)

12. Does Paul know whom he is writing to? What is Paul's plan, and what is he asking for? Does Paul present these things clearly?

_____

_____

_____

13. What do you think Paul means in verse 24 when he says, "and to be helped on my way there by you?"

_____

_____

_____

While working for the Lord, Paul makes plans, he shares the plans clearly, and asks his friends to join him.

14. How would you describe the relationship between Paul and his readers? Have they supported Paul in the past? Are they a group that Paul has been ministering to?

_____

_____

_____

Paul defends his apostleship

¹Am I not free? Am I not an apostle? Have I not seen Jesus our Lord? Are you not my work in the Lord? ²If I am not an apostle to others, at least I am to you, for you are the confirming sign of my apostleship in the Lord. ³This is my defense to those who examine me. ⁴Do we not have the right to financial support? ⁵Do we not have the right to the company of a believing wife, like the other apostles and the Lord's brothers and Cephas? ⁶Or do only Barnabas and I lack the right not to work? ⁷Who ever serves in the army at his own expense? Who plants a vineyard and does not eat its fruit? Who tends a flock and does not consume its milk? ⁸Am I saying these things only on the basis of common sense, or does the law not say this as well? ⁹For it is written in the law of Moses, "Do not muzzle an ox while it is treading out the grain." God is not concerned here about oxen, is he? ¹⁰Or is he not surely speaking for our benefit? It was written for us, because the one plowing and threshing ought to work in hope of enjoying the harvest. ¹¹If we sowed spiritual blessings among you, is it too much to reap material things from you? ¹²If others receive this right from you, are we not more deserving? But we have not made use of this right. Instead we endure everything so that we may not be a hindrance to the gospel of Christ. ¹³Don't you know that those who serve in the temple eat food from the temple, and those who serve at the altar receive a part of the offerings? ¹⁴In the same way the Lord commanded those who proclaim the gospel to receive their living by the gospel. ¹⁵But I have not used any of these rights. And I am not writing these things so that something will be done for me. In fact, it would be better for me to die than—no one will deprive me of my reason for boasting! ¹⁶For if I preach the gospel, I have no reason for boasting, because I am compelled to do this. Woe to me if I do not preach the gospel! ¹⁷For if I do this voluntarily, I have a reward. But if I do it unwillingly, I am entrusted with a responsibility. ¹⁸What then is my reward? That when I preach the gospel I may offer the gospel free of charge, and so not make full use of my rights in the gospel. (1 Cor. 9:1–18, NET)

15. What point is Paul making in verses 4 and 6?

16. Paul asks a question in verse 7. What is his point?

17. What are the material things Paul is speaking about in verse 11?

18. Explain Paul's comment in verse 12. How would the gospel be hindered?

_____

_____

_____

19. Explain verse 14.

_____

_____

> ⁵For I consider that I am not at all inferior to the most eminent apostles. ⁶Even though I am untrained in speech, yet I am not in knowledge. But we have been thoroughly manifested among you in all things. ⁷Did I commit sin in humbling myself that you might be exalted, because I preached the gospel of God to you free of charge? ⁸I robbed other churches, taking wages from them to minister to you. ⁹And when I was present with you, and in need, I was a burden to no one, for what I lacked the brethren who came from Macedonia supplied. And in everything I kept myself from being burdensome to you, and so I will keep myself. (2 Cor. 11:5–9)

20. Explain verse 8.

_____

_____

21. Explain verse 9.

_____

_____

_____

Paul was not supported fully by making tents when he ministered to the Corinthians; he actually had help from other churches.

Other New Testament verses that reflect supporting missionaries

> ⁵Dear friend, you demonstrate faithfulness by whatever you do for the brothers (even though they are strangers). ⁶They have testified to your love before the church. You will do well to send them on their way in a manner worthy of God. ⁷For they have gone forth on behalf of "The Name," accepting nothing from the pagans. ⁸Therefore we ought to support such people, so that we become coworkers in cooperation with the truth. (3 Jn. 1:5–8; NET)

22. In verse 5, John said faithfulness is demonstrated by caring for the worker/messenger. What could this look like?

_____

_____

23. In verse 6, how could they send them on their way in a manner worthy of God? What could this include?

_____

_____

24. In verse 8, "therefore" connects two thoughts. What are they and what is the result?

_____

_____

_____

25. When we support a worker/messenger, we share in the work they are doing and co-labor with them. Where our money goes we go. We are coming into agreement with the truth by supporting messengers of truth. In what way could this truth be helpful as you raise support?

_____

_____

_____

_____

_10_I have great joy in the Lord because now at last you have again expressed your concern for me. (Now I know you were concerned before but had no opportunity to do anything.) _11_I am not saying this because I am in need, for I have learned to be content in any circumstance. _12_I have experienced times of need and times of abundance. In any and every circumstance I have learned the secret of contentment, whether I go satisfied or hungry, have plenty or nothing. _13_I am able to do all things through the one who strengthens me. _14_Nevertheless, you did well to share with me in my trouble. _15_And as you Philippians know, at the beginning of my gospel ministry, when I left Macedonia, no church shared with me in this matter of giving and receiving except you alone. _16_For even in Thessalonica on more than one occasion you sent something for my need. _17_I do not say this because I am seeking a gift. Rather, I seek the credit that abounds to your account. _18_For I have received everything, and I have plenty. I have all I need because I received from Epaphroditus what you sent—a fragrant offering, an acceptable sacrifice, very pleasing to God. _19_And my God will supply your every need according to his glorious riches in Christ Jesus. (Phil. 4:10–19, NET)

26. In verse 10, what is the source of Paul's joy? Describe the relationship between Paul and the Philippians.

27. What do you think Paul means in verse 10b?

28. Paul is presenting them with an opportunity to express their love. How?

29. In verse 11, is Paul writing out of desperate need?

30. How often did the Philippians help Paul?

31. In verse 15, what did the Philippians share in?

32. Was Paul receiving support just from the people he was ministering to?

33. What is Paul saying in verse 17?

_____

_____

34. What does Paul say about their giving?

_____

35. How does God feel about their giving?

_____

12Indeed, the signs of an apostle were performed among you with great perseverance by signs and wonders and powerful deeds. 13For how were you treated worse than the other churches, except that I myself was not a burden to you? Forgive me this injustice! 14Look, for the third time I am ready to come to you, and I will not be a burden to you, because I do not want your possessions, but you. For children should not have to save up for their parents, but parents for their children. 15Now I will most gladly spend and be spent for your lives! If I love you more, am I to be loved less? 16But be that as it may, I have not burdened you. Yet because I was a crafty person, I took you in by deceit! 17I have not taken advantage of you through anyone I have sent to you, have I? 18I urged Titus to visit you and I sent our brother along with him. Titus did not take advantage of you, did he? Did we not conduct ourselves in the same spirit? Did we not behave in the same way? (2 Cor. 12:12–18, NET)

36. What point do you think Paul is making with verse 13?

_____

_____

37. Do you think there were positive experiences the Corinthians and Paul missed out on because of a lack of giving and receiving? If so, what were they?

_____

_____

38. Do you think Paul is grieved to the point of repentance or do you think he is being a bit sarcastic? How does your answer change things?

_____

_____

_____

¹⁷Elders who provide effective leadership must be counted worthy of double honor, especially those who work hard in speaking and teaching. ¹⁸For the scripture says, "Do not muzzle an ox while it is treading out the grain," and, "The worker deserves his pay." (1 Tim. 5:17–18, NET)

39. What do you think is meant by the phrase "double honor"?

_____

_____

40. How would you describe an "elder"? Are they pastors or apostles?

_____

_____

41. In verse 18, why is Paul quoting an Old Testament verse? What point is he communicating to Timothy?

_____

_____

¹³Make every effort to help Zenas the lawyer and Apollos on their way; make sure they have what they need. ¹⁴Here is another way that our people can learn to engage in good works to meet pressing needs and so not be unfruitful. (Titus 3:13–14, NET)

42. Notice the language Paul uses: "Make every effort . . . make sure they have what they need." What could this look like? List several examples.

_____

_____

_____

43. Is Paul saying that supporting a gospel worker is a good work and therefore fruitful?

_____

_____

44. Are only apostles to be supported? Explain.

_____

_____

Paul takes up an offering for the saints

¹Now concerning the collection for the saints, as I have given orders to the churches of Galatia, so you must do also: ²On the first day of the week let each one of you lay something aside, storing up as he may prosper, that there be no collections when I come. ³And when I come, whomever you approve by your letters I will send to bear your gift to Jerusalem. ⁴But if it is fitting that I go also, they will go with me. ⁵Now I will come to you when I pass through Macedonia (for I am passing through Macedonia). ⁶And it may be that I will remain, or even spend the winter with you, that you may send me on my journey, wherever I go. ⁷For I do not wish to see you now on the way; but I hope to stay a while with you, if the Lord permits. ⁸But I will tarry in Ephesus until Pentecost. ⁹For a great and effective door has opened to me, and there are many adversaries. ¹⁰And if Timothy comes, see that he may be with you without fear; for he does the work of the Lord, as I also do. ¹¹Therefore let no one despise him. But send him on his journey in peace, that he may come to me; for I am waiting for him with the brethren. (1 Cor. 16:1–11)

At this point, Paul is not talking about support for himself, but taking up an offering for the saints. We still have some things to learn from the way he does it.

Notice Paul is looking ahead and writing in advance.

45. What is Paul's plan? Is he 100% clear on all his plans? Does he share about the work he is doing?

46. What is Paul asking the Corinthians to do? What is he asking for Timothy? Why should they support Timothy?

¹⁵And with this confidence I intended to come to you first so that you would get a second opportunity to see us, ¹⁶and through your help to go on into Macedonia and then from Macedonia to come back to you and be helped on our way into Judea by you. (2 Cor. 1:15–16, NET)

Paul may still be talking about the offering for the saints.

47.   What is Paul's plan and what is he asking? Was Paul asking for himself?

_____

_____

_____

48.   How many things is Paul asking for? Is Paul asking for a "one-time gift"?

_____

_____

_____

Notice Paul has a pattern: vision, plan, share, and ask (hint: this is a good pattern!)

Paul does not hem-haw around. He comes right out and asks them to help him get to Judea. Most of this passage is about the offering for the saints, but Paul seems to add his own personal ministry in there as well.

Homework assignment

Read through all the class notes, and read through the questions and comments following each set of verses. Write out your answers and your own observations.

After you have completed the above, answer the following questions.

1.   Are only apostles worthy of support? Who is worthy?

_____

_____

2.   How would you define a worker? Are people in supportive roles workers as well?

_____

_____

_____

3.   How many different places and times does Paul ask for help?

_____

_____

4. Describe our role as a "worker" and God's role as "provider." What are some of the requirements and conditions of a worker? If we meet the conditions, what does God promise?

_____

_____

_____

5. Read and meditate on 1 Corinthians 9:1–14. What are your observations? List them. Does this passage give you confidence in raising support? Why or why not?

_____

_____

_____

6. Describe interdependence (body life). Why do you think that God does it this way?

_____

_____

_____

After doing the Bible study above, conclusions can be drawn from Scripture concerning support and about workers, messengers, and leaders receiving support. Summarize your conclusions and include the main points from the Old Testament Study and the New Testament Study.

7. Summary.

_____

_____

_____

_____

_____

_____

_____

_____

HOMEWORK ASSIGNMENT #6

Create Your Name List

Checklist

☐ Did you enter all the names into TNTMPD?

☐ How many names do you have written down so far? _____ (It should be more than 200)

☐ Did you start dividing them into 3 groups?

Homework assignment

1. Read through the notes covered in class.

2. TNTMPD is free software that will help you manage all of your contacts. Go online to www.tntware.com and download it. The software is both Mac and PC friendly.

3. Once you have downloaded TNTMPD, start to load your contact information and begin to work with the system. Work with it each day; this is a powerful and helpful tool.

4. Export the contact list from TNTMPD once you have more than 200 names, and print out and submit your name list.

Build your contact list

Make a list of people who you know by name. If you know their names and they know your name, put them on the list. If you think about who you would invite to your wedding or who may show up to your funeral, you know between 200–300 people or more. This list will include unsaved people, people who you think can't or won't give, people who like you, and people who don't. (See Before Your Campaign section for a helpful guide, "Strategy Brainstorming per Location.")

This is not your mailing list or your ask list: this is a list of people you know. We will talk later about what to do with the contact list. For now, write their names down, even if you don't have their contact information yet.

1. Once you have your list, arrange it into 3 categories:

   » Group A: Your best relationships. Could do coffee or lunch almost anytime.

   » Group B: People you know. If you ran into them at the store, you could easily talk for 5–10 minutes.

   » Group C: All other relationships that are not in groups A or B.

   If you have a large number of contacts in different cities, you may want to make a list per location (e.g. the Buffalo list, the Denver list).

2. Start praying for the people on your list. Ask the Lord to bless them, to stir hearts, and to connect you with those hearts.

3. If you do not have a computer, you will need to create a system of some sort to organize your contacts. Do whatever works for you. Your system should have all of your contacts in one place. You should break down your contacts into Groups A, B, and C, and have all of their contact information. This system should also help you keep track of the type and frequency of your contacts. Be prepared to show your system to your coach. If it's just a rough draft that's fine, but you need to show it to your coach.

4. Keep notes on each of your contacts, adding the information to TNTMPD (if using this system). Dates, ages, children's names, line of work, points of interest, prayer needs, church history, and so forth. All of this information will help you connect and communicate in the future. Be sure to follow up on prayer requests.

Contact idea list

This list may help you brainstorm and remember people you actually do know. Look at each line and think through the categories.

- » Advertising agencies
- » Apartment manager
- » Auto mechanic
- » Avon lady
- » Baker
- » Basketball team
- » Bank personnel
- » Barber
- » Beautician
- » Bible bookstore owner or manager
- » Bible study or prayer group
- » Boy or Girl Scout leader
- » Brother
- » Building contractors
- » Butcher
- » Children's teachers
- » Christian business people
- » Christmas card list
- » Church choir director
- » Church directory
- » Church friends
- » Church missions committee
- » Church staff
- » Civic clubs
- » Coaches
- » Community leaders
- » Computer programmers
- » Corporate executives

- » Dentist
- » Dental assistant
- » Doctor/office nurses
- » Family attorney
- » Farmers/ranchers
- » Fast food restaurants
- » Florist
- » Former customers
- » Former employees
- » Former college professors
- » Former high school teachers
- » Former salesmen
- » Foundations
- » Fraternity
- » Friends of the family
- » Groups that share missions interest
- » High school & college friends
- » Hospital chaplains
- » Hospital personnel
- » House church networks
- » Insurance agent
- » Kiwanis Club
- » Jaycees
- » Mayor/civic leaders
- » Men's breakfast groups
- » Military personnel
- » Missionary societies
- » Mom's groups

- » Neighborhood watch
- » Neighbors/former neighbors
- » Newspaper personnel
- » Parents
- » Parents' address book
- » Parents' Christmas card list
- » Parents' employers
- » Parents' employees
- » Parents' business contacts
- » Pastors
- » People you have led to Christ
- » Prayer chain
- » PTA
- » Real estate agent
- » Referrals
- » Relatives

- » Retired people
- » School activities
- » Secretary/receptionist
- » Self-employed friends
- » Service men
- » Shoe salesman
- » Sister
- » Sunday school class
- » Tax accountant
- » Teammates
- » Telephone book
- » TV and radio stations
- » Veterinarian
- » Yearbooks
- » Wedding list
- » Women's clubs

HOMEWORK ASSIGNMENT #7
Financial Vision Plan

Homework assignment

1. The electronic Financial Vision Plan form is an Excel spreadsheet. You must have compatible software to use this electronic form.

2. Electronic instructions:

    a. Download attachment from email.

    b. Open file.

    c. Insert your financial information in the editable boxes on the right side of the page.

    d. Save.

    e. Print it and submit the printed copy.

HOMEWORK ASSIGNMENT #8a

Your Vision Statement

Now that you have taken time to pray and wrestle through some tough questions, you should have an idea of your ministry vision/assignment. You may even know what you're not called to. Remember, vision is having a clear understanding of what the Lord Jesus is asking of you and knowing what you must do to obey and stand before the Lord without regret.

Look back through your journal and the answers to your questions. Write out a one-sentence ministry vision statement of what you need to do as it relates to your spiritual occupation. It does not need to be long or detailed, but should communicate the basics of your ministry vision. You can break your one-sentence ministry vision statement into three parts:

» **Calling/assignment** (e. g., as messenger, proclaimer, or shepherd to serve, teach, train, equip, etc.)

» **To whom** (e. g., young adults, children, the house of prayer, the Body of Christ, nations)

» **Unto** (e. g., wholeheartedness; maturity in Christ; transformation of Atlanta, the US, nations)

Example: "I am called to teach, train, and equip the younger generation unto wholeheartedness."

Vision, Obstacles, and Goals Worksheet

Vision statement

_____

_____

_____

_____

Top five obstacles

What are the top five obstacles that stand in the way of your vision being fulfilled?

Examples may include the lack of training, finances, ailments, debt, lack of biblical understanding, family or personal circumstances, lack of a particular skill, fear, pride, lack of motivation, or lack of accountability.

1

2

3

4

5

Obstacle #1

List the action steps to overcome this obstacle.

1. _____

   _____

   _____

2. _____

   _____

   _____

3. _____

   _____

   _____

4. _____

   _____

   _____

5. _____

   _____

   _____

Obstacle #2

List the action steps to overcome this obstacle.

6. _____

_____

_____

7. _____

_____

_____

8. _____

_____

_____

9. _____

_____

_____

10. _____

_____

_____

Obstacle #3

_____

List the action steps to overcome this obstacle.

11. _____

_____

_____

12. _____

_____

_____

13. _____

_____

_____

14. _____

_____

_____

15. _____

_____

_____

Obstacle #4

_____

List the action steps to overcome this obstacle.

16. _____

    _____

    _____

17. _____

    _____

    _____

18. _____

    _____

    _____

19. _____

    _____

    _____

20. _____

    _____

    _____

Obstacle #5

List the action steps to overcome this obstacle.

21.

22.

23.

24.

25.

HOMEWORK ASSIGNMENT #9a

Write Your Letter: First Draft

Checklist

☐ Did you read through your notes from this session?

☐ Did you write the first rough draft of your letter?

assignment is Temporary!!

Homework assignment

1. Read through your class notes.

2. Start writing the first rough draft of your letter by hand on the attached page provided. Utilize the letter outline template found on the next two pages. Be sure your letter can answer the following questions:

   a. Did you get your reader's attention?

   b. Have they been brought up to date on your life?

   c. Did you communicate your ministry vision and transition to full-time, vocational ministry?

   d. Have you shared a little about the organization and where you will serve?

   e. Have you invited them to partner with your ministry through prayer and financial partnership?

Be a father love, care. Shepard.

Broad, General. [long-term]

I am a full-time worker, not called to NYC. only

I'll what is the thing I can't get away from?

many ways

what is the one thing I needed to do with my life — ??

4,000 words

Letter outline template

Catchy opening line, headline, or hook:

Personal address:

One page –
One side –
One Topic –
One person – as IF

Bring them up to date:

Announcement of vision
and
(Invitation) ask ...

ask, letter
(personal)
X
newsletter

Impersonal
X
personal

Your calling, including how you were called:

the way
business man

Off – white
paper.

"I'm raising of my
voice for those who don't
a voice"...

never –
(idear friends and
+ emily.
– as many as you
know ...

Read more
newspaper.

The ministry's vision and value; your work and role at the ministry:

don't use unique language. use bible language.

to put

the

"dear Billy white" on it.

app → Mail merge.

Invitation to share in your calling. Be sure they know you will be contacting them soon:

— Paragun.

6 — 7 lines

LETTERS with the paper

Handwritten PS:

Build a compline

even as a church!

So good!

→ OASIS → business legitimate!

PART 2

video 27

→ How my mission fits their mission.

→ be general in my role.

(no → afterschool, english service)

(global God in a global plan / redemption)

→ avoid sharing budgets.

POST card →D

[through organization]

- UPS online

- POSTcards.com
  VISTa PRINT.

- glossy PHOTO

- [white in the back]

always blue ink

HOMEWORK ASSIGNMENT #9b

Write Your Letter: Second Draft

Checklist

☐ Did you write (type out) the second rough draft of your letter?

☐ Did you print out a copy of your letter to turn in?

Homework assignment

Using your first rough draft as the foundation, begin the process of writing your second draft. Overall, your second draft should be smoother, clearer, and better communicated. Eliminate jargon and overly charismatic language. Move through each paragraph, studying what you really want to say, and choose your words wisely to make your point. Don't be afraid to let them hear your heart. Your assignment, your ministry organization's vision and values, and the invitation to financial partnership should all be very clear.

Your second draft should be typed and a printed copy turned in. Pay attention to line spacing, use of white space, and font type and size. Make your headline or hook considerably larger than the body text. Use one-inch margins all around.

Remember to give the reader as much information as you can about your journey, your assignment, the ministry's vision and values, and the work you plan to do.

Again—here's what your letter should cover:

1. Did you get your reader's attention?

2. Have they been brought up to date on your life?

3. Did you communicate your ministry vision and transition to full-time, vocational ministry?

4. Have you shared a little about the organization? Rewrite the following in a conversational style for the third section of your letter and be sure to include your role at the ministry, highlighting either your calling or team ABC Ministries.

   Note: Typically it is easier to address the vision and the values of the ministry organization and to secondarily weave in your calling or your role there. For example:

   ABC Ministries is an evangelical missions organization that is committed to praying for the release of the fullness of God's power and purpose, as we actively win the lost, heal the sick, feed the poor, make disciples, and impact society—family, education, government, economy, arts, media, religion, etc. Our vision is to work in relationship with the Body of Christ to engage in the Great Commission, as we seek to walk out the two great commandments to love God and people.

5. Have you invited them to partner with your ministry through prayer and financial partnership?

11 After many years in full-time ministry, I have learned few things...

How can I write, especially, IF I have been in the field.

Written Phone Call: Yes

Write out your phone conversation following the outline that you learned in class (see below). Ask them for an appointment. They will say yes. Then walk through time and location. End the conversation reiterating the time and location details.

For all of your script homework use the following script format to write out your conversation.

Me:

My potential partner:

Me:

My potential partner:

Written Phone Call: No, With an Additional Ask

Write out your phone conversation following the outline you learned in class. Ask them for an appointment. They will say no. Assure them that there is no financial obligation and express your desire to share about what God is doing. Ask for the appointment again. If they say yes, then direct the conversation toward time and location. End the conversation reiterating the time and location details. If they say no, move toward the newsletter. (You get to choose whether they say yes or no to the second ask.)

Use the script format.

Written Phone Call: Have Not Read the Letter Yet

Write out your phone conversation following the outline that you learned in class. When you ask if they read your letter, they will reply no. Express your desire and excitement for them to read the letter and to learn about what God is doing in your life. Ask if three or four days will give them enough time to read the letter. Be proactive by setting up a follow-up time and date.

Use the script format.

HOMEWORK ASSIGNMENT #10d
Practice Phone Calls: Yes

Checklist

☐ Did you complete all the mock calls?

☐ Did you complete the call log?

☐ Did you fill out the feedback and self evaluation summaries?

Homework assignment

To complete the assignment, you must do the following:

1. Make at least five mock calls, asking for the face-to-face appointment. Connect with at least four different people for these calls.

2. Record your phone calls by using a voice recorder or a voice note app on your cell phone. After your role-play, use your recordings to evaluate your progress. Make changes where necessary.

3. Use the phone script outline (provided below) for your mock phone calls. Familiarize yourself with it to the point of having it memorized.

4. Once the outline is memorized, make mock phone calls to mock prospective partners. Pick someone in your Partnership Development training group or a close friend. Make the call, stay "in character," and walk through all the points of the outline. Then talk about it afterwards. Make your calls with the outline in front of you.

    Note: If you are calling a friend who is not in your PD training, make arrangements ahead of time rather than trying to explain the assignment and role-play in the same call.

5. When you talk about it afterwards, always ask for feedback. It should not take more than three minutes per call, plus a couple of minutes for feedback. Track your calls in the mock calls log (provided below).

6. Provide a summary of the feedback you received from your mock calls in the feedback summary section below.

Phone script outline

1. Identify yourself; let them know who is calling.

2. Be sure you are talking with the right person.

3. Ask if it's a good time to call, respond accordingly, and be sensitive.

4. Make a little small talk or general conversation.

5. Transition ("Hey, Jim, the reason I am calling is that I recently sent you a letter . . . " [Briefly explain vision and summarize]. "Did you have a chance to read it?")

6. Ask for an appointment to share.

7. Finalize details (date, time, and place).

8. Say thank you.

9. Wrap up your conversation.

Mock call log

1. Name: _____   # of dials before connecting: _____

2. Name: _____   # of dials before connecting: _____

3. Name: _____   # of dials before connecting: _____

4. Name: _____   # of dials before connecting: _____

5. Name: _____   # of dials before connecting: _____

Feedback summary

_____

_____

_____

_____

_____

Self-evaluation summary

_____

_____

_____

_____

_____

HOMEWORK ASSIGNMENT #10e

Practice Phone Calls: Various Responses

Checklist

☐ Did you complete all the mock calls?

☐ Did you complete the call log?

☐ Did you fill out the feedback and self-evaluation summaries?

Homework assignment

To complete the assignment, you must do the following:

1. Make at least ten mock calls, asking for the face-to-face appointment. Connect with at least five or six different people for these calls.

2. Record your phone calls by using a voice recorder or a voice note app on your cell phone. After your role-play, use your recordings to evaluate your progress. Make changes where necessary.

3. Use the phone script outline (provided below) for your mock phone calls. Familiarize yourself with it to the point of having it memorized.

4. Once the outline is memorized, make mock phone calls to mock prospective partners. Pick someone in your partnership development training group or a close friend. Make the call, stay "in character," and walk through all the points of the outline. Then talk about it afterwards. Make your calls with the outline in front of you.

    Note: If you are calling a friend who is not in your PD training, make arrangements ahead of time rather than trying to explain the assignment and role-play in the same call.

5. When you talk about it afterwards, always ask for feedback. It should not take more than three minutes per call, plus a couple of minutes for feedback. Track your calls and responses in the mock call log (provided below).

6. Have a mix of phone calls with various responses. This will take a little planning, so talk with your role-playing partner ahead of time. You don't have to do them all, but mix it up. Utilize this list of potential responses:

    » "Not a good time to talk."
    » "We can't give right now."
    » "Tell me all about your ministry."
    » "Yes, but I can't meet right now."

    » No answer; voice mail.
    » "Is this about money?"
    » "No."

7. Provide a summary of the feedback you received from your mock calls in the feedback summary section below.

Phone script outline

1. Identify yourself; let them know who is calling.

2. Be sure you are talking with the right person.

3. Ask if it's a good time to call, respond accordingly, and be sensitive.

4. Make a little small talk or general conversation.

5. Transition (Hey, Jim, the reason I am calling is that I recently sent you a letter [vision and summary]. Did you have a chance to read it?)

6. Ask for an appointment to share.

7. Finalize details (date, time, and place).

8. Say thank you.

9. Wrap up your conversation.

Mock call log

1. Name: _____ # of dials: _____ Response: _____

2. Name: _____ # of dials: _____ Response: _____

3. Name: _____ # of dials: _____ Response: _____

4. Name: _____ # of dials: _____ Response: _____

5. Name: _____ # of dials: _____ Response: _____

6. Name: _____ # of dials: _____ Response: _____

7. Name: _____ # of dials: _____ Response: _____

8. Name: _____ # of dials: _____ Response: _____

9. Name: _____ # of dials: _____ Response: _____

10. Name: _____ # of dials: _____ Response: _____

Feedback summary

_____

_____

_____

_____

_____

Self-evaluation summary

HOMEWORK ASSIGNMENT #11a

Thinking It Through

Work through the following questions and answer in two or three full sentences.

1. When did you first realize the Lord might be inviting you to serve in a full-time ministry? What were the circumstances (i.e., season of life, where, who did the Lord use, what did the Lord use, and how did He speak to you)?

2. Describe how you went from "I *think* I've been called to full-time ministry" to "I *know* I'm called to full-time occupational ministry." Has this happened yet?

3. If during a face-to-face appointment a potential partner were to ask you, "How do you know that the Lord is leading you into full-time ministry?" how would you answer?

4. If someone were to ask you, "Why serve at ABC Ministries in Kansas City, when you could serve here in our city?" what would you say?

5. What *compels* you to stay employed as a missionary versus going back to the marketplace?

HOMEWORK ASSIGNMENT #11b
Appointment Script

Checklist

☐ Did you read through your notes?

☐ Did you write out one page of greeting conversation and one page of building rapport?

Greeting conversation

You have just entered an appointment in someone's home or in a public place. You have little or no relationship with this person. Greet him or her warmly and help set the tone of your meeting. Be prepared to carry the first couple of minutes of the greeting time by yourself. Write out at least one page of your greeting conversation below.

Building rapport

Now that you've had a couple of minutes for greeting, you need to build a little rapport. Be prepared and use the F.O.R.M. model. Write out at least one page of rapport conversation below.

Appointment Script: Yes

Checklist

☐ Did you write out one page for each response to your invitation to be on your ministry team?

You asked for partnership, and they said yes

You have been in a partnership appointment and just invited them to be a part of your ministry team. They said YES! Write out one page, picking up the conversation at, "Yes, we would like to partner with you." Include walking all the way through the partnership details—how much, how often. Then move towards *excited friends*, but only give a sentence or two of the excited-friends conversation.

No, but with hope

The appointment invitation just received a no, but it was a hopeful no. Write out one page responding correctly and asking if you may revisit the topic in the future.

No, with another ask

You have just done the invitation ask, but the answer was no. Now ask about a special gift. Start writing from "Mr. Smith, will you partner with me in ministry?"

Appointment Script: Excited-Friends Ask

Checklist

☐ Did you write out the excited-friends ask and the phone call to the excited friend?

Excited-friends ask

Your appointment ask has ended with a yes or a very positive, excited no. Now you want to ask about excited friends. Pick the conversation up with "Mr. Smith, there is another way you could help with our ministry." Write one to two pages.

_____

_____

_____

_____

_____

_____

_____

_____

_____

_____

Phone conversation with an excited friend

You have received the name of a potential excited friend. Write out a two-minute phone conversation with the person. Your partner has sent either an electronic message, a written letter of introduction, or phoned them ahead of time. Choose one as you write a script below. Your handwritten conversation should include the following:

1. Ask for the excited friend by their full name.

2. Be sure to identify yourself, mentioning your mutual friend.

3. Ask if this is a good time to talk.

4. Refer to the contact method (letter, phone, or an electronic message).

5. Give a short (fifteen-second) introduction of the ministry you are with, and ask if they have heard about it.

6. Give a further one-minute explanation about the ministry.

7. Share that many are excited about what God is doing.

8. Request an appointment with them.

9. Respond appropriately.

10. Ask for either their email or mailing address so that you can send a little information about yourself and the ministry you are with to maximize your appointment time.

11. Remain flexible. Set a time, date, and location.

12.   Lastly, give them a physical description of yourself and ask for their description so that you can recognize each other.

13.   Say thank you and share your excitement. For example, "Thank you, Mr. Smith. I look forward to sharing with you about how the Lord is using ABC Ministries."

HOMEWORK ASSIGNMENT #12a
Practice Appointment #1

Checklist

☐ Did you read through your notes?

☐ Did you complete Practice Appointment #1?

☐ Did you summarize the feedback you received?

Practice appointment #1

Use your appointment outline and the scripts you wrote to get started and to keep on track. Because of time constraints, only cover greeting, building rapport, and transition.

Record your mock appointments by using a camcorder or a video camera app on your cell phone.

Ask for feedback, watch the video together, and make notes from the feedback.

Feedback summary

_____

_____

_____

_____

_____

_____

HOMEWORK ASSIGNMENT #12b

Practice Appointment #2: Including Ask

Checklist

☐ Did you read through your notes?

☐ Did you complete Practice Appointment #2?

☐ Did you summarize the feedback you received?

Practice appointment #2

Use your appointment outline and the scripts you wrote to get you started and keep you on track. Because of time, skip greeting, building rapport, and transition. Start with the body of your presentation, working all the way through the ask. Be sure to wrap up the amount, partnership card (mock), and giving instructions (mock).

Your role-play partner gets to choose the response.

Record your mock appointments by using a camcorder or a video camera app on your cell phone.

Ask for feedback, watch the video together, and make notes from the feedback.

Feedback summary

_____

_____

_____

_____

_____

_____

_____

Practice Appointment #3: Excited Friends

Checklist

☐ Did you read through your notes?

☐ Did you complete Practice Appointment #3?

☐ Did you summarize the feedback you received?

Practice appointment #3

Use your appointment outline and the scripts you wrote to get you started and to keep you on track. Because of time, skip all of the appointment, and start at excited friends. Walk through the excited-friends process, the ask, the writing names down, and determining the follow-up communication (include your partner, but steer the conversation).

Your role-play partner gets to choose the response.

Record your mock appointments by using a camcorder or a video camera app on your cell phone.

Ask for feedback, watch the video together, and make notes from the feedback.

Feedback summary

_____

_____

_____

_____

_____

_____

_____

Practice Phone Call: Excited Friends

Checklist

☐ Did you read through your notes for Appointment: Excited Friends?

☐ Did you summarize the feedback you received?

To complete the assignment, you must do the following:

1. Make at least seven mock calls, asking an excited friend for a face-to-face appointment. Connect with at least four different people for these calls.

2. Record your phone calls by using a voice recorder or a voice note app on your cell phone. After your role-play, use your recordings to evaluate your progress. Make changes where necessary.

3. Use the phone call outline with an excited friend (see Lesson 11 notes) for your mock phone calls. Familiarize yourself with it to the point of having it memorized.

   a. Ask for the excited friend by their full name.

   b. Be sure to identify yourself, mentioning your mutual friend.

   c. Ask if this is a good time to talk.

   d. Refer to the contact method (letter, phone, or an electronic message).

   e. Give a short (fifteen-second) introduction of the ministry you are with, and ask if they heard about it.

   f. Give a further one-minute explanation about the ministry.

   g. Share that many are excited about what God is doing.

   h. Request an appointment with them.

   i. Respond appropriately.

   j. Ask for either their email or mailing address so that you can send a little information about yourself and the ministry you are with to maximize your appointment time.

   k. Remain flexible. Set time, date, and location.

   l. Lastly, give them a physical description of yourself and ask for their description.

   m. Say thank you and share your excitement. For example, "Thank you, Mr. Smith. I look forward to sharing with you about how the Lord is using ABC Ministries."

Feedback summary

HOMEWORK ASSIGNMENT #13
Vision of Being Properly Funded

Checklist

☐ Did you read through your notes?

☐ Did you complete all the questions?

Take the following questions to the prayer room and spend some time meditating and reflecting on them. Dialogue with the Lord, pay attention to your heart responses, and write down your answers.

There is no need to spend a considerable amount of time looking for the "will of the Lord." We are looking for what is in your heart to do and what you would do if you had proper funding.

1. How different would your life look if you were properly funded (stress, emotions, giving, prayer, ministry, household, transportation)?

2. How could your prayer time be different, if your prayer was around stewardship and not around your lack?

3. What long-term plans could you make with your family if you were properly funded?

4. What ministry plans could you make and commit to if you were properly funded?

_____

_____

_____

5. How would your marriage and other relationships be affected if you had a decent salary and were not in constant lack?

_____

_____

_____

6. What could your fully-funded missionary life communicate to people around you?

_____

_____

_____

7. If you had a decent salary, how much more ministry could be done that is not currently being done?

_____

_____

8. Who could you disciple?

_____

9. Who could you bless?

_____

10. Who could you support—short term or long term?

_____

11.   What mission trip would you take if you already had the money?

_____

_____

12.   What new initiatives would you start?

_____

_____

13.   How could you touch the poor, the orphan, and the widow?

_____

_____

Campaign Resources

CAMPAIGN RESOURCE

Where to Begin

What is your calling, your spiritual occupation?

- » What would you do if money or circumstances were not a problem?

- » What must you do to stand before the Lord without regret, in terms of service assignment?

- » What is God asking you to do in this current season, as His servant? What must you do to obey?

- » Write out your vision and pray. Keep doing this until you can state your vision in a sentence or two.

List of names

1. **Create a list of names**

   - » If you know their names and they know yours, put them on the list – regardless of age, income, and giving history.

   - » You may not ask everyone on the list, but write them down anyway.

2. **Divide your list into three groups: A, B, and C**

   - » Group A: your best relationships and those you feel are most likely to partner with you, if you were to ask them

   - » Group B: acquaintances and causal friends who you're not sure what would happen if you were to ask them

   - » Group C: those you don't have much contact with currently

3. **Create a plan**

   - » Reach everyone on your list, in the most personal and practical way.

   - » Create a schedule to connect with everyone on your list. Using a combination of emails, Facebook, postcards, and phones calls. Connect in a way that's appropriate to the level of relationship.

   - » Reach out to them often.

Pray for

- » Everyone on your list

- » Your calling

- » Wisdom

> » Hearts to be stirred

> » Connection with those hearts

Educate yourself about partnership development

> » Study Partnership Development training notes

> » Read books

> » Search online

Start the contact process

> » Start with your home church, if possible

> » Attend prayer meetings, visit small groups, post strategically on Facebook, go to church functions, attend weddings and parties

Start writing your letter

> » Review PD training session 9 Letter and Postcard

> » Write your letter, comprised of four main parts:

>> i. Mention full-time ministry, that God has called you, your excitement

>> ii. Your need to raise up a team for prayer and financial support

>> iii. Invitation

>> iv. You will be contacting them soon

> » Handwrite a postscript (PS) at the bottom of the letter

> » Send your letters

>> i. Only send as many letters in a week as you can schedule appointments in a week

>> ii. Don't send 40 letters, as you could not possibly have that many appointments in a week

>> iii. Schedule 15–20 appointments in a week (maximum)

>> iv. Send slightly more letters than appointments

>> v. Don't start sending letters until you are ready to have appointments

Send your postcards

> » Hand-written; 2–3 sentences long

> » Convey excitement, calling, partnership or invitation, looking forward to share

Make your calls

- » Call at peak times
- » Confirm you have the right person and that it is a good time to talk
- » Make small talk; listen well
- » Ask if they had a chance to read your letter
    - i. If they have read your letter, move towards the appointment
    - ii. If they have not read the letter, shut down the call, and be proactive and set a time you will call back in 4–5 days
- » Don't tell your story on the phone
- » Be flexible and do what works for them
- » Confirm time and location
- » After the call, update the partner profile and send appointment reminder, if there is time

Go to your appointment

1. Prepare for the appointment
    - » Make sure you have your appointment kit
    - » Make sure you have all of your appointment materials
    - » Make sure you have the appointment location address, directions, and time
    - » Go through your pre-appointment checklist and review notes
2. Go to your appointment (do not be late!)
3. Small talk—be a friend, listen well
4. Sharing—you can use your letter as an outline
5. Answer questions—be flexible, but stay on track and listen well
6. Invitation—look them in the eye, ask if they would partner with you in ministry (do not draw back), and wait for their answer
7. Respond accordingly
8. Have them fill out partner response card, and share giving instructions
9. Fellowship
10. Send thank-you card after your appointment, regardless of the outcome

Post-appointment

» Follow up with any appointments where a decision was not made

» Start sending them your newsletter

» Expand your team

» Follow up with your team with letters, calls, postcards, and face-to-face visits

» Pastor your team well

Helpful reminders

» Practice calls and appointments (see PD training notes for mock examples)

» Start weeks ahead of time, plan well, and stay organized, as this will assist you with managing the process and help keep you on track

CAMPAIGN RESOURCES

Before Your Campaign

»   Vision, Obstacles, and Goals Worksheet

»   PD Strategy Brainstorming per Location

»   Grouping Your Contacts

»   PD Campaign Calendar

»   Instructions for Hosting a Small Group

»   Recommendation Letters and Emails

BEFORE YOUR CAMPAIGN

Vision, Obstacles, and Goals Worksheet

Vision statement

Top five obstacles

What are the top five obstacles that stand in the way of your vision being fulfilled?

Examples may include the lack of training, finances, ailments, debt, biblical understanding, family or personal circumstances, lack of a particular skill, fear, pride, lack of motivation, lack of accountability.

1

2

3

4

5

Obstacle #1

_____

List the action steps to overcome this obstacle.

1. _____

   _____

   _____

2. _____

   _____

   _____

3. _____

   _____

   _____

4. _____

   _____

   _____

5. _____

   _____

   _____

Obstacle #2

_____

List the action steps to overcome this obstacle.

1. _____

   _____

   _____

2. _____

   _____

   _____

3. _____

   _____

   _____

4. _____

   _____

   _____

5. _____

   _____

   _____

Obstacle #3

_____

List the action steps to overcome this obstacle.

1. _____

   _____

   _____

2. _____

   _____

   _____

3. _____

   _____

   _____

4. _____

   _____

   _____

5. _____

   _____

   _____

Obstacle #4

_____

List the action steps to overcome this obstacle.

1. _____

   _____

   _____

2. _____

   _____

   _____

3. _____

   _____

   _____

4. _____

   _____

   _____

5. _____

   _____

   _____

Obstacle #5

_____

List the action steps to overcome this obstacle.

1. _____

_____

_____

2. _____

_____

_____

3. _____

_____

_____

4. _____

_____

_____

5. _____

_____

_____

BEFORE YOUR CAMPAIGN ————————————

Strategy Brainstorming Per Location

A successful campaign starts 3 months prior to your campaign!

Campaign Strategy for location: _____

People I know:

Churches that I attended?

Name: _____   Pastor: _____

Name: _____   Pastor: _____

Name: _____   Pastor: _____

Churches that my friends go to?

Name: _____   Pastor: _____

Name: _____   Pastor: _____

Name: _____   Pastor: _____

Name: _____   Pastor: _____

Name: _____   Pastor: _____

Name: _____   Pastor: _____

Name: _____   Pastor: _____

Small group members?

_____   _____   _____

_____   _____   _____

_____   _____   _____

_____   _____   _____

_____   _____   _____

Family friends?

_____   _____   _____

_____   _____   _____

_____   _____   _____

_____   _____   _____

_____   _____   _____

_____   _____   _____

_____   _____   _____

School friends? (high school, college, etc.)

_____   _____   _____

_____   _____   _____

_____   _____   _____

_____   _____   _____

_____   _____   _____

_____   _____   _____

Christian social group and activity friends?
(sports leagues, clubs, hobbies, children's school, etc.)

_____   _____   _____

_____   _____   _____

_____   _____   _____

Former coworkers?

_____   _____   _____

_____   _____   _____

_____   _____   _____

_____   _____   _____

_____   _____   _____

_____   _____   _____

_____   _____   _____

Former neighbors?

_____   _____   _____

_____   _____   _____

_____   _____   _____

_____   _____   _____

_____   _____   _____

Christian business owners who you are connected with?

_____   _____   _____

_____   _____   _____

_____   _____   _____

_____   _____   _____

Spouse's contacts:

Chuches that my spouse attended?

Name:_____ Pastor:_____

Name:_____ Pastor:_____

Name:_____ Pastor:_____

Churches that friends of my spouse go to?

Name:_____ Pastor:_____

Name:_____ Pastor:_____

Name:_____ Pastor:_____

Name:_____ Pastor:_____

Name:_____ Pastor:_____

Name:_____ Pastor:_____

Name:_____ Pastor:_____

Former small group members of spouse?

_____ _____ _____

_____ _____ _____

_____ _____ _____

_____ _____ _____

_____ _____ _____

Family friends of spouse?

_____   _____   _____

_____   _____   _____

_____   _____   _____

_____   _____   _____

_____   _____   _____

_____   _____   _____

School friends of spouse?

(high school, college, etc.)

_____   _____   _____

_____   _____   _____

_____   _____   _____

_____   _____   _____

_____   _____   _____

_____   _____   _____

Christian social group and activity friends of spouse?

(sports leagues, clubs, hobbies, children's school, etc.)

_____   _____   _____

_____   _____   _____

_____   _____   _____

Former coworkers of spouse?

_____ _____ _____

_____ _____ _____

_____ _____ _____

_____ _____ _____

_____ _____ _____

_____ _____ _____

_____ _____ _____

_____ _____ _____

Former neighbors of spouse?

_____ _____ _____

_____ _____ _____

_____ _____ _____

_____ _____ _____

_____ _____ _____

Christian business owners spouse is connected with?

_____ _____ _____

_____ _____ _____

_____ _____ _____

_____ _____ _____

Ministries & network:

Ministries and churches to connect with?

Name: _____   Leader: _____

Name: _____   Leader: _____

Name: _____   Leader: _____

Excited ministries that share in our excitement and concern for the same issues?

Name: _____   Leader: _____

Name: _____   Leader: _____

Name: _____   Leader: _____

Name: _____   Leader: _____

Name: _____   Leader: _____

Name: _____   Leader: _____

Name: _____   Leader: _____

Small group gathering:

Potential hosts for small group gatherings?

Name: _____   Phone: _____

Name: _____   Phone: _____

Name: _____   Phone: _____

Name: _____   Phone: _____

Name: _____   Phone: _____

Name: _____   Phone: _____

Name: _____   Phone: _____

Name: _____   Phone: _____

Name: _____   Phone: _____

Name: _____   Phone: _____

Name: _____   Phone: _____

Name: _____   Phone: _____

BEFORE YOUR CAMPAIGN
Grouping Your Contacts

Contact schedule

Each week you will do the assigned task below. Following this schedule will help you to contact the maximum amount of people in the shortest time.

	Week 1	Week 2	Week 3	Week 4	Week 5	Week 6	Week 7	Week 8	Week 9
Group 1	Letter	Post-card	Phone Call	Appt	Follow Up				
Group 2		Letter	Post-card	Phone Call	Appt	Follow Up			
Group 3			Letter	Post-card	Phone Call	Appt	Follow Up		
Group 4				Letter	Post-card	Phone Call	Appt	Follow Up	
Group 5					Letter	Post-card	Phone Call	Appt	Follow Up

Group 1

Location: _____

	Name	Phone Number	Letter	Post-card	Phone Call	Appt Date/Time	Follow up	Results	Comments
1									
2									
3									
4									
5									
6									
7									
8									
9									
10									
11									
12									
13									
14									
15									

Group 2

Location: _____

	Name	Phone Number	Letter	Post-card	Phone Call	Appt Date/Time	Follow up	Results	Comments
1									
2									
3									
4									
5									
6									
7									
8									
9									
10									
11									
12									
13									
14									
15									

Group 3

Location: _____

	Name	Phone Number	Letter	Post-card	Phone Call	Appt Date/Time	Follow up	Results	Comments
1									
2									
3									
4									
5									
6									
7									
8									
9									
10									
11									
12									
13									
14									
15									

Group 4

Location: _____

	Name	Phone Number	Letter	Post-card	Phone Call	Appt Date/Time	Follow up	Results	Comments
1									
2									
3									
4									
5									
6									
7									
8									
9									
10									
11									
12									
13									
14									
15									

Group 5

Location: _____

	Name	Phone Number	Letter	Post-card	Phone Call	Appt Date/Time	Follow up	Results	Comments
1									
2									
3									
4									
5									
6									
7									
8									
9									
10									
11									
12									
13									
14									
15									

Group 6

Location: _____

	Name	Phone Number	Letter	Post-card	Phone Call	Appt Date/Time	Follow up	Results	Comments
1									
2									
3									
4									
5									
6									
7									
8									
9									
10									
11									
12									
13									
14									
15									

Group 7

Location: _____

	Name	Phone Number	Letter	Post-card	Phone Call	Appt Date/Time	Follow up	Results	Comments
1									
2									
3									
4									
5									
6									
7									
8									
9									
10									
11									
12									
13									
14									
15									

Group 8

Location: _____

	Name	Phone Number	Letter	Post-card	Phone Call	Appt Date/Time	Follow up	Results	Comments
1									
2									
3									
4									
5									
6									
7									
8									
9									
10									
11									
12									
13									
14									
15									

Group 9

Location: _____

	Name	Phone Number	Letter	Post-card	Phone Call	Appt Date/Time	Follow up	Results	Comments
1									
2									
3									
4									
5									
6									
7									
8									
9									
10									
11									
12									
13									
14									
15									

Group 10

Location: _____

	Name	Phone Number	Letter	Post-card	Phone Call	Appt Date/Time	Follow up	Results	Comments
1									
2									
3									
4									
5									
6									
7									
8									
9									
10									
11									
12									
13									
14									
15									

Group 11

Location: _____

	Name	Phone Number	Letter	Post-card	Phone Call	Appt Date/Time	Follow up	Results	Comments
1									
2									
3									
4									
5									
6									
7									
8									
9									
10									
11									
12									
13									
14									
15									

Group 12

Location: _____

	Name	Phone Number	Letter	Post-card	Phone Call	Appt Date/Time	Follow up	Results	Comments
1									
2									
3									
4									
5									
6									
7									
8									
9									
10									
11									
12									
13									
14									
15									

BEFORE YOUR CAMPAIGN

Campaign Calendar

Month of:

Location 1: _____ Date: _____

Location 2: _____ Date: _____

	Sunday	Monday	Tuesday	Wednesday	Thursday	Friday	Saturday
# of letters: ___ for group: ___ # of postcards: ___ for group: ___ # of contacts to call to schedule appt: ___ # of appt scheduled: ___ # of followup appt: ___ # of appt with Group B & C: ___							
# of letters: ___ for group: ___ # of postcards: ___ for group: ___ # of contacts to call to schedule appt: ___ # of appt scheduled: ___ # of followup appt: ___ # of appt with Group B & C: ___							
# of letters: ___ for group: ___ # of postcards: ___ for group: ___ # of contacts to call to schedule appt: ___ # of appt scheduled: ___ # of followup appt: ___ # of appt with Group B & C: ___							
# of letters: ___ for group: ___ # of postcards: ___ for group: ___ # of contacts to call to schedule appt: ___ # of appt scheduled: ___ # of followup appt: ___ # of appt with Group B & C: ___							
# of letters: ___ for group: ___ # of postcards: ___ for group: ___ # of contacts to call to schedule appt: ___ # of appt scheduled: ___ # of followup appt: ___ # of appt with Group B & C: ___							

Hosted Small Group Schedule

Name: _____ Phone: _____ Date: _____

Name: _____ Phone: _____ Date: _____

Name: _____ Phone: _____ Date: _____

Name: _____ Phone: _____ Date: _____

Name: _____ Phone: _____ Date: _____

Speaking Engagement

Organization Name: _____ Date: _____

Pastor: _____ Phone: _____

Organization Name: _____ Date: _____

Pastor: _____ Phone: _____

Organization Name: _____ Date: _____

Pastor: _____ Phone: _____

Organization Name: _____ Date: _____

Pastor: _____ Phone: _____

Organization Name: _____ Date: _____

Pastor: _____ Phone: _____

Intentional Church or Home Group Visit

Ministry Name: _____ Date: _____

Leader: _____ Phone: _____

Ministry Name: _____ Date: _____

Leader: _____ Phone: _____

Ministry Name: _____ Date: _____

Leader: _____ Phone: _____

Ministry Name: _____ Date: _____

Leader: _____ Phone: _____

Ministry Name: _____ Date: _____

Leader: _____ Phone: _____

BEFORE YOUR CAMPAIGN

Instructions For Hosting A Small Group

Dear _____,

Thank you for your willingness to be a part of what the Lord is doing through this ministry. Your prayers and support enable us to serve in full-time occupational ministry. We are currently building our partnership team with friends, family, and people we have met through ministry. There is a way you can help us build our team. We have found that one of the most effective ways to do this is by having a friend like you host a cookout or dessert gathering where we have a chance to meet your friends. Hosting a small group is a lot of fun and simple when we work together.

Your role as a host

1. **Send a pre-written letter to 5–7 friends.**

    A. We have a pre-written letter of invitation for you to send to your guests. It is written as though it is from you. We will provide the letter, envelopes, and stamps for you. Feel free to edit it as you see fit.

    B. Send the letter of invitation approximately three weeks before the small group gathering.

2. **Make a few phone calls.**

    A. One week after you have sent the invitations, call your invited guests to confirm their attendance.

    B. When you call them, draw their attention to the invitation letter and ask if they had a chance to read it. If they have not read the letter, remind them that it is an invitation to a cookout/dessert at your house and that you can call them back in a few days to confirm their attendance.

    C. In today's culture, some people respond to texts and social media more than live phone calls. If you're having a hard time getting a hold of the guest by phone, feel free to contact them via text or social media (private messages).

    D. Don't worry if not all your invitees are able to attend. Any family unit we get to meet that we didn't personally know before is a great help to us.

3.   **Host a cookout or dessert.**

   A.   The gathering would be at your house, and it will mostly be a meet and greet. There will be no major presentation of our mission, and there will be no solicitation of funds. **It's not a sales party.**

   B.   We do ask that you take some time to personally introduce us to each of the guests throughout the night. When you introduce us to your friends, you can share with them that we are missionaries you support and that you are excited about our mission. We'll take it from there.

4.   **Follow up**

   A.   Contact the guests a few days after the gathering by phone, in person, through social media, or even email.

   B.   When you contact them simply ask them if we have their permission to contact them and share more about our mission.

   C.   Afterwards, we will contact you to see who is willing to be contacted by us, and you can send us their contact information.

Our role

   1.   We will provide the letter, envelopes, and stamps for you.

   2.   We will provide the food, snacks, or dessert.

   3.   We will come early to help you set up and clean up afterward.

By following these four simple steps, you will greatly help us to build up and strengthen our partnership team. Thank you for being willing and for running alongside us in the furtherance of the kingdom of God.

Many blessings to you,

BEFORE YOUR CAMPAIGN
Recommendation Letters & Emails

Example of a partner sending a recommendation letter ahead your phone call

Hi *(name of excited friend)*,

I want to introduce you to friends of ours, Rob and Rhonda Parker. We've known Rob and Rhonda personally for years, and we share a common heart and passion for Jesus.

Rob and Rhonda are full-time ministry workers with ABC Ministry. ABC Ministry is a missions base committed to intercession, worship, evangelism, training, equipping young adults, being mindful of the poor, and other acts of justice. All of the work revolves around and flows out of a prayer meeting that began fifteen years ago and continues to this day.

We have been prayer and financial partners with Rob and Rhonda in ministry for over five years, and we have thoroughly enjoyed being connected with them. They are trustworthy, faithful, and encouraging to our life in the Lord!

We want to personally recommend Rob and Rhonda's ministry to you. We think you would enjoy them and their ministry as much as we have. Rob will be contacting you by phone in a few days and would like to have an opportunity to meet with you and share further about the ministry.

I am excited about their work, and I think you will be too.

Many blessings on you,

(name of your partner)

(Your partner could insert some ministry materials in this letter. Provide these materials for your partner.)

Example of a written communication you could send to an excited friend before you call them

Hi *(name of excited friend)*,

Greetings in the name of Jesus!

My name is John Doe and we have a mutual friend, Sally Singer. My wife, Jane, and I have known Sally for about ten years now and first met her in a home group through our church. We, like Sally, have a heart and passion for Jesus and His coming kingdom. My wife and I were recently sharing with Sally about the ministry that we serve and she said that you would be excited to hear about how the Lord is (workin; reaching the poor; and so on) at ABC Ministries in Kansas City.

Picture of yourself

We are full-time ministry staff at the ABC Ministries in Kansas City. ABC Ministries is a missions base committed to advancing the Kingdom of God through worship, evangelism, training, equipping young adults, mindfulness of the poor, and other acts of justice.

It is a great privilege to serve the Lord Jesus and prepare the earth for His coming. We, like the other staff members at ABC Ministries—and many other missions organizations as well—have this privilege and responsibility to develop a team of financial partners who make it possible for us do this work of the ministry. Sally and I are currently developing our team of partners. We would be grateful for an opportunity to share with you how the Lord is moving through ABC Ministries and the work we do. We will be calling you in a few days to ask you for an appointment.

We have also enclosed some information about our ministry and we look forward to speaking with you soon.

Many blessings to you,

(your name)

Letter could also include a ministry picture that is self-explanatory

Example of an email from a partner who has been on your team a while

Possible subject line: *Touching the poor, inner city, and youth with the love of Christ*, or *Equipping a generation of young leaders.*

Dear *(name of excited friend)*,

It was good to see you last week and catch up a bit. We love you and your family!

I want to introduce you to friends of ours, Rob and Rhonda Parker. We've known Rob and Rhonda personally for years, and we share a common heart and passion for Jesus.

Rob and Rhonda are full-time gospel workers with ABC Ministries. ABC Ministries is a missions base committed to intercession, worship, evangelism, Christian education and training, equipping young adults, being mindful of the poor, and other acts of justice. All of the work revolves around and flows out of a prayer meeting that began fifteen years ago and continues to this day.

Like many other missions organizations, ABC staff members have the privilege and responsibility to develop a team of financial partners who make it possible for them do the work of the ministry. We have joined their team of prayer and financial partners and are grateful for the opportunity to invest in their work of (the Great Commission, equipping of young adults, etc.).

Rob and Rhonda are currently building their partnership team. We thought you would be encouraged to hear about their ministry, and we suggested they contact you. We are planning to share your contact information with them, unless you object, otherwise they will be contacting you soon.

If you have any questions, please do not hesitate to email or call.

Many blessings to you,

(name of partner sending email)

Example of an email from a new ministry partner

Possible subject line: *A great opportunity for the kingdom of God* or, *Advancing the kingdom through prayer and missions.*

Dear *(name of excited friend)*,

It was good to see you at the basketball game last week; the kids are having a great season!

The other day we met with a dear family who are staff members with ABC Ministries—Rob and Rhonda Parker. ABC Ministries is a missions base committed to intercession, worship, evangelism, Christian education and training, equipping young adults, being mindful of the poor, and other acts of justice. All of the work revolves around and flows out of a prayer meeting that began fifteen years ago and continues to this day.

Like many other missions organizations, ABC staff members have the privilege and responsibility to develop a team of financial partners who make it possible for them to do the work of the ministry. We have joined their team of prayer and financial partners and are grateful for the opportunity to (sow into the kingdom, equip young adults, reach the lost, help fulfill the Great Commission).

Rob and Rhonda are currently building their partnership team. We thought you would be encouraged to hear about their ministry, and we suggested they contact you. We plan to share your contact information with them, unless you object, otherwise they will be contacting you soon.

If you have any questions, please feel free to contact me.

(name of new partner sending email)

Last paragraph could also read:

Rob and Rhonda are currently building their partnership team. We thought you would be encouraged to hear about their ministry. May we share your contact information with them so that you would have an opportunity to hear about this impactful ministry?

We look forward to your reply

CAMPAIGN RESOURCES

During Your Campaign

» Partnership Commitment Cards

» Giving Instructions

» Excited Friends Brainstorm

» Gathering Contact Information Cards

» Weekly Run Sheet

» *Instructions for Hosting a Small Group**

» *Recommendation Letters and Emails**

*You can find these materials in the "Before Your Campaign" section and continue to use them during your campaign.

DURING YOUR CAMPAIGN

Partnership Commitment Cards

Yes! I'd like to partner with you.

Ministry logo

First name(s) _____ Last name _____

Email _____ Cell phone _____ – _____ – _____

Home phone _____ – _____ – _____ Work phone _____ – _____ – _____

Street _____

City _____ State _____ Zip code _____

Yes, I commit to partner with you in your ministry by giving: $_____

Frequency of gift ☐ Monthly ☐ Special Gift

☐ Annually ☐ Other: _____

Signature _____

Yes! I'd like to partner with you.

Ministry logo

First name(s) _____ Last name _____

Email _____ Cell phone _____ – _____ – _____

Home phone _____ – _____ – _____ Work phone _____ – _____ – _____

Street _____

City _____ State _____ Zip code _____

Yes, I commit to partner with you in your ministry by giving: $_____

Frequency of gift ☐ Monthly ☐ Special Gift

☐ Annually ☐ Other: _____

Signature _____

Yes! I'd like to partner with you.

Ministry logo

First name(s) _____ Last name _____

Email _____ Cell phone _____ – _____ – _____

Home phone _____ – _____ – _____ Work phone _____ – _____ – _____

Street _____

City _____ State _____ Zip code _____

Yes, I commit to partner with you in your ministry by giving: $_____

Frequency of gift ☐ Monthly ☐ Special Gift

☐ Annually ☐ Other: _____

Signature _____

DURING YOUR CAMPAIGN

Giving Instructions Cards

ABC Ministry logo

Giving Instructions for *SALLY SINGER*
For Tax-Deductible Giving

Make your partnership check payable to "ABC Ministry"
Mail to: Sally Singer
PO BOX 12345
Kansas City, MO 64134

Please leave the memo line blank; my name should not appear anywhere on the check. If my name is on the check anywhere you may not receive a giving receipt for tax benefits.
Contributions to ABC Ministry are income tax deductible to the extent allowable under applicable law. Contributions to ABC Ministry are made with the understanding that ABC Ministry has complete discretion and control over the use of all donated funds.

ABC Ministry logo

Giving Instructions for *SALLY SINGER*
For Tax-Deductible Giving

Make your partnership check payable to "ABC Ministry"
Mail to: Sally Singer
PO BOX 12345
Kansas City, MO 64134

Please leave the memo line blank; my name should not appear anywhere on the check. If my name is on the check anywhere you may not receive a giving receipt for tax benefits.
Contributions to ABC Ministry are income tax deductible to the extent allowable under applicable law. Contributions to ABC Ministry are made with the understanding that ABC Ministry has complete discretion and control over the use of all donated funds.

ABC Ministry logo

Giving Instructions for *SALLY SINGER*
For Tax-Deductible Giving

Make your partnership check payable to "ABC Ministry"
Mail to: Sally Singer
PO BOX 12345
Kansas City, MO 64134

Please leave the memo line blank; my name should not appear anywhere on the check. If my name is on the check anywhere you may not receive a giving receipt for tax benefits.
Contributions to ABC Ministry are income tax deductible to the extent allowable under applicable law. Contributions to ABC Ministry are made with the understanding that ABC Ministry has complete discretion and control over the use of all donated funds.

Excited Friends Brainstorming Sheet

Excited friends of: _____

#	Name	Email	Phone	Contact Method	Memo	Contacted
1						
2						
3						
4						
5						
6						
7						
8						
9						
10						
11						
12						
13						
14						
15						

DURING YOUR CAMPAIGN

Gathering Contact Information Cards

Date _____ Location _____

Name(s) _____

Email _____

Home phone _____–_____–_____

Cell phone _____–_____–_____

Address _____

_____

Memo _____

_____

Date _____ Location _____

Name(s) _____

Email _____

Home phone _____–_____–_____

Cell phone _____–_____–_____

Address _____

_____

Memo _____

_____

Date _____ Location _____

Name(s) _____

Email _____

Home phone _____–_____–_____

Cell phone _____–_____–_____

Address _____

_____

Memo _____

_____

Date _____ Location _____

Name(s) _____

Email _____

Home phone _____–_____–_____

Cell phone _____–_____–_____

Address _____

_____

Memo _____

_____

Date _____ Location _____

Name(s) _____

Email _____

Home phone _____–_____–_____

Cell phone _____–_____–_____

Address _____

_____

Memo _____

_____

Date _____ Location _____

Name(s) _____

Email _____

Home phone _____–_____–_____

Cell phone _____–_____–_____

Address _____

_____

Memo _____

_____

DURING YOUR CAMPAIGN

Weekly Run Sheet

Looking forward to the week of: _____

Mail Letters: • How many? ___ • To which group? ___ • What day will they be in the mail? ___

Mail Post Cards: • How many? ___ • To which group? ___ • What day will they be in the mail? ___

Make Phone Calls:

- Start your next call list (the group you sent postcards to last week).
- Call those you haven't gotten a hold of the last 3 weeks.

Send reminders for the appointments you are having in the next 5-7 days.

Appointments in the next 7 days:

- How many one-on-one appointments? _____ • How many relationship building with B & C group? ___
- Send a simple reminder (email, voicemail, text, etc.) for appointments within 48 hours of your appointment.
- Restock your appointment kit
  - ▫ Partnership Response Cards ▫ Budget Sheet ▫ Giving Instructions ▫ Thank You Cards
  - ▫ Self-addressed stamped envelopes ▫ Materials about your ministry ▫ Partner Profiles
  - ▫ Small Gift (Optional) ▫ Breath Mints ▫ Pens ▫ Current Newsletter

Excited Friends

- Review your Excited Friends list. • Determine who you need to contact this week
- Contact and follow up accordingly.

Small Groups

- Contact your small group hosts for this week. Go over last minute details.
- Make preparations according to PD Training Manual "Multiple Strategies" section.
- Look at your calendar and your "PD Campaign Strategy per Location" brainstorm. Who can host a small group for you? Contact them and send them the "Small Group Hosting" instructions.

Churches

- What speaking engagements do you have this week at which local churches?
- Gather contact info, including mailing addresses, for the churches you're going to speak at.
- Send appreciative reminders for upcoming church speaking engagements.
- If you haven't already, send thank you notes to previous church speaking engagements.
- Contact pastors and leaders for future speaking engagements.
- Prepare church packets: to drop off during regular business hours at 5-7 churches or ministries. Address them accordingly
  - ▫ Cover Letter ▫ Ask Letter ▫ Spiritual Resume ▫ Ministry Literature
- Follow up with the packets dropped off last week.

Follow Up

- When necessary, follow up with last week's appointments.
- Send thank you cards to any of last week's appointments that you have forgotten.
- Review follow up dates with appointments that ended with "undecided." Review call back phone dates.
- Review second appointments dates. Contact accordingly.

Relationship Building with Non-Partners

- Review your B and C groups, pastors, and leaders. Note that anyone you meet as a result of church engagement, small groups, or excited friends, becomes part of your B or C group.

- Schedule 4-6 hours this week for relationship building. Connect with these contacts via postcard, phone call, social media, text, or face-to face. Aim for 3-4 one-on-one appointments for relationship building this week.

- Review your social events calendar this week. Plan to attend social functions such as weddings, cookouts, picnics, city-wide church events etc.

- Review your home church events calendar and plan to attend social functions such as church pot-lucks, church work days, etc.

- Do not schedule more than two events per week. New ask one-on-one appointments take priority.

CAMPAIGN RESOURCES

After Your Campaign

»   Tracking Monthly Partnership

»   Thank-You Chart

»   Cultivating Relationship Chart

»   83 Ways To Say Thank You

AFTER YOUR CAMPAIGN

Tracking Monthly Partnership

Example Chart

Partner	Pledge	Jan	Feb	Mar	Apr	May	Jun	Jul	Aug	Sep	Oct	Nov	Dec	Total
James	$300	300	300	300	/	600	300	/	600	300	300	300	350	3650
Paul	50	50	150*	50	50	50	50	50	50	50	/	100	50	550
David	$150	150	150	150	150	150	150	150	150	150	150	150	150	1800
Jenn	35	35	35	/	70	35	35	35	35	/	70	35	35	420
Ashley	200	200	200	200	200	/	/	600	200	200	200	200	200	2400
Hannah	50	50	50	50	50	50	50	50	50	50	50	50	50	600
Daniel	100	100	100	100	100	100	100	100	100	100	200*	100	100	1100
Jane	130	130	/	130	130	130	130	/	260	130	130	130	130	1430
Sam	75	75	75	75	75	/	150	75	75	75	75	75	75	900
Ken	200	200	200	200	200	200	200	200	200	200	200	200	200	2400
Eunice	60	60	60	60	/	60	60	60	60	60	60	60	60	660
Jess	40	40	40	40	40	40	40	/	40	40	40	40	40	440
SUM	1390	1390	1210	1355	1065	1415	1265	1320	1820	1355	1275	1440	1440	16350

» Acknowledge every gift with a thank-you.

» Acknowledge any increase or extra.

» If any increase or extra is significant, it ought to be acknowledged with a phone call.

» If a regular monthly partner misses a month, notate it. If they miss the next month, immediately call.

Monthly Giving Income Chart

Year: _____

Partner	Pledge	Jan	Feb	Mar	Apr	May	Jun	Jul	Aug	Sep	Oct	Nov	Dec	Total
SUM														

AFTER YOUR CAMPAIGN
Thank-You Chart

Example Chart

Partner	Jan	Feb	Mar	Apr	May	Jun	Jul	Aug	Sep	Oct	Nov	Dec
James	E	E	**P**	E	E	**C**	E	E	**P**	E	E	**C**
Paul	E	E	**P**	E	E	**C**	E	E	**P**	E	E	**C**
David	E	E	**P**	E	E	**C**	E	E	**P**	E	E	**C**
Jenn	E	E	**P**	E	E	**C**	E	E	**P**	E	E	**C**
Ashley	**P**	E	E	**C**	E	E	**P**	E	E	**C**	E	E
Hannah	**P**	E	E	**C**	E	E	**P**	E	E	**C**	E	E
Daniel	**P**	E	E	**C**	E	E	**P**	E	E	**C**	E	E
Jane	**P**	E	E	**C**	E	E	**P**	E	E	**C**	E	E
Sam	**C**	E	E	**P**	E	E	**C**	E	E	**P**	E	E
Ken	**C**	E	E	**P**	E	E	**C**	E	E	**P**	E	E
Eunice	**C**	E	E	**P**	E	E	**C**	E	E	**P**	E	E
Jess	**C**	E	E	**P**	E	E	**C**	E	E	**P**	E	E

Pattern: E, E, P, E, E, C

E = Email

P = Postcard

C = Call

Thank-you chart

Partner	Jan	Feb	Mar	Apr	May	Jun	Jul	Aug	Sep	Oct	Nov	Dec

AFTER YOUR CAMPAIGN
Cultivating Relationship Chart

Group	%	Week 1	Week 2	Week 3	Week 4	Week 5	Week 6	Week 7	Week 8	Week 9	Week 10	Week 11	Week 12
		Jan				Feb				Mar			
		1st Wk	2nd Wk	3rd Wk	4th Wk	1st Wk	2nd Wk	3rd Wk	4th Wk	1st Wk	2nd Wk	3rd Wk	4th Wk
A Group	15%		ME	C							E		
	15%		ME		C							E	
	15%		ME			C							E
	15%		ME				C						
	15%		ME					C					
	15%		ME						C				
	10%		ME							C			
B Group	13%		ME	E								C	
	13%		ME		E								C
	13%		ME			E							
	13%		ME				E						
	13%		ME					E					
	13%		ME						E				
	13%		ME							E			
	13%		ME								E		
C Group	10%		ME	E									
	10%		ME		E								
	10%		ME			E							
	10%		ME				E						
	10%		ME					E					
	10%		ME						E				
	10%		ME							E			
	10%		ME								E		
	10%		ME									E	
	10%		ME										E

ME = Mass email   **C** = Phone call   **E** = Personal email   **P** = Postcard

		Week 13	Week 14	Week 15	Week 16	Week 17	Week 18	Week 19	Week 20	Week 21	Week 22	Week 23	Week 24
		Apr				May					June		
		1st Wk	2nd Wk	3rd Wk	4th Wk	1st Wk	2nd Wk	3rd Wk	4th Wk	5th Wk	1st Wk	2nd Wk	3rd Wk
A Group	15%					E							P
	15%						E						
	15%	E						E					
	15%		E						E				
	15%			E						E			
	15%				E						E		
	10%											E	
B Group	13%							E					
	13%								E				
	13%	C								E			
	13%		C								E		
	13%			C								E	
	13%				C								E
	13%					C							
	13%						C						
C Group	10%	E										C	
	10%		E										C
	10%			E									
	10%				E								
	10%					E							
	10%						E						
	10%							E					
	10%								E				
	10%									E			
	10%										E		

ME = Mass email   **C** = Phone call   **E** = Personal email   **P** = Postcard

Week 25	Week 26	Week 27	Week 28	Week 29	Week 30	Week 31	Week 32	Week 33	Week 34	Week 35	Week 36	Week 37
June	Jul				Aug				Sept			
4th Wk	1st Wk	2nd Wk	3rd Wk	4th Wk	1st Wk	2nd Wk	3rd Wk	4th Wk	1st Wk	2nd Wk	3rd Wk	4th Wk
						C						
P							C					
	P							C				
		P							C			
			P							C		
				P							C	
					P							C
		P								E		
			P								E	
				P								E
					P							
						P						
							P					
E								P				
	E								P			
								E				
									E			
C										E		
	C										E	
		C										E
			C									
				C								
					C							
						C						
							C					

		Week 38	Week 39	Week 40	Week 41	Week 42	Week 43	Week 44	Week 45	Week 46	Week 47	Week 48
		Sept	Oct					Nov				Dec
		5th Wk	1st Wk	2nd Wk	3rd Wk	4th Wk	5th Wk	1st Wk	2nd Wk	3rd Wk	4th Wk	1st Wk
A Group	15%	E		ME					E			HOLIDAY GREETING CARD
	15%		E	ME							E	HOLIDAY GREETING CARD
	15%			ME & E								HOLIDAY GREETING CARD
	15%			ME	E							HOLIDAY GREETING CARD
	15%			ME		E						HOLIDAY GREETING CARD
	15%			ME			E					HOLIDAY GREETING CARD
	10%			ME				E				HOLIDAY GREETING CARD
B Group	13%			ME			E					HOLIDAY GREETING CARD
	13%			ME				E				HOLIDAY GREETING CARD
	13%			ME					E			HOLIDAY GREETING CARD
	13%	E		ME						E		HOLIDAY GREETING CARD
	13%		E	ME								HOLIDAY GREETING CARD
	13%			ME & E								HOLIDAY GREETING CARD
	13%			ME	E							HOLIDAY GREETING CARD
	13%			ME		E						HOLIDAY GREETING CARD
C Group	10%			ME								
	10%			ME								
	10%			ME								
	10%			ME								
	10%			ME								
	10%	E		ME								
	10%		E	ME								
	10%			ME & E								
	10%			ME								
	10%			ME								

ME = Mass email   **C** = Phone call   **E** = Personal email   **P** = Postcard

Week 49	Week 50	Week 51	Week 52
Dec			
2nd Wk	3rd Wk	4th Wk	5th Wk
YEAR-END ASK			
YEAR-END ASK			
YEAR-END ASK			
YEAR-END ASK			
YEAR-END ASK			
YEAR-END ASK			
YEAR-END ASK			
YEAR-END ASK			
YEAR-END ASK			
YEAR-END ASK			
YEAR-END ASK			
YEAR-END ASK			
YEAR-END ASK			
YEAR-END ASK			
YEAR-END ASK			
CHRISTMAS LETTER			
CHRISTMAS LETTER			
CHRISTMAS LETTER			
CHRISTMAS LETTER			
CHRISTMAS LETTER			
CHRISTMAS LETTER			
CHRISTMAS LETTER			
CHRISTMAS LETTER			
CHRISTMAS LETTER			
CHRISTMAS LETTER			

A Pattern: P, E, C, E, E, ME

B Pattern: E, C, E, P, E, E

C Pattern: E, E, P, E

AFTER YOUR CAMPAIGN ——————————
83 Ways To Say Thank You

It is important to say thank you well and often to your partnership team. Say it right away— each month for every gift by email, card, or phone—even mentioning the dollar amount. Specifying the amount makes a personal connection and shows that you are paying close attention—that they aren't just another name on a long list. If you don't say it within twenty-four hours, it's the same as not saying it.

At the top of the list of reasons why partners stop supporting missionaries is not hearing from them often enough, as well as not feeling important, acknowledged, and valued by them. People want to know that their gift was received and appreciated. Be sure to thank them for each gift, but you don't have to mention the amount every time.

Below are 83 different ways you could say thank you, compiled and adapted from the work of Sandy (Buschman) Weyeneth[1] and Alan Sharpe[2]. Adjust them to fit your situation. Some of the phrases (which are underlined) are more appropriate for first-time gifts or partners who give occasionally and randomly, so they may not be the best for regular, steady partners.

1. _____ and I are excited that as you *"honor the Lord from your wealth and from the first of all your produce,"* He will take care of you! And through your gifts, He is taking care of us, too.

2. Thank you for your gift last month. It encouraged me.

3. It's a privilege to serve the Lord here in _____. Thank you for standing with us.

4. I never get tired of thanking the Lord for you and your partnership in ministry. Thank you for all that you do.

5. When David commissioned Solomon to build the house of the Lord, *"the people rejoiced because they had offered so willingly and made their offering to the Lord with a whole heart."* I thank God for your willingness and wholeheartedness in partnering with us in ministry.

6. It's a joy to serve the Lord in ministry with you.

7. We are grateful for your support these past years. You have freed us to focus on raising up and training young college students for campus ministry.

8. We rejoice that you faithfully partnered with us this past year. It meant a lot to us.

9. Students at _____ are bombarded with pressures and opportunities to have sex outside marriage. Your giving helps us reach them with the truth that only Jesus can satisfy our craving for genuine love. We value your partnership.

10. I am filled with thanks to our Father, as you stand with us and make this ministry possible.

———————————

[1]   #1-47 from *"50 Ways of Saying 'Thank You' to Your Giving Partners."* Weyeneth, Sandy (Buschman), 1995. Used by permission. Sandy Weyeneth, of The Navigators, is the author of *Writing Exceptional Missionary Newsletters.*

[2]   #48-81 from *"51 Ways to Say Thank-you in a Fundraising Letter."* Sharpe, Alan. Used by permission. Alan Sharpe is a fundraising consultant, writer and evangelical Christian. Learn more at www.raisersharpe.com

11. We praise God that you, *"do not neglect doing good and sharing."* We appreciate how you share your gifts with us unto Him.

12. We often remember you in prayer and thank God for the important part you have played in our work.

13. I appreciate your readiness and willingness to give. Thank you.

14. Your giving is a ministry of His grace to us. Blessings to you.

15. You are a continual source of joy and encouragement to us as you pray and give so faithfully. Thank you.

16. We thank God for you and pray the Lord will *"supply and multiply your seed for sowing and increase the harvest of your righteousness."*

17. At our Bible study last night, _____ asked how he could know Jesus is God. Thank you for helping to make it possible to reach (businessmen, students, etc.) like _____.

18. Each time your gift comes, I realize that your prayers back it up. That is such an encouragement! Thank you.

19. The Lord overwhelms us with joy through your faithfulness to us. Thank you.

20. It thrills me to receive your gifts these past (months, years). May His grace be yours in abundance.

21. As Paul said to the Philippians, I say to you. Your gifts are *"a fragrant offering, a sacrifice acceptable and pleasing to God."*

22. Your prayers and gifts often cause me to praise God for His goodness.

23. Each month you bring a smile to my face, as I'm reminded of your partnership. Thank you for your $_____ gift.

24. We appreciate your trust in God and decision to partner with us. We couldn't do it without friends like you.

25. I just returned from _____ where I taught about how to help a new believer. Your support helped make this possible. Thank you for investing in equipping laborers for Christ.

26. You are a vital part of our lives and ministry. Thank you.

27. Each time we see your gift, we stop and thank the Lord for you!

28. What a pleasure to partner with you, as God changes lives here in ____. Your gifts are touching lives like_____. She is understanding more and more of the gospel and learning to trust. Thank you for your help!

29. We appreciate your friendship and partnership. We love you.

30. Often we are reminded of how precious you are to us. We appreciate you and your generous heart.

31. We feel such gratitude to the Lord for the way He touches hearts to be a part of this ministry. Thank you for your part!

32. As I write this, my heart is filled with gratitude for all you mean to me and for your help to make this ministry possible.

33. We realize you have many choices of where to give your money. Thank you for partnering with us in reaching _____ with the gospel.

34. Thank you for standing with me with your prayer and finances. It is an honor to be in partnership with you.

35. Your prayers make a difference in our lives and work. Your faithful support is so helpful and encouraging. We hope you know what a joy you are to us.

36. It encourages me that you keep praying and giving. Thank you.

37. We love you and are grateful for your partnership.

38. I am glad that the Lord brought you into my life and for your continued support.

39. Your partnership makes it possible to serve the Lord in the task of _____. Thank you!

40. _____ and I feel humbled and glad that you are part of our ministry team. Many thanks to you!

41. You truly are partners with us in this work. Thank you for laboring with us.

42. You are part of a team that "holds the ropes" for us while we "rappel" into the fatherless neighborhoods of _____. Your giving is a glorious gift to us!

43. You are storing up treasure in heaven as you give to the Lord through this ministry to families.

44. As Hebrews 6:10 says, "God is not unjust so as to overlook your work and the love *that you have shown for his name in serving the saints, as you still do*" (ESV).

45. I appreciate your sacrifice to partner so generously with this work.

46. Thank you for standing with me and enabling me to invest in young adults like _____. He is growing into an excellent leader.

47. I deeply appreciate you and your heart to give.

48. In response to your recent gift to our ministry, I join with the people of Afghanistan in saying, "shúker." Thank you.

49. We are so grateful to you for your recent gift. Thank you!

50. I received your check in the mail today. Thank you for your partnership in ministry.

51. I had to simply praise the Lord this morning when I received your gift in the mail. Bless you!

52. Thank you for your continued partnership. Here's what you're doing: [list impact].

53. Your gift of $100 arrived today and will soon be hard at work, helping us provide fresh drinking water to the people of Nanbitu. Thank you. (Adjust to your ministry.)

54. Thank you for your continued, faithful partnership with us in ministry.

55. I have to admit I am overjoyed by your recent generosity. Thank you for your $ ____ gift. (You might use this when someone sends a gift for the first time or when a partner sends a special gift.)

56. What a delight it was for all of us here at [The ABC Mission] to learn that you have included us in your will. May the Lord reward you richly for remembering the poor and destitute with your bequest!

57. I greatly appreciate your kindness to our ministry.

58. I put the phone down just now after talking with you and simply had to put in writing how excited we all are to be receiving your $ ____ toward our [ABC] ministry.

59. Simply put, if it wasn't for faithful partners like you, our ministry wouldn't exist. So, thank you for supplying the funds that we need to make a difference in the lives of teenagers who struggle with eating disorders right here in our own city. (Adjust to your own ministry.)

60. For your generosity, I thank you.

61. Your gift of $_____ raised our spirits. Thanks to your generosity, we are now able to [list the impact here].

62. Your recent gift reminds me of how much we depend on your generosity and moral support to accomplish our mission.

63. Thank you for your gift. Your kind gesture will help us. So I thank you today. The children will thank you in January!

64. Two things thrill me about your recent gift to [ABC] ministry—your generosity and the your continued confidence in us and our mandate.

65. Your gift, which arrived this morning, will help us reach [insert name of group] for Jesus. Thank you so much!

66. I was looking through our files the other day and realized that you have been supporting our ministry for 20 years come the end of this month. So, this is a personal letter from me and the people we serve. Thank you for your faithfulness.

67. This is just a quick note, but it comes from my heart, as I head out the door for my flight to India. Thank you for your recent gift. Your generosity will make an immediate difference in the lives of [insert]. I am going to make sure to keep you up to date on [insert].

68. "Use where needed most." Those four words on your recent $_____ gift has changed the life of one youngster forever. His name is Billy, and after we prayed for him, Jesus completely healed him—he is no longer blind! Thank you.

69. The Bible says that the Lord loves a cheerful giver, and so do we! Thank you for your generosity.

70. For your gift, for your prayers, and for your steadfast commitment to the work of the Lord in Kansas City, I thank you.

71. I shared Thanksgiving Dinner with 100 wonderful street people last night. Thank you for your support. See the enclosed photographs.

72. Martin Luther said that if you want to change the world you should pick up your pen. I see from this morning's mail that you picked up your pen last Friday. Your gift has changed the world of one here in _____ who I will call John.

73. You are a treasure to us. Thank you again for standing [linking arms] with us.

74. Thanks to your kindness and generosity, as I write, 100 blankets are being loaded on a plane, headed to the New Hope Orphanage in Johannesburg. They have warmed many hearts around here already. (Adjust to your own situation.)

75. I must run, but let me conclude with a final heartfelt THANK YOU for remembering _____ and the difference you make in [his/her/their] [life/lives].

76. You'll see that everyone here at the office has signed this thank-you letter. That's because we are so amazed by your faithful partnership over the years.

77. We are humbled by your recent expression of support for our work. Thank you.

78. Someone once said that whatever we possess becomes of double value when we share it with others. I'm looking around at the difference your financial support has made to our ministry, and I know that statement is true. So, I'm writing you this brief note to express our thanks—for you and for your partnership in ministry.

79. Let me explain how your $ _____ a month has helped us.

80. The nice thing about writing thank-you letters is that we are blessed twice—when we receive your gift and again when we remember it in writing. I hope you are doubly blessed in the giving and when I describe the difference your gift is making in our [describe project here].

81. Thank you for your partnership.

82. Thank you.

83. Thank you for your continued, consistent care. You have loved us well.

CAMPAIGN RESOURCES
Other Resources

- » My Confession
- » Challenges to Partnership
- » Please Do's & Please Don'ts

My Confession

I have been called into full-time ministry. I must respond by giving myself fully to this work; therefore, I will raise the ministry team needed to accomplish my assignment. My life and ministry will bring glory to God. My obedience to Jesus is what really matters. Because I love Him, I will obey Him. My life is all I have to give.

God is able to supply all of my needs, and He will primarily supply through other people. There are people who, upon hearing about my assignment, will gladly partner with me to prepare the earth for the Lord's return. My ministry will be an answer to prayer for many; they have been praying for "laborers in the harvest," and here I am. God has a partnership team waiting for me; I must move forward and discover the team He has prepared for me.

I cannot do God's part, and He will not do my part. Therefore, I will be excellent in all areas of ministry, starting with my partnership development. Raising the team that God has for me will be excellent training for ministry. I am not laboring in vain. Every call I make and every appointment I go to will build character, teach me, train me, prepare me, and make me a better servant of the gospel. I will work hard; I will be diligent; I will stick to the strategy; I will always move forward; I will communicate clearly; I will articulate my assignment well; and I will give it one hundred percent and allow God to do His part.

I am providing an excellent stewardship opportunity for the Body of Christ. I will not believe the lies of the devil. God has called me, and He has a team for me. I am developing a team for the sake of the gospel and for the glory of His name. There are plenty of resources for the task at hand; God would not commission me if there was not adequate supply.

My partnership team will mean much more than just finances. I will not treat them like an ATM machine, but rather as the brothers or sisters that they are. I am determined to love them well. I will walk in the second commandment with everyone on my team and with everyone I meet. God is giving me real friends who understand partnership, and we will all work together to partner with Him in His global mission.

Father, thank You for my assignment, and thank You for the wisdom of biblical partnership.

Challenges to Partnership Development

Eleven things that can hinder partnership development

1. Lack of knowledge

For most people the skills needed for partnership development do not come naturally. We need to be properly trained. Our most natural instincts in these areas are often not helpful. Take time to educate yourself in the area of partnership development. Read through these notes several times, and talk about partnership with your coworkers. If you are called to full-time missions work, *take the time to get the right training so that you can serve in your calling for a lifetime.*

2. Lack of tools

Any job has tools, and living as a missionary with a partnership team is no different. Take the time to gather the proper team-building tools and develop your skills with them.

3. Ineffective or inconsistent efforts

Mass mailings, social media, and emails are often our first thoughts of how to raise funds, but these mediums are often ineffective. Take time to be properly trained in effective communication. Once trained we need to be consistent in our efforts. Good partnership development habits flow out of a lifestyle and are not an occasional event.

4. No plan

Partnership development is not a natural thing, especially in the beginning. You have to be intentional about building your team. It takes time; you must set aside the proper time to get it done. Have a plan laid out for letters, postcards, phone calls, and appointments that will reach all of your contacts in an effective time frame. Hold yourself to your plan. You are never too busy to develop partners.

5. Bad theology

For many their thoughts of money, missions, and funding missionaries are developed by fear, mission traditions, and culture, not the Scriptures. We must have our minds renewed and have a kingdom mindset in funding the Great Commission. Currently, there is a powerful stronghold on the mind of much of the Church. Many Christians, including missionaries, have a wrong concept of money, wealth, poverty, etc. Even the powerful testimonies of "by faith alone" or stories of miraculous provision can be counterproductive. These stories are the exception not the rule. What God rarely does we should rarely do, and what God does regularly we should regularly do. Practice the biblical principle of sharing your vision and asking others to join you. There are thousands of people who have tried the no-ask approach who are no longer in missions.

6. **Pride**

Sometimes we can be very creative and spiritual when it comes to explaining our lack. But often at the root it is pride. Often we can be fiercely independent and it is seen as a virtue. God has placed us within a spiritual family, and we function best when we are interdependent on one another. Interdependence requires humility, but pride brings God's resistance. Don't draw back from financial partnership; ask God for the grace to do it humbly.

7. **Fear**

Fearing failure and rejection, being concerned at the possibility of being controlled or manipulated by supporters, fearing what our family might think, and worrying about always being in need, etc., are signs that we are still under an unbiblical stronghold. We need to have our mind renewed.

8. **Lack of personal giving**

As born-again believers we should tithe. Tithing is worship and good stewardship, and empowers ministry. Because God has been generous toward us we should be the most generous people on the earth. Additionally there is the simple principle of sowing and reaping. We can't expect to reap if we haven't sown. Tithing as well as a dozen other financial responsibilities from Scripture are not suddenly relaxed because we are missionaries. We must be doers of the Word.

> *Honor the LORD with your wealth and with the first fruits of all your produce; then your barns will be filled with plenty, and your vats will be bursting with wine. (Prov. 3:9-10, ESV)*

> *One gives freely, yet grows all the richer; another withholds what he should give, and only suffers want. Whoever brings blessing will be enriched, and one who waters will himself be watered. (Prov. 11:24-25, ESV)*

> *You shall give to him freely, and your heart shall not be grudging when you give to him, because for this the LORD your God will bless you in all your work and in all that you undertake. (Deut. 15:1,0 ESV)*

9. **Lack of confidence**

Clarity is confidence. We must have clarity and conviction about our ministry. We must believe that partnership is God's preferred way to fund His workers. And we must believe that God has a team for us. When you have confidence in these three areas then you will be able to share and invite with confidence, and this will lead to others having confidence to partner with you. Confidence may be your most important asset.

10. **Wrong motives**

We should always walk in humility, embracing the Sermon on the Mount teaching and loving our neighbor as ourselves. We should first seek the kingdom and its righteousness, and then all we need will be added to us.

> *Whoever closes his ear to the cry of the poor will himself call out and not be answered. (Prov. 21:13, ESV)*

Whoever loves pleasure will be a poor man; he who loves wine and oil will not be rich. (Prov. 21:17, ESV)

²¹Beloved, if our heart does not condemn us, we have confidence before God; ²²and whatever we ask we receive from him, because we keep his commandments and do what pleases him. (1 John 3:21-22, ESV)

¹Blessed is the man who walks not in the counsel of the wicked, nor stands in the way of sinners, nor sits in the seat of scoffers; ²but his delight is in the law of the LORD, and on his law he meditates day and night. ³He is like a tree planted by streams of water that yields its fruit in its season, and its leaf does not wither. In all that he does, he prospers. (Ps. 1:1-3, ESV)

11. ## Lack of passion

Without clarity and conviction about your ministry, you will not press through the challenges of developing financial partnership. Without a holy conviction you will lack the diligence needed to build your team. A lack of passion about your ministry will lead to a low volume of fruit.

Do not be slothful in zeal, be fervent in spirit, serve the Lord. (Rom. 12:1,1 ESV)

Pray and ask the Holy Spirit to show you any areas of your life where you are not lining up properly with the Word of God. Repent and ask the Lord for grace to obey.

Six failures of partnership development

1. ### Failure to do a face-to-face meeting

Face-to-face meetings are your best form of communication. Meetings give you a chance to build relationship with a brother or sister in Christ and share your vision with them. Most will give because they are asked to give. They don't mind being asked, and they will really appreciate you asking them at a face-to-face meeting. By this they feel valued and respected.

In my personal training experience about 33-36% of the people approached for partnership say yes. When the face-to-face meeting is replaced by a video meeting it drops to 8%. When done through mass mailing or social media it drops to about 1%.

2. ### Failure to make the phone call

The first call is the toughest, but after that it becomes really fun. This is your chance to share a little of the excitement you have for your new ministry. This is your chance to invite your friend to talk a little more. *Don't back away; people want to hear how the Lord is moving.*

Do not allow time to lapse between your letter, postcard, and phone call. Start making your calls seven days after mailing your postcard. I have seen many well prepared missionaries trip and stumble at the phone call. It's the first time in the process where we actually have to talk to a real person. Pray. When the day comes, pick up the phone and dial as fast as you can, and don't stop until you have made several calls.

3. **Failure to secure the appointment**

Sometimes when we call a friend and the call is going really well and we both are excited and having fun, we can simply forget to schedule an appointment. At other times appointments can be cancelled because we failed to give multiple points of contact or our communications were not clear and the person didn't really understand what we were asking of them. Remember to give them enough points of contact and state very clearly why it is you want to meet.

When on the phone, treat them with respect; be flexible to their schedule, meet them at their convenience. Don't use strong or manipulative language, but always remain proactive. Be sure they have heard your excitement. You may want to send an appointment reminder by text, email, or postcard.

4. **Failure to give a personable and personal presentation**

It's important that early on in the appointment we take time to build rapport with the person. Get to know them; ask them about their family, their work, or hobbies. Ask them about their church; try to hear their level of involvement. Show that you care by listening well and asking secondary questions. At this stage you want them talking way more than yourself.

When it comes time for you to share, be conversational rather than presentational. Be sure this part is also organic and natural. Remember you are simply sharing what the Lord is doing through you and your organization. Be sure to share the why behind the ministry and not just what you do. People will make their decision based on why not what.

In the event that you are using some sort of media, keep it short (under three minutes). Before the meeting, make sure all batteries are charged and videos are queued. Don't overly trust in media to tell your story or to do the ask for you; no one can tell your story better than you.

5. **Failure to ask for partnership**

Don't chicken out. If you're afraid to ask the partnership question, it may be that you are still under a stronghold. Having a biblical understanding of partnership will make it much easier to ask. Remember, you are inviting them to be a part of your team—a way for them to join the Lord in what He is doing in the earth. *Many people will say yes when they are asked, but very few will say yes without being asked.*

Be clear and ask, *"John and Jane, would you partner with me in ministry?"* and then wait for an answer. Don't speak for them. Let them be the next to speak.

6. **Failure to follow up**

If you have given a clear presentation and made a clear invitation to partner with you in ministry, there is a really good chance that they will say yes. In the event that they cannot say yes right away, ask if you may contact them in a few days once they have had more time to pray. **Don't leave it open-ended—name a specific date when you will contact them.** *"Could I contact you on Monday the 7th? Would that be enough time for you?"*

Follow through on all the steps. If you are having trouble connecting by phone, stay with it and don't give up. Be sensitive. Don't give up.

If they have said yes to partnership, but they are not going to start their support until you are in your field of service, then the above still applies. Thank them and set a date. *"John and Jane, thank you for partnering with us in ministry; we look forward to your official start date of May 9th. May I go ahead and start sending you our newsletter?"* Then, follow up the appointment, at least once a month, with a newsletter, card, or email thanking them and *mentioning the start date a week prior.*

Partnership Development mistakes to avoid

» Trying to develop a partnership plan that does not meet face to face or that does not hear no. You are going to hear no.

» Trying to tell your story by social media, video, phone, or some other means rather than face to face.

» In an effort to try and save time, you do a group ask instead of individual asks.

» Asking for financial partnership by social media, email, or in a newsletter.

» Having a low level of faith and low expectations.

» Not having a plan for making all your calls and appointments.

» Lack of diligence.

» Presuming that people don't want to partner with you rather than just inviting them to be a part of your team. Don't make the decision for them.

» Trying to "raise funds" instead of building a "ministry team."

» Starting your partnership development without proper understanding and proper training.

» Being busy with ministry activities and responsibilities and not giving proper time for partnership development.

» Failing to invite them into financial partnership because of fear; instead you only ask them to be a prayer partner. Assessing someone's financial capabilities and making decisions for them instead of asking and letting them make their own decisions.

» Launching out into full-time ministry before you have been proper trained and before you have completed your team.

» Starting your partnership development without accountability and encouragement from a coach.

» Settling for a less than proper budget.

» Not ministering to your team well (lack of communication, gratitude, and personal attention).

» Not being prepared for your face-to-face meetings.

» Not following through on calls before and after appointments.

Reminders for partnership development

Things to keep in mind

There is a process to raising sufficient prayer, encouragement, and financial partnership to enable a missionary to serve full-time in their field. Just as consistent prayer and encouragement are crucial to your ministry, consistent financial support is also necessary.

Few workers look forward to the fundraising element of missions. Remembering a few things may help you:

1. ### God has called you

   Because God has called you, He will also provide the support that you need. You can't do His part, and He won't do your part. A worker is worthy of a wage. The support is there. Your job is to gather the provision the Lord already has for you.

2. ### You are not asking for money for yourself

   You are quite capable of supporting yourself through work here or back home, but that's not what you came here for. Instead, *you are raising money for a ministry*—a ministry that would not happen in the same way, if you were to stay at home. Jesus, the apostles, and Paul, most of the time, trusted in the provision of God that came through other people. "*The worker deserves his wages,*" (Lk. 10:7, NIV).

3. ### Most missionaries look back on the process of building a team as being very positive and even fun!

   It builds a prayer team for your ministry. When people support you and your ministry, they will pray for you. Prayer follows finance.

   » Raising a partnership team will build your own faith.

   » Your partnership team will strengthen the movement you are called to. Your organization is only as strong as it has properly funded and fully available people.

   » Team building trains you for other areas of ministry.

   » Partnership development creates friendships that might not have otherwise happened.

   » Partnership development provides a platform for the gospel and your organization.

   » Partnership development requires humility and promotes interdependence (Body life).

4. ### Focus on relationships and ministry—not money

   We must develop partners to do what God has called us to, but the money is incidental. Our emphasis will be on building, maintaining, and deepening personal relationships with friends who are or may become ministry partners—not on seeking funds.

   Focus all of your contact time, ***prior** to partnership development*, on building relationship. Be sure to connect by phone, email, text, postcard, and face-to-face appointments over lunch or coffee. You may invite them to see the work that you are doing.

Don't use your letters or an email to ask for money or talk about how great your need is. When you do ask for financial partnership, it will be in face-to-face appointments.

5. **Partnership development is a very significant ministry (yes, ministry!).**

Most Christians are not called to full-time ministry. Partnering with others who are called through prayer, encouragement, and finances could very well be the best or only ways for them to connect with global missions.

The "house of prayer message" is not yet common in most churches. Therefore, your opportunity to share with individuals is a chance to encourage them with God's heart, with what He is doing world-wide, and how they can participate.

OTHER RESOURCES

The Please Do's & Please Don'ts

Please do

»   Remember that people give to people

»   Ask and ask repeatedly

»   Say thank you well and often (ingratitude is a partnership killer)

»   Nurture supportive relationships

»   Remember the purpose of the phone call is to ask for an appointment, not to ask for partnership

»   Always remain in a proactive position; take the lead in the process

»   Be persistent with the process and stick to the plan

»   Be prepared

»   Think through every meeting before you go

»   Develop rapport with your prospective partners

»   Learn to communicate the vision the Lord has put in you

»   Ask for what you want, not what you think they can or will give

»   Clearly ask for partnership and then wait for the reply

»   Ask for one thing at a time; don't lump several things together in one request

»   Be faithful with all of your follow up

»   Always have a grateful heart

»   Schedule your time—or else someone or something will

»   Have a plan for every goal

Please do not

»   Please do *not* start partnership development unprepared—lack of training, faith, savings, time, transportation

»   Please do *not* tell your story over the phone, but face-to-face

»   Please do *not* deviate from the four-step process

»   Please do *not* focus on money or else you will miss great opportunities and be stressed out

»   Please do *not* think that letters, postcards, and other materials will do all the work for you

» Please do *not* ask groups to partner with you; ask individuals to partner with you

» Please do *not* presume who will or will not give; you never know how God will work in someone

» Please do *not* allow emotions, circumstances, or appearances to determine whether or not you ask

» Please do *not* take shortcuts

» Please do *not* ask for "one-time gifts," but ask for a "special gift"

» Please do *not* ask for prayer partnership only because you're lacking the confidence and boldness to ask for financial partnership

» Please do *not* do partnership development without prayer

» Please do *not* fear hearing a "no," as most of the time it's due to temporal circumstances

» Please do *not* forget to remind partners of what their giving is accomplishing

» Please do *not* start full-time ministry until you are fully funded

INTERNATIONAL HOUSE *of* PRAYER

· ·

24/7 LIVE WORSHIP AND PRAYER

ihopkc.org/prayerroom

· ·

Since September 19, 1999, we have continued in night-and-day prayer with worship as the foundation of our ministry to win the lost, heal the sick, and make disciples, as we labor alongside the larger Body of Christ to see the Great Commission fulfilled, and to function as forerunners who prepare the way for the return of Jesus.

By the grace of God, we are committed to combining 24/7 prayers for justice with 24/7 works of justice until the Lord returns. We believe we are better equipped to reach out to others when our lives are rooted in prayer that focuses on intimacy with God and intercession for breakthrough of the fullness of God's power and purpose for this generation.

INTERNATIONAL
HOUSE *of* PRAYER
UNIVERSITY

MINISTRY • MUSIC • MEDIA • MISSIONS

• •

ENCOUNTER GOD. DO HIS WORKS. CHANGE THE WORLD.

ihopkc.org/ihopu

• •

International House of Prayer University (IHOPU) is a full-time Bible school which exists to equip this generation in the Word and in the power of the Holy Spirit for the bold proclamation of the Lord Jesus and His return.

As part of the International House of Prayer, our Bible school is built around the centrality of the Word and 24/7 prayer with worship, equipping students in the Word and the power of the Spirit for the bold proclamation of the Lord Jesus and His kingdom. Training at IHOPU forms not only minds but also lifestyle and character, to sustain students for a life of obedience, humility, and anointed service in the kingdom. Our curriculum combines in-depth biblical training with discipleship, practical service, outreach, and works of compassion.

IHOPU is for students who long to encounter Jesus. With schools of ministry, music, media, and missions, our one- to four-year certificate and diploma programs prepare students to engage in the Great Commission and obey Jesus' commandments to love God and people.

> "What Bible School has 'prayer' on its curriculum? The most important thing a man can study is the prayer part of the Book. But where is this taught?
>
> Let us strip off the last bandage and declare that many of our presidents and teachers do not pray, shed no tears, know no travail. Can they teach what they do not know?"
>
> –Leonard Ravenhill, *Why Revival Tarries*

International House of Prayer University, 12901 S. US Highway 71, Grandview, MO 64030
(816) 763-0243 | info@ihopu.org

International House *of* Prayer
INTERNSHIPS

INTRO TO IHOPKC • FIRE IN THE NIGHT
ONE THING INTERNSHIP • SIMEON COMPANY

ihopkc.org/internships

Internships exist to see people equipped with the Word of God, ministering in the power of the Holy Spirit, engaged in intercession, and committed to outreach and service.

Our four internships are three to six months long and accommodate all seasons of life. The purpose of the internships is to further prepare individuals of all ages as intercessors, worshipers, messengers, singers, and musicians for the work of the kingdom. While each internship has a distinctive age limit, length, and schedule, they all share the same central training components: corporate prayer and worship meetings, classroom instruction, practical ministry experience, outreach, and relationship-building.

Biblical teaching in all of the internships focuses on intimacy with Jesus, ministry in the power of the Holy Spirit, the forerunner ministry, evangelizing the lost, justice, and outreach. Interns also receive practical, hands-on training in the prophetic and healing ministries.

Upon successful completion of a six-month internship or two three-month tracks, some will stay and apply to join IHOPKC staff.

Our IHOPKC Leadership Team

Our leadership team of over a hundred and fifty men and women, with diversity of experience, background, and training, represents twenty countries and thirty denominations and oversees eighty-five departments on our missions base. With a breadth of experience in pastoral ministry, missions work, education, and the marketplace, this team's training in various disciplines includes over forty master's degrees and ten doctorates.

International House of Prayer Missions Base, 3535 E. Red Bridge Road, Kansas City, MO 64137
(816) 763-0200 | internships@ihopkc.org

MIKE BICKLE
TEACHING LIBRARY
—— *Free Teaching & Resource Library* ——

This International House of Prayer resource library, encompassing more than thirty years of Mike's teaching ministry, provides access to hundreds of resources in various formats, including streaming video, downloadable video, and audio, accompanied by study notes and transcripts, absolutely free of charge.

You will find some of Mike's most requested titles, including *The Gospel of Grace; The First Commandment; Jesus, Our Magnificent Obsession; Romans: Theology of Holy Passion; The Sermon on the Mount: The Kingdom Lifestyle*; and much more.

We encourage you to freely copy any of these teachings to share with others or use in any way: "our copyright is the right to copy." Older messages are being prepared and uploaded from Mike's teaching archives, and all new teachings are added immediately.

Visit mikebickle.org

International House of Prayer Missions Base, 3535 E. Red Bridge Road, Kansas City, MO 64137
(816) 763-0200 | info@ihopkc.org | ihopkc.org